American Public Opinion on the Iraq War

American Public Opinion on the Iraq War

OLE R. HOLSTI

The University of Michigan Press

Ann Arbor

Published in the United States of America by
The University of Michigan Press
Manufactured in the United States of America
⊗ Printed on acid-free paper

2014   2013   2012   2011   4   3   2   1

A CIP catalog record for this book is available from the British Library.

Library of Congress Cataloging-in-Publication Data

Holsti, Ole R.
        American public opinion on the Iraq War / Ole R. Holsti.
            p.   cm.
        Includes bibliographical references and index.
        ISBN 978-0-472-11704-8 (cloth : alk. paper) — ISBN 978-0-472-03480-2
    (pbk. : alk. paper) — ISBN 978-0-472-02782-8 (ebk.)
        1. Iraq War, 2003– —Public opinion.   2. United States—Foreign
    relations—2001–2009—Public opinion.   3. Public opinion—United States.
    I. Title.
        DS79.767.P83H65   2011
        956.7044'31—dc22

                                                              2011014838

For
Maija, Brad, Aksel, and Mikko
Kal and Marilyn
All my students, 1962–2009

Contents

Tables and Figures

Preface

When a prospectus for this book was sent out to external reviewers, one of them raised a very telling question: "What makes the author believe that the Iraq War will be finished by mid-2010?" We have now reached early 2011 and several observations are in order. The outgoing George W. Bush administration signed an agreement with the Nuri al-Maliki government in November 2008 calling for the withdrawal of all American forces from Iraq by the end of 2011. Although sectarian violence has declined since the near–civil war of 2006–7, it continues to take a heavy toll on Iraqi civilians, and the important elections scheduled for January 2010 had to be postponed for two months owing to continuing disagreements among sectarian groups. After the elections were held in March, the various parties were unable to form a ruling coalition until November 2010. At the same time, the monthly total of American military casualties reached a postinvasion low of three—all in noncombat incidents—in December 2009. On August 2, 2010, President Obama declared that U.S. combat brigades would be withdrawn by the end of the month, "as promised and on schedule," and the withdrawal was in fact completed in a timely manner. That said, one of the most prescient analysts of the war, Thomas E. Ricks, forecast that what he has called "the American military adventure in Iraq" will persist long beyond the date stipulated by the Bush–al-Maliki agreement, and indeed, that we may be only halfway through our active engagement in Iraq.

Whatever the accuracy of the Ricks forecast, because the focus of this book is on public opinion, 2010 represents a reasonable end point. The evidence of public disenchantment and deep partisan divisions aroused by the war, as described in the chapters that follow, is unlikely to change significantly, barring dramatic and unforeseen developments on the ground in Iraq. Moreover, the economic consequences of the financial collapse of 2008 and the war in Afghanistan have displaced Iraq at the top of public attention, and as a consequence, the major survey organizations have sharply curtailed polling on the Iraq War. Stated differently, it seems unlikely that the vast volume of survey data on Iraq generated during the 2003–9 period will be matched in the future.

In undertaking this book, I have been beneficiary of the talents, kindness, and insights of many friends and colleagues. Andy Bell, Peter Feaver, and Tim Lomperis and three anonymous external reviewers for the University of Michigan Press read the entire manuscript and offered a good deal of useful advice on how to improve it. Andy Bell also formatted figures 2.1 through 2.5 and assisted with the index. Michael Cobb was an especially insightful discussant on a paper at the 2008 American Political Science Association conference. Richard Sobel, Bethany Barratt, and Peter Furia provided useful comments on an early draft of chapter 2. Lecture audiences at Catholic University in Belo Horizonte, Brazil, and at the Catholic University of Brasilia, the University of Brasilia, and Brigham Young University raised a number of thought-provoking questions that required me to sharpen the analysis. Juliano Cortinhas, who arranged my trip to Brasilia, also made a number of useful suggestions. Elizabeth Kelly, an undergraduate at Duke University, was an exceptional research assistant who always went well beyond the assigned tasks to find a new source of valuable information.

Anne Marie Boyd, whose title of research secretary did not fully describe the range of her many talents, worked with me during the initial stages of this project. It was our fourth book together. Kathy Tutson and Laura Satterfield later provided exceptionally valuable assistance in typing and formatting the manuscript. Finally, my ability to complete this project owes a great deal to the professional expertise and kindness of Dr. Heather Gilbert and Dr. Joseph Moore.

This is my fourth book with the University of Michigan Press. It has always been a pleasure to work with the staff of the UMP. Melody Herr, Acquisitions Editor, offered exceptional support since the inception of this project, and Janice Brill provided outstanding copyediting.

I am deeply grateful to all of the above for their valuable contributions. Any remaining deficiencies must, alas, be laid at my doorstep.

The triple dedication is to my beloved daughter, son-in-law, and two grandsons; to my brother and his lovely wife; and to the thousands of students I have known—and learned a great deal from—at Stanford, the University of British Columbia, the University of California at Davis, and, since 1974, at Duke.

Introduction

Having entered into its ninth year in March 2011, the conflict in Iraq is now America's third longest war, behind only the Vietnam and Afghanistan conflicts, exceeding in length even the Revolutionary War, Civil War, and World War II. It has also established a record in another significant respect; it has generated far more surveys of public attitudes than any previous conflict. Political scientist John Mueller described the 1991 Gulf War to expel Iraq from Kuwait as "the mother of all polling events,"[1] but it has long since relinquished that title to the conflict that began with a U.S.-led invasion of Iraq on March 19, 2003. Although the United States has played by far the most important role in Iraq, the war has also become the topic of vast numbers of surveys in scores of other countries.[2]

Although the final chapter has yet to be played out on the ground in Iraq, and full access to the archives will not be available for years—if ever—the war has also generated an immense literature, including some exceptionally insightful studies by military analysts, Washington-based correspondents, area experts, and many others.[3] In addition, we now have several memoirs by Bush administration officials, including by the president, defense secretary Donald Rumsfeld, and White House adviser Karl Rove. Others are sure to follow.[4]

This book focuses on American public opinion about the Iraq War. The availability of vast amounts of survey data is not, however, sufficient reason for undertaking a detailed analysis of public opinion. Indeed, from the "realist" perspective on international relations, there would be several strong reasons for believing that public opinion would be largely acquiescent and thus irrelevant during both the run-up to the 2003 invasion and in subsequent policies for dealing with the postwar situation in Iraq: It was a war initiated against a regime headed by the almost universally hated Saddam Hussein; and it was launched less than two years after the September 11 terrorist attacks that had, at least in their initial aftermath, unified the American public behind the administration's policies, including the invasion of Afghanistan to topple the Taliban regime that had provided a home for Osama bin Laden and his al Qaeda terrorist organization. Almost from its first days in office the Bush administration had made regime change in Baghdad a high priority. After the September 11 attacks it launched a vigorous overt and covert campaign to persuade the public that removal of the Saddam Hussein regime in Baghdad would not only eliminate the imminent threat of Iraqi weapons of mass destruction and sever its ties to the al Qaeda terrorists who had carried out the September 11 attacks, but it would also represent a major step in bringing peace and stability to the Middle East region. In short, that perspective would have suggested that in any analysis of the Iraq War, some interesting probes might be undertaken about administration efforts to "manufacture consent" for its policies, but on balance public opinion would most likely otherwise be viewed as a residual category.

The invasion of Iraq in 2003 was a "war of choice" initiated by an administration whose leaders harbored few if any doubts about its favorable military outcome and its salutary longer-range consequences, for Iraq, for the Middle East region, and for vital American security interests. Had events on the ground followed the script confidently outlined by President George Bush, Vice President Dick Cheney, Defense Secretary Donald Rumsfeld, Paul Wolfowitz, and other top administration leaders during the months leading up to the invasion, a swift military victory over Iraq's poorly equipped and poorly led military would have been the prelude to an outpouring of gratitude for the American liberators by the vast majority of Iraqis. It was an article of faith among these officials that various groups in Iraq, having been freed from the grips of the tyrannical Sunni-dominated Saddam Hussein regime in Baghdad, would put national interests ahead of sectarian ones in creating a viable post-Saddam Iraq. Consequently, after a relatively brief transitional period during which the American military would help maintain internal security, a new leadership and a stable democratic civic order would emerge in Iraq. Whatever infrastructure damage had been incurred during the war could easily be covered by Iraq's vast oil resources. Most if not all American forces could then be withdrawn safely.

The war and its outcome were also intended to serve as a test case for and a vindication of Rumsfeld's transformation of military doctrine: American superiority in military and information technology would be used to achieve rapid victory with limited forces, followed by quick withdrawal to avoid getting bogged down in postwar nation-building. It would thus simultaneously drive a stake through the heart of policies advocated by Rumsfeld's bitter rival within the administration, Secretary of State Colin Powell. According to the Powell Doctrine, military interventions abroad must meet a number of requirements, including the use of massive force at the outset, support from Congress and the American public, and a viable exit plan.

In a letter to Colonel Theodore Roosevelt, leader of the famed Rough Riders who fought in the Spanish-American War, future Secretary of State John Hay described that conflict as "a splendid little war." Had the Iraq War followed the administration's scenario, it might well have been depicted in similar terms. In that case, the role of American public opinion would hardly have been a high priority in analyses of the war and its implications for American foreign and defense policy. Research might have probed such questions as the level of support for taking military action against Iraq, the degree to which that support was contingent upon gaining the approval of NATO allies and/or the UN Security Council, the extent to which policy differences fell along or across party lines, the effects of the Iraq issue on the 2002 midterm elections, and the like. Quite predictably, a low-cost victory resulting in removal of Saddam Hussein from power in Baghdad, followed by a rapid withdrawal of American forces, would have gained very strong public support. Most polling organizations that had been posing questions about Iraq would soon be turning their attention to other issues.

Instead of a "splendid little war" that yielded important short-term and long-term benefits at very limited cost in blood and treasure, the invasion of Iraq triggered one of the longest, costliest, and most controversial conflicts in American history, the final outcome of which remains uncertain. It has thus given rise to a wide range of important questions about the conduct of American foreign and defense policies. As noted above the war has generated an unprecedented number of public opinion surveys, many of which were conducted or commissioned by media organizations. The voluminous data generated by these surveys provides significant opportunities for analyzing a wide range of questions concerning American public opinion and foreign policy.

OVERVIEW

Chapter 1 describes the long and convoluted course of events that constituted American relations with Baghdad during several decades prior to the 2003 invasion of Iraq. That relationship covered virtually the entire gamut of possibilities, including an extended period of nonrecognition, an informal alliance, and war. The two countries had no diplomatic relations between 1967 and the mid-1980s. During the long war triggered by Iraq's invasion of Iran in 1980, not only were diplomatic relations restored, but the United States was a major supplier of military equipment and vital military intelligence that enabled Iraq to avoid defeat at the hands of its larger and more populous neighbor. When in 1990 Iraq invaded another of its neighbors—Kuwait—the George H. W. Bush administration led an impressive international coalition that crushed Iraqi military forces and expelled them from Kuwait but stopped short of toppling the Saddam Hussein regime. That decision, and the subsequent controversies about whether Iraq was in compliance with postwar prohibitions against acquiring weapons of mass destruction, set the stage for the George W. Bush administration when it came to office in January 2001.

Chapter 2 opens with a discussion of the domestic and international politics of the Iraq issue between the inauguration of the George W. Bush administration and the U.S.-led invasion of Iraq twenty-six months later. It then turns to survey responses to five central questions that were frequently posed by several major polling organizations: Did the United States do the right thing in invading Iraq? How well is the war effort going? Has the Iraq War made the United States safer, especially from terrorist attacks? Was the situation in Iraq worth going to war over? How long should American forces remain in Iraq, and under what circumstances should they be reduced or withdrawn? In each case results from three polling organizations are presented and analyzed in order to reduce the risk of results that are heavily dependent on the sampling designs and question wording of any single organization. Additional analyses include other, less-frequently asked questions about U.S. policy in Iraq. The discussion explores the extent to which changes in public opinion reflect events on the ground as against, for example, vigorous administration public relations efforts to manufacture support for the war. This issue will be revisited in chapter 5 in assessing the impact of the almost unprecedented multipronged efforts to generate public support for its policies.

Chapter 3 addresses one of the oldest myths about public opinion, usually propounded by officials of whatever party or political persuasion is in power, that "politics stops at the water's edge." A brief summary of some previous wars involving the United States reveals that partisan differences have often marked debates about policies in times of war. The analysis examines in more detail the nature and extent of partisan differences generated by the war in Iraq. It explores public responses to questions of *values* (for example, should the United States have invaded Iraq?); *fact* (for example, did Saddam Hussein have weapons of mass destruction and an intimate working relationship with al Qaeda prior to the September 11 attacks on New York and Washington?); and *prescription* (for example, under what circumstances and in what time frame, if any, should American forces in Iraq be reduced or withdrawn?).

Even prior to the September 11 terrorist attacks and the Iraq War, some expert analysts predicted that the end of the Cold War would mark the demise of American public support for multilateral internationalism. For example, the distinguished historian Arthur M. Schlesinger's lament on this score appeared in a widely cited 1995 article, "Back to the Womb?"[5] In the light of disenchantment with American policy in Iraq, chapter 4 places views on the war in a broader context, addressing some issues that might shed light on the future conduct of foreign affairs. Have views on the war spilled over into other opinions about the country's proper international role, the nature of threats to vital national interests, the importance of various international goals that the United States might pursue, and the circumstances that would warrant the deployment of American forces into conflict situations abroad? In sum, has the Iraq experience led substantial numbers of Americans to rethink the active international role that has broadly characterized this country's foreign policy since the Japanese attack on Pearl Harbor on December 7, 1941, that brought the United States into World War II?

Chapter 5 turns to the important but difficult questions of the impact, if any, that public opinion may have had on American foreign policy. Because archival evidence and interviews with top officials after they have left office— the best sources for assessing the impact of public opinion—are not available for such ongoing issues as the Iraq War, the analysis must of necessity be anecdotal and incomplete rather than comprehensive and conclusive. The discussion describes how the administration dealt with public opinion, first during the months prior to the invasion of Iraq and then during the post-Saddam era. Although the administration largely enjoyed a free pass from the media and Congress during the run-up to the war, its top leaders argued repeatedly that the American media were consumed with powerful anti-administration and antiwar biases that seriously damaged the war effort. In response, it undertook very vigorous overt and covert public relations programs to "educate" the public on justifications for the war and its intimate connection to the most vital national security interests, including the "global war on terrorism" (GWOT). The discussion then reviews evidence about the impact of the Iraq War on the four U.S. elections since the 9/11 terrorist attacks.

The concluding chapter places the findings in a broader context. It addresses several questions that arise from the Iraq War, including the role of public opinion in foreign policy, the media, and possible postwar "stab in the back" myths.

To what extent and how does this case contribute to our understanding of the important but often elusive relationship between public opinion and foreign policy? The evidence suggests that even in the face of vigorous public relations efforts by administration officials, public opinion, in the aggregate, seemed to reflect a sensible appraisal of events on the ground. In short, the charge that public opinion is fickle and subject to random changes rooted in little more than moods and whims receives scant support in this case. The evidence also confirms hypotheses about bipartisanship and the circumstances under which administrations are likely to "go public" in foreign policy confrontations.

There are various conceptions of the proper role of the media in democratic governance, ranging from the watchdog fourth estate role to that of the faithful conveyor of information provided by the government. How did the often-conflicting demands of the media and government officials play out in the Iraq War? How might some recent media developments—the vast increase in the types of media outlets as well as the serious difficulties facing the print media—affect public opinion on foreign affairs?

Should the Iraq War fail to result in at least minimal success—a relatively stable country in which the sectarian groups tolerate each other and that lives at peace with its neighbors—is there any danger that a new stab-in-the-back explanation will develop to account for the shortfalls? Is it possible that the war, assessments of which have been divided by partisan differences of historic proportions, will give rise to sharply divergent postmortems that could have the same corrosive effects as the debates on the "lessons of Vietnam" had for some years following the end of that conflict?

CHAPTER 1

Prelude: The United States and Iraq before the Iraq War

During the quarter century prior to the American-led invasion of Iraq in March 2003 the two countries had experienced almost the full gamut of relations, from being quasi allies to going to war against each other. Although the United States was officially neutral during the long and bloody Iran-Iraq War (1980–88), Washington in fact provided the Baghdad regime with vital material and intelligence assistance sufficient to avert an Iranian victory. Arguably it prevented the overthrow of the Saddam Hussein regime because a victorious Iran would have been unlikely to leave Saddam in power. But only a short time later, after Iraq invaded Kuwait in August 1990, supported by a series of United Nations Security Council Resolutions, including one urging members the "use of all necessary means" to force Iraqi withdrawal from Kuwait, Washington led a coalition of 34 countries that crushed Saddam Hussein's forces while expelling them from Kuwait.

Once a part of the Ottoman Empire, Iraq was one of several countries created when the map of the Middle East was redrawn, largely by the French and British Foreign Offices, after World War I. Britain installed a Hashemite monarch, King Faisal I, in Iraq—or as it was sometimes called, Mesopotamia—and governed the country under a League of Nations mandate until 1932. Although Iraq had formally achieved independence in October 1932 and had joined the League of Nations, Britain maintained military bases there. By the Anglo-Iraqi Treaty of 1930, Britain was granted the right to maintain air forces in Iraq for 25 years. As a consequence of a six-week Anglo-Iraq war in the spring of 1941, in which the German Luftwaffe intervened on the side of Iraq, Britain reoccupied Iraq until two years after the end of World War II. London continued to play a significant role in the affairs of the country until a revolution led by General Abdul Karim Kassim in 1958 overthrew and killed King Faisal II in a massacre at his palace on July 14, 1958. Five years later, the popular General Kassim was killed in a bloody coup. Another coup in 1968, in which Saddam Hussein played an important role, brought the pan-Arab Baath Party to power in Baghdad.

Unlike Great Britain, the United States had historically played a relatively limited role in the Middle East, but that changed significantly during and after World War II. President Roosevelt made Saudi Arabia eligible for Lend-Lease aid and declared that because of its oil, the defense of Saudi Arabia was a vital national interest. His interior secretary, Harold Ickes, was concerned that the United States was running out of oil, and he published an article with that title in *American Magazine*. In 1945 FDR met King Abdul Aziz aboard the USS *Quincy* in the Suez Canal, furthering ties to Saudi Arabia. After the war, Washington raced Moscow to be the first to recognize Israel after its birth in April 1948, and it has consistently championed the right of Israel to exist, although there have been occasional differences about its proper borders and a host of other issues, including expanding settlements in the occupied territories in the West Bank. The Central Intelligence Agency played an active role in the politics of a number of countries. In 1949 the CIA installed a pro-American military officer, Col. Adib Shishkali, as leader of Syria. After his regime was overthrown, Syria entered into a short-lived merger with Egypt under the name of the United Arab Republic.

At the behest of the British, in 1953 the American Central Intelligence Agency played the lead role in overturning the elected Mossadeq government that had nationalized foreign oil holding in Iran, and in returning the Mohammad Reza Pahlavi (hereafter the Shah) to power in Tehran. Iran had demanded an equal share rather than the one-sixth it had been receiving of the oil revenues from the giant Anglo-Persian Oil Company. When negotiations broke down, Iran nationalized the firm. Prime minister Winston Churchill had approached the Truman administration about an invasion to regain control of the oil company and its huge refinery, but Truman flatly rejected the overture. Washington attempted to promote further negotiations on the issue, but British foreign minister Anthony Eden was adamantly opposed. Believing that his knowledge of Persian literature gave him special insight into Iranians, he told Secretary of State Dean Acheson that "they [Iranians] were rug merchants and that's all they were. You should never give in and they would always come around and make a deal if you stayed firm." When Eden suggested a joint coup to overthrow Mossadeq, Acheson told him that it was the British who were behaving like rug merchants.[1]

After Dwight Eisenhower assumed the presidency in 1953, Churchill tried again, pointing out that American support for London in Iran would be a quid pro quo for British participation in the Korean War. After an initial lack of enthusiasm for acting in support of the British, Eisenhower relented. When Secretary of State John Foster Dulles was persuaded that Mossadeq was favorably inclined toward Iran's small Tudeh communist party, he threw his support behind such a plan. Mossadeq had in fact excluded communists from his government and, according to Henry Grady, the former American ambassador to Iran, Mossadeq "has the backing of 95 to 98 percent of the people of the country."[2] Dulles's younger brother, Allen, was head of the CIA. Led by Kermit Roosevelt, grandson of America's 26th president, the CIA undertook Operation Ajax wherein they used large cash handouts to various groups of thugs, and charges that Mossadeq was a tool of the communists, to generate sufficient chaos in Tehran to topple the government and to permit the weak-willed Shah, who had left the country, to return from abroad and to resume power. Some in the CIA, including Director Allen Dulles, came to view the Iran undertaking as its finest hour and a blueprint for how to deal with other recalcitrant regimes. Others in the CIA were less sure.[3]

Three years later, Egypt nationalized the Suez Canal in response to Dulles's withdrawal of aid for building the Aswan Dam on July 26, 1956. Egypt's purchase of arms from Czechoslovakia and its threat to seek alternative financing from the Soviet Union triggered Dulles's action. The Aswan project was likely to result in increased cotton production by Egypt, giving rise to some opposition in Congress, especially among cotton state members. International negotiations failed to resolve the canal issue. In the meanwhile Israel, Britain, and France agreed on a plan wherein Israel would invade the Sinai, followed by British and French forces, ostensibly to separate the Egyptian and Israeli forces and to take control of the canal. When Egypt failed to respond to a British and French ultimatum, the invasion plan went into effect.

The invasion found no favor in Washington. The Eisenhower administration used its immense financial and economic power—including a threat to sell its large sterling bond holdings—to coerce the invading forces to withdraw. Secretary of State Dulles pointedly asserted that the American action represented a final and decisive break with support for traditional colonialism. Not the least reason for American displeasure was the fact that the Suez crisis took the world's attention away from the brutal, nearly simultaneous Soviet invasion of Hungary. At the suggestion of Lester Pearson of Canada, a United Nations Emergency Force was created to maintain peace in the region. Pearson won the Nobel Peace Prize for his efforts. According to the 1957 Eisenhower Doctrine, the United States asserted the right to intervene in the area in case of a threat from international communism.

The July 1958 revolution that removed Faisal II from power in Iraq led to concerns in Washington about spreading turmoil in the Middle East that might engulf Lebanon, at that time a major regional banking center and sometimes considered "the Switzerland of the Middle East." The pro-Western government of President Camille Chamoun called for American assistance, citing threats of a civil war pitting Maronite Christians against Muslims. Washington invoked the Eisenhower Doctrine to justify the deployment of army and marine forces to Lebanon. The 14,000 troops were withdrawn three months later. President Chamoun resigned and was replaced by Fuad Chehab. The Macmillan government in London urged Washington to help roll back the coup against King Faisal II in Iraq but Eisenhower declined to do so as long as the new government in Baghdad, whatever its domestic policies, posed no threat to vital American interests, including continued flow of oil.

As a result of American support for Israel in the Arab-Israeli war in 1967, Baghdad broke diplomatic relations with Washington, and in 1972 it nationalized oil interests. The Baath regime brought Communists into the government after it had signed a 15-year Treaty of Friendship and Cooperation with the USSR. In light of those developments, Washington viewed Iraq as a Soviet ally. In the meanwhile, Saddam Hussein, an ambitious and brutal leader, but also considered a modernizer as a result of some domestic reforms, rose through Baath party ranks and had become the de facto ruler of the country well before formally assuming the presidency in 1979. Iraq began a nuclear enrichment program with French help, but before its Osirak nuclear reactor was completed it was destroyed by an Israeli air strike on June 7, 1981.

A revolution in Iran saw the overthrow in 1979 of the Mohammad Reza Shah Pahlevi government and its replacement by a fundamentalist Islamic regime led by the Ayatollah Ruhollah Mussaui Khomeini. Khomeini had been among the witnesses to the 1953 coup that returned the Shah to power in Iran. While in exile, Khomeini had lived in Iraq's holy city of Najaf for four years but at the behest of the Iranian government he had been expelled and had lived in Paris prior to the upheaval that brought him to power in Tehran. This was but one source of tension between the neighboring Islamic countries. Both populations were predominantly Shiite, but Sunnis dominated the largely secular Saddam Hussein regime. Sensing that Iran had been weakened by postrevolutionary turmoil, Saddam launched an invasion of Iran in September 1980 to settle a long-standing border dispute involving the Shatt al-Arab waterway that runs into the Persian Gulf. After some initial military successes by the invading forces, Iran was able to turn the tide and put Iraqi forces on the defensive.

The war between the two Middle Eastern neighbors placed Washington in an awkward position. Before the Islamic revolution, Iran had been a cornerstone of American policy in the Middle East, and Iraq was viewed as ally of the Soviet Union. Iran enjoyed special access to American arms sales, and both Republican and Democratic presidents had hailed the Shah as a statesman and friend. In the wake of the disastrous Vietnam War, the so-called Nixon Doctrine allocated significant security responsibilities to major regional powers, of which Iran was one of the most important. According to Nixon, "I just wish that there were more leaders around the world with his foresight . . . and his ability to run, basically, let's face it, a virtual dictatorship in a benign way." Jimmy Carter described Iran as "an island of stability in a sea of turmoil."[4]

When the Shah, living in exile following his ouster, requested permission to enter the United States for cancer treatment, he had a powerful ally in Henry Kissinger, who used all his influence to accommodate the Shah. In the tumultuous post-Shah environment in Iran, some officials in Washington worried about the safety of the American Embassy. The CIA Iran branch chief had assured his colleagues in Tehran that an attack on the U.S. Embassy there was unlikely: "The only thing that could trigger an attack would be if the Shah was let into the United States—and no one in this town is stupid enough to do that."[5] When President Carter caved in and allowed the Shah into the country, his grave doubts about the wisdom of doing so notwithstanding, Iranian militants invaded the American Embassy and held its personnel hostage for 444 days. Some Iranians may have justified that action, while contrary to the most basic norms regulating relations between countries, as a legitimate response to fears that the United States would try to restore the Shah to power, as it had done in 1953. Writing in 2004, a veteran CIA analyst described the embassy takeover as "an act of vengeance" for the 1953 coup.[6] In short order, Iran had been transformed from a staunch ally into a country that most Americans could love to hate. Television networks ended their nightly newscasts with a scoreboard showing the number of days that the Iranians had held American diplomats hostage, and T-shirts depicting the Ayatollah in the worst possible terms enjoyed brisk sales.

The prospect of an Iranian victory and the possible transformation of Iraq into a clone of Iran—a fundamentalist and revolutionary Islamic regime—led Washington to rethink its policy toward Iraq. In 1979 Iraq had been added to a State Department list of countries sponsoring terrorist activities, including support for the militant Abu Nidal organization,[7] and in 1980 the Defense Intelligence Agency reported that Iraq had been "actively acquiring chemical weapons capacity since the mid-1970s."[8] Two years later the Reagan administration removed Iraq from that list, without consulting Congress, thus making Iraq eligible to buy "dual-use" technology—that is, technology with both civilian and military applications, including heavy trucks, helicopters, and high-speed computers. The administration approved the sale of 60 Hughes helicopters, and the secretaries of commerce and state lobbied the National Security Council to permit the sale of ten Bell helicopters, ostensibly for crop spraying. With little effort, those aircraft could be—and were—used to spray poison gas on Iranian forces and Kurdish groups in the north of the country. In 1983 the State Department asserted that Iraq continued to support groups on its terrorist list, and a CIA report revealed that Iraq had used mustard gas against Iran. State Department officials recommended discussing the use of chemical weapons, in order to deter further use and "to avoid unpleasantly surprising Iraq through public positions we may have to take on the issue."[9]

Later that year, President Reagan sent Donald Rumsfeld, at that time an executive at the pharmaceutical firm G. D. Searle, to Baghdad as an official representative of the administration. On December 20, 1983, Rumsfeld met with top Iraqi officials, including Saddam Hussein, and he participated in a highly publicized photo opportunity shaking hands with Saddam. In a 90-minute meeting, the two discussed common U.S.-Iraqi interests, including U.S. efforts to cut off arms sales to Iran and opposition to an outcome of the war with Iran that "weakened Iraq's role or enhanced interests and ambitions of Iran." The wide-ranging agenda of their discussions made no mention of chemical weapons, although the issue did come up in passing at a later meeting with foreign minister Tariq Aziz.[10]

After Iraq expelled the Abu Nidal organization to Syria, Rumsfeld returned to Baghdad the following year. By late 1984 diplomatic relations between Iraq and the United States were restored despite growing evidence of Iraqi use of chemical weapons. But even prior to restoration of formal relations, the United States had been providing Iraq with substantial assistance for its bloody war with Iran and to suppress its own domestic Kurdish groups in the northern part of the country. Pursuant to the administration's policy of increasing support for Iraq, the State Department urged the U.S. Export-Import Bank to provide Iraq with financial credits. With the expulsion of the Abu Nidal organization, the financing was intended to signal belief in Iraq's financial viability and to "go far to show our support for Iraq in a practical, neutral context."[11] A State Department official informed the House Committee on Foreign Affairs that it had not objected to the sales that included 2,000 heavy-duty trucks, noting pointedly that they were built not only in Michigan but also in five other states. When asked if the trucks were intended for military purposes, in an early version of "don't ask–don't tell," the official responded, "we presumed that this was Iraq's intention, but had not asked."[12] Aside from its own sale of dual-use equipment, Washington encouraged Jordan, Saudi Arabia, Kuwait, and Egypt to transfer various kinds of weapons to Iraq, and President Reagan personally asked the Italian prime minister to ship arms to Iraq.

By the following year there was ample evidence from multiple sources, including American intelligence, that Iraq was guilty of violating the 1925 Geneva Protocol against the use of chemical weapons. Seven UN missions conducted between 1986 and 1988, including medical examinations of Iranian poison gas victims, added to the case against Baghdad. In the meanwhile, the United States was providing important satellite intelligence to Baghdad that, among other uses, helped Iraq to "calibrate" its employment of mustard gas against Iranian forces. American determination to assist Baghdad seemed almost impervious to Iraq's actions. In a 1984 press briefing a State Department spokesperson stated that Iraq's use of chemical weapons would not change American interest in closer relations with the Saddam Hussein regime. Shortly later, an internal State Department paper discussed the sale of "certain categories of dual-use items to Iraqi nuclear entities," and indicated that preliminary results favored expanding such trade. According to American intelligence, between August 1983 and March 1988 there were at least ten documented Iraqi uses of chemical weapons against Iranians and three against Kurds, with deaths ranging up to 10,000 per attack.[13]

Washington's rather convoluted relationships in the war between Iraq and Iran became even more complex when the al-Shira's Lebanese newspaper revealed on November 2, 1986, that the United States had delivered advanced TOW (tube-launched, optically tracked, wire-guided) missiles to Iran in September 1985 (508 missiles) and January 1986 (4,000 missiles). After the revelation, Washington stated that its purpose was to enable the release of some American hostages held by groups believed to be controlled by Tehran, but another goal was to use the funds from the arms sales secretly to fund Contra rebels fighting the government in Nicaragua, in contravention of a congressional prohibition against military support of the Contras.

In light of the overwhelming evidence that Iraq was guilty of using chemical weapons, the House of Representatives in 1985 moved to restore Iraq to the State Department terrorist list. The effort died, however, after Secretary of State George Shultz intervened to oppose it. Indeed, arms sales continued at an accelerated pace. The Commerce Department approved exports of computers valued at one million dollars that helped Iraq develop ballistic missiles, as well as equipment for upgrading of Baghdad's SCUD missiles that could reach military bases in Saudi Arabia and Israeli civilian centers in Tel Aviv and Haifa. While it jumps ahead of the story, it is worth pointing out that such SCUD attacks in fact took place during the 1990–91 Gulf War.

Shortly after evidence of especially brutal Iraqi attacks against its own Kurdish population, the Senate unanimously passed the "Prevention of Genocide Act of 1988" that cut off U.S. loans, military and nonmilitary assistance, credits, credit guarantees, items subject to export controls, and imports of Iraqi oil. The State Department expressed its opposition to the Senate measure as well as to a companion House of Representatives bill. Efforts toward legislative compromise failed, and the bills died at the end of the session.

The United Nations Security Council brought forth six resolutions—numbers 552, 582, 588, 612, 619, and 620—concerning the use of chemical weapons. Although Iran was clearly the target of most such attacks, the Security Council resolutions did not condemn Iraq directly but used more neutral language, such as "condemns resolutely the use of chemical weapons in the conflict between the Islamic Republic of Iran and Iraq." When on March 21, 1986, the Security Council president proposed to issue a statement condemning the frequent Iraqi use of chemical weapons, the United States voted against it, and four important U.S. allies—Australia, Great Britain, France, and Denmark—abstained, but owing to the favorable votes of the remaining ten Security Council members, the statement represented the first formal Security Council criticism of Iraqi actions.

The end of the Iraq-Iran War with a formal cease-fire on August 20, 1988, did not reduce, much less terminate, American aid to Baghdad. By 1989, when all international banks had cut off loans to Iraq, President Bush issued National Security Directive 26 mandating closer links between Washington and Baghdad, and one billion dollars of agricultural loan guarantees. According to that directive, "Normal relations between the United States and Iraq would serve our longer-term interests and promote stability in both the Gulf and the Middle East. The United States Government should propose economic and political incentives for Iraq to moderate its behavior and to increase our influence with Iraq." After warning that Iraq's illegal use of chemical weapons would lead to economic and political sanctions, NSD 26 suggested that, "as a means of developing access to and influence with the Iraqi defense establishment, the United States should consider sales of non-lethal forms of military assistance."[14] At the same time, Richard Haass and Robert Kimmitt, National Security Council and State Department officials, respectively, told the Commerce Department not to single out Iraq for restrictions on exports of dual-use technology. Indeed, when an American firm raised questions about the possible Iraqi use of its products for nuclear weapons and ballistic missiles, it was told that an Iraqi written guarantee about civilian use would suffice and thus that the shipment to Iraq was acceptable.

By the spring of 1990 there were indications of a serious dispute between Iraq and neighboring Kuwait. Iraq demanded payments for costs associated with its long and costly war against Iran, and it accused Kuwait of stealing Iraqi oil by "slant drilling." Baghdad also claimed that Kuwait was historically the "19th province of Iraq." On July 25, Saddam Hussein summoned American ambassador April Glaspie to his office on very short notice. She had only one half hour to prepare for the meeting with Saddam and foreign minister Tariq Aziz. Transcripts of their conversation reveal that she asserted, "We have no opinion on your Arab-Arab conflicts, such as your dispute with Kuwait. Secretary Baker has directed me to emphasize the instructions, first given to Iraq in the 1960s, that the Kuwait issue is not associated with America."[15]

Earlier that spring, five visiting American senators, led by Senate Republican leader Robert Dole, stated the problem in relations between Washington and Baghdad could be traced to Iraq suffering from a major "public relations deficit" in the United States. They assured Saddam that Voice of America had fired the author of a pro–human rights editorial that had offended the Iraqi leader, and that the Bush administration would oppose any legislation to invoke sanctions again Iraq. They reminded him, moreover, that "we condemned" the 1981 Israeli air attack on Iraq's nuclear facilities. In the meanwhile American aid had continued, uninterrupted by the possibility of conflict between Iraq and Kuwait. As late as July 31, the CIA stated that an invasion was unlikely despite satellite photos showing that two divisions of the elite Iraqi Republican Guard had massed on the Kuwait border. President Bush's telephone calls to the president of Egypt, the king of Saudi Arabia, and the emir of Kuwait reassured him that Saddam would not invade.[16]

Whether Saddam Hussein had been lulled by Ambassador Glaspie's statement, backed by Secretary of State Baker, and the long record of generous
American aid into thinking that Washington would look the other way in case
of an attack on Kuwait is source of considerable conjecture, and it cannot either
be proved or disproved. If Saddam Hussein persuaded himself that his "best
case" scenario—American acquiescence to his aggression in Kuwait—and reality were identical, he would certainly not be the first or only leader to engage in
such self-delusions, especially about politics in the Middle East. In the event, after stating that diplomacy had failed, Iraq invaded Kuwait on August 2, 1990,
and overran it within two days. The previous day, the Bush administration had
approved the sale of advanced data transmission devices worth $695,000.

The invasion of Kuwait instantly transformed relations between Washington and Baghdad. British prime minister Margaret Thatcher was in Washington at the time, and she urged President Bush to act immediately: "This is no
time to go wobbly, George." Until her resignation as prime minister in November 1990, Thatcher was opposed to taking the issue to the United Nations as doing so might serve as a constraint on policy options, including the use of
force.[17] President Bush had much better insight into the situation, however, as
unilateral action without the support of Security Council resolutions would
have made it impossible to form the impressive anti-Iraq coalition that ultimately included Egypt and Turkey, as well as eight other predominantly Muslim countries. All forms of aid to Iraq were cut off, and on August 6 the president demanded a complete withdrawal of all Iraqi forces from Kuwait. Two
days later he sent substantial U.S. military forces to Saudi Arabia to deter any
possible Iraqi attack on its oil-rich neighbor. Although there were reports that
Iraqi forces were massing on the Saudi frontier, satellite photos failed to
confirm that. Within days, the United States and its allies instituted a naval
blockade of Iraq, and the military was ordered to block exports of Iraqi oil and
all shipments other than food to Iraq. In the largest troop deployment since the
Vietnam War, American forces numbering in the tens of thousands landed in
Saudi Arabia. Fearing that the United States was not a reliable ally, and citing
President Reagan's withdrawal of American troops from Lebanon after the
deadly bombing of the marine barracks in 1983 as support for that doubt, the
Saudi government was initially unenthusiastic about any deployment of U.S.
forces into the kingdom. The Saudis acquiesced only after intensive discussions
in Washington and Riyadh with top American officials. As another very public
signal of American resolve, the president called 40,000 reservists to active duty.

The UN Security Council also took action immediately after the invasion of Kuwait. Security Council Resolution 660 on the day of the invasion, citing Articles 39 and 40 of the UN Charter, asserted that the Security Council:

1. Condemns the Iraqi invasion of Kuwait;
2. Demands that Iraq withdraw immediately and unconditionally all its forces to the positions in which they were located on 1 August 1990;
3. Calls upon Iraq and Kuwait to begin immediate intensive negotiation for the resolution of their differences and supports all efforts in this regard, and especially those of the League of Arab States;
4. Decides to meet again as necessary to consider further steps with which to ensure compliance with the present resolution.

In the meanwhile Washington and Moscow issued an important joint statement: "We must demonstrate beyond any doubt that aggression cannot and will not pay." Secretary of State Baker said that this statement, even more than destruction of the Berlin Wall, indicated that the Cold War was over.[18] Saddam Hussein's response was to link any Iraqi retreat with Israeli withdrawal from the West Bank and Gaza.

By Resolution 661 the Security Council added economic sanctions against Iraq and reaffirmed the right of self-defense under Article 51 of the Charter. Before the end of the month, Security Council Resolution 665 gave the United States and its allies the right to enforce an economic embargo on Iraq. A month later, yet another Security Council resolution (number 670) extended the economic blockade to include air traffic. In its most significant resolution (number 674) to that point, at the end of October the Security Council warned that further actions would follow if Iraq failed to withdraw its forces from Kuwait.

Security Council Resolution 678 of November 29 essentially issued an ultimatum to Iraq. Citing all 11 of its resolutions since the invasion (numbers 660–62, 664–67, 669, 670, 674, and 677), it stated that the Security Council:

1. Demands that Iraq comply fully with resolution 660 and all subsequent relevant resolutions, and decides, while maintaining all its decisions, to allow Iraq one final opportunity, as a pause of goodwill, to do so;
2. Authorizes Member States co-operating with the Government of Kuwait, unless Iraq on or before 15 January 1991 fully implements, as set forth in paragraph 1 above, the above-mentioned resolution, to use all

necessary means to uphold and implement resolution 660 and all subsequent relevant resolutions and to restore international peace and security in the area;

3. Requests all States to provide appropriate support for the actions undertaken in pursuance of paragraph 2 of the present resolution.

The key phrase—"to use all necessary means"—was inserted in lieu of "to use force" in the second paragraph to assuage Soviet and Chinese objections. In either case the meaning of the ultimatum was unambiguous.

Despite a clear expression of support from the Security Council, the political situation within the United States became somewhat murkier as the crisis developed during the autumn. Although Iraq had only recently been a quasi–American ally during its war with Iran, and the United States was entering into the midterm election season, the large deployment of American forces to Saudi Arabia initially elicited only muted domestic opposition. In many ways, Saddam Hussein was his own worst enemy; for example, he was shown on television pretending to be concerned about the welfare of one of his young international hostages. On October 3, the Senate approved a resolution backing the president's actions. Two weeks later, however, the Foreign Relations Committee demanded that the president gain congressional approval for any military action against Iraq.

Two days after the congressional elections, in which the Democrats increased their strong majority in the House by 7 seats (to 267 members) and their narrower margin in the Senate by 1 seat (to 55 members), President Bush ordered the deployment of additional troops to the Persian Gulf area, bringing the total to more than 400,000, in order to provide "adequate offensive military options." The transformation of the American deployment in the area, from a large force serving as a deterrent against a possible Iraqi attack on Saudi Arabia—Operation Desert Shield—into a much larger one with the capabilities of attacking the Iraqi forces totaling approximately 450,000, triggered considerable controversy in the domestic political arena. In response to demands by congressional leaders of both parties for a special session to deal with the issue, the president told members of Congress that he would consult them prior to using force against Iraq. House Democrats passed a nonbinding resolution demanding that any offensive action against Iraq be conditioned on formal congressional approval.

In the meanwhile, various diplomatic moves, including a meeting between Secretary of State James Baker and Iraqi foreign minister Tariq Aziz on January

9 in Geneva, failed to resolve the issue. Saddam Hussein stated that all foreign hostages could leave Iraq, but he otherwise failed to meet demands by Washington and the UN Security Council to withdraw his forces from Kuwait.

In the light of Iraqi intransigence on Kuwait, the ball was back in the court of the U.S. Congress and the United Nations. On January 12, 1991, both houses authorized the use of force against Iraq. In the closest votes since the War of 1812, the resolution passed the House by a margin of 250–183, and the vote in the Senate was an even closer 52–47. But even in the absence of a favorable vote, there is little doubt that the president would have gone ahead with the attack on Iraq.[19] In his view, the congressional vote was an act of support rather than authorization; for the latter, he could cite the various Security Council resolutions. Three days later the UN Security Council issued a final ultimatum for Iraqi withdrawal from Kuwait.

Operation Desert Storm began on January 17 with air attacks on Iraq. Significantly, the 34-nation coalition opposing Iraq included 10 Islamic countries—Afghanistan, Bahrain, Egypt, Morocco, Oman, Pakistan, Qatar, Saudi Arabia, Turkey, and the United Arab Emirates—thereby undercutting the Iraqi thesis that the conflict was essentially a "clash of civilizations" in which they represented the Islamic world against Western imperialism. Egypt, the most important of the Islamic coalition members, received forgiveness of its $7 billion debt to the United States. Iraq launched several attacks of SCUD missiles into Israel in the hopes of provoking Israel into joining the conflict, an action that surely would have fractured the coalition opposing Iraq. Washington effectively restrained Tel Aviv.

During the opening days of the Gulf War, coalition air forces undertook an extensive aerial bombing campaign aimed at damaging Iraqi infrastructure, reducing Baghdad's ability to resupply its forces in Kuwait, and attacking SCUD missiles sites. The aerial campaign also decimated the Iraqi air force. Iraq lost numerous MIG aircraft, and an even larger number of them fled to Iran to avoid being shot down. Not surprisingly, Iran failed to return the aircraft to the country with which it had fought a bloody war that had ended less than three years earlier, and only much later were the air crews permitted to return to Iraq.

The ground phase of the war began on February 24. By numbers alone, the ground forces were fairly evenly matched as Iraq was estimated to have deployed about 450,000 men, including their highly trained Republican Guard brigades, but coalition forces had the advantage of almost total air superiority. Rather than attacking Iraqi units occupying Kuwait directly, American, British, and French forces surprised Iraq by executing an effective "left hook" attack to the west of Kuwait. The Iraqi invaders began retreating from Kuwait within two days, setting fire to oil fields as they left. Air attacks inflicted heavy casualties on retreating forces along what became known as "the highway of death." American, British, and French units pursued the Iraqis to within 150 miles of Baghdad. At that point, one hundred hours after the start of ground operations, President Bush ordered a cease-fire, and on April 6 he declared that Kuwait had been liberated.

The military phase of the conflict was a success for the coalition. American military casualties were far lower than some prewar estimates with 294 deaths, of which 149 were battle-related. According to Congress, the war was estimated to have cost the United States $61.1 billion, but some $52 billion of that total was paid by others, including contributions of $36 billion from Gulf states, $10 billion from Japan, and $6.6 billion from Germany.[20]

That success notwithstanding, the war left a legacy of controversies, notably arising from President Bush's decision to stop military operations short of Baghdad, thus permitting the Baathist Saddam Hussein regime to remain in power. There was widespread belief in the administration that the military in Baghdad would probably overthrow Saddam because his policies had visited a military disaster upon Iraq. During the following decade the CIA was involved in various efforts to organize a coup against Saddam, but its efforts were unsuccessful.

In the light of subsequent events, it is worth describing how important U.S. policymakers subsequently assessed and justified that decision. Shortly after the end of hostilities, then-defense secretary Dick Cheney made this statement.

> If you're going to go in and try to topple Saddam Hussein, you have to go into Baghdad. Once you've got Baghdad, it's not clear what you do with it. It's not clear what kind of government you would put in place of the one that's currently there. Is it going to be a Shia regime, a Sunni regime, or a Kurdish regime? Or one that tilts toward the Baathists, or one that tilts toward the Islamic fundamentalists? How much credibility is that government going to have if set up by the United States military when it's there? How long does the United States military have to stay to protect the people that sign on for the government, and what happens to it once we leave?[21]

Even a year later, when it had become clear that the Saddam Hussein regime was reverting to its brutal ways by attacking its Shias in the south and Kurds in the north of the country, Cheney continued to be an articulate advocate of the cease-fire decision. He spoke to a staunchly conservative audience at the Discovery Institute in Seattle.

> I would guess that if we had gone in there, I would still have forces in Baghdad today. We'd be running the country. We would not have been able to get everybody out and bring everybody home. And the final point that I think needs to be made is this question of casualties, and while everybody was tremendously impressed with the low cost of the conflict, for the 146 Americans who were killed in action and for their families, it wasn't a cheap war. And the question in my mind is, how many additional American casualties is Saddam worth? And the answer is, not that damned many. So, I think we got it right, both when we decided to expel him from Kuwait, but also when the President made the decision that we'd achieved our objectives and were not going to get bogged down in the problems of trying to take over and govern Iraq.[22]

Most important, in their joint memoir published some years later, the president and Brent Scowcroft, his national security adviser, addressed this issue.

> Trying to eliminate Saddam, extending the ground war into an occupation of Iraq, would have violated our guideline about not changing objectives in midstream, engaging in "mission creep," and would have incurred incalculable human and political costs. Apprehending him was probably impossible. We had been unable to find Noriega in Panama, which we knew intimately. We could have been forced to occupy Baghdad and, in effect, rule Iraq. The coalition would instantly have collapsed, the Arabs deserting it in anger and other allies pulling out as well. Under the circumstances, there was no viable "exit strategy" we could see, violating another of our principles. Furthermore, we had been self-consciously trying to set a pattern for handling aggression in the post–Cold War world. Going in and occupying Iraq, thus unilaterally exceeding the United Nations' mandate, would have destroyed the precedent of international response to aggression that we hoped to establish. Had we gone the invasion route, the United States could conceivably still be an occupying power in a bitterly hostile land. It would have been a dramatically different—and perhaps barren—outcome.[23]

UN Security Council Resolution 687 on April 3, 1991, established the terms of the peace, economic sanctions, and Iraqi disarmament. Baghdad was to provide a full listing of all its weapons of mass destruction, and UNSCOM (United

Nations Special Commission) inspectors were to determine that the arms had in fact been surrendered. In 1994 the Iraqi National Assembly and Saddam Hussein officially recognized the sovereignty of Kuwait, and shortly thereafter UN Security Council Resolution 986 established the "Oil for Food" Program whereby Iraq was permitted to sell oil and use the proceeds for the purchase of food and other nonmilitary goods to improve the lives of its citizens.

During the dozen years following the Gulf War, the Saddam Hussein regime played a game of cat and mouse on the WMD issue. In November 1997 Iraq ordered all UNSCOM inspectors to leave the country. Shortly after their departure they were allowed to return. A year later Iraq stopped all cooperation with UNSCOM, but when faced with the threat of an American missile strike, it agreed to resume cooperation. In late 1999 the United States and Britain bombarded Iraq air defense capabilities—Operation Desert Strike—in response to Iraq's failure to cooperate fully with UNSCOM. At the same time, UN Security Council Resolution 1284 of December 17, 1999 created an UN inspection commission, UNMOVIC (United Nations Monitoring, Verification and Inspection Commission), to replace UNSCOM, but Iraq rejected the resolution.

In response to Iraq's persistently uncooperative behavior, Congress passed the "Iraq Liberation Act in 1998." It stated, "It should be the policy of the United States to support efforts to remove the regime of Saddam Hussein from power in Iraq and to promote the emergence of a democratic government to replace that regime." The act, which passed by a vote of 360–35 in the House and unanimously in the Senate, authorized the expenditure of $97 million for military education and training for Iraqi opposition organizations. It also concluded with a very important limitation: "Nothing in this Act shall be construed to authorize or otherwise speak to the use of United States Armed Forces in carrying out this Act."[24] Nevertheless, in December 1998 the United States and United Kingdom launched Operation Desert Fox, a four-day bombing campaign against Iraqi R&D installations, weapons depots, Republican Guard barracks, and other military sites. Marine General Anthony Zinni, head of Central Command, was in charge of Desert Fox. Republican critics charged President Clinton with ordering the operation to divert attention from his impeachment arising from the Monica Lewinsky scandal.

CONCLUSION

When the George W. Bush administration came to office in January 2001 it inherited a relationship with Iraq that had been marked by a long and highly convoluted history. The Gulf War had brought to a sudden end the highly optimistic assumption of the Reagan and first Bush administrations that massive American aid would buy Baghdad's support for U.S. goals in the Middle East, especially serving vital American interests by providing an effective counterweight to contain the influence and ambitions of the fundamentalist regime in Iran, and perhaps even by reducing support for terrorist groups in the region.

However, the successful military operations to liberate Kuwait, while leaving Saddam Hussein in power, left a legacy of unresolved issues. When outgoing president Clinton met with Bush for two hours in January 2001 to discuss national security challenges that the incoming president would have to confront, he listed the following in order of importance.

Osama bin Laden and al Qaeda
The absence of a Middle East peace
The nuclear standoff between India and Pakistan
Pakistan's ties to both the Taliban and al Qaeda
North Korea

Only then did he mention Iraq. In a related briefing, Clinton's national security adviser told his successor, Condoleezza Rice, "You're going to spend more time during the next four years on terrorism generally and al Qaeda specially than any other issue."[25]

Despite this advice from the outgoing administration—or perhaps because of it—at the first meeting of his Cabinet, the new president made it clear that his administration would give high priority to reversing his father's decision to declare a cease-fire short of the gates of Baghdad.[26]

CHAPTER 2

Public Opinion on the War in Iraq

The American invasion of Iraq, buttressed by a much smaller contingent of British forces, began 26 months after the Bush administration took office. The president and three of his top advisers—Vice President Dick Cheney, Secretary of Defense Donald Rumsfeld, and the latter's top deputy, Paul Wolfowitz—placed regime change in Baghdad at the top of their foreign policy agendas from the beginning. Cheney, Rumsfeld, and Wolfowitz had served in the elder President Bush's administration during the 1990–91 Gulf War. Although they had not dissented from the president's decision in 1991 to leave Saddam Hussein in power rather than to deal with the uncertainties and burdens that a post-Saddam Iraq might impose on the United States, during the eight-year period between the two Bush administrations they had become outspoken advocates of an active American policy to "finish the job" in Iraq. They joined the Project on a New American Century, a conservative group organized by William Kristol and Robert Kagan in 1997, which had a regime change in Baghdad as one of its primary goals. In a letter dated January 26, 1998, to President Clinton, they asserted that the Saddam Hussein regime represented "a threat more serious than any we have known since the end of the Cold War," and that the policy of containment of Iraq was steadily eroding.

> Given the magnitude of the threat, the current policy, which depends for its success upon the steadfastness of our coalition partners and upon the cooperation of Saddam Hussein, is dangerously inadequate. The only acceptable strategy is one that eliminates the possibility that Iraq will be able to use or threaten to use

weapons of mass destruction. In the near term, this means a willingness to undertake military action as diplomacy is clearly failing. In the long term, it means removing Saddam Hussein and his regime from power. That now needs to become the aim of American foreign policy. We urge you to articulate this aim, and to turn your Administration's attention to implementing a strategy for removing Saddam Hussein from power. . . .We believe the U.S. has the authority under existing UN resolutions to take the necessary steps, including military steps, to protect our vital interests in the Gulf. In any case, American policy cannot continue to be crippled by a misguided insistence on unanimity in the UN Security Council.[1]

The Iraq issue came up at the first meeting of the new administration's National Security Council, and at its second meeting Secretary of Defense Rumsfeld raised the issue of removing Saddam Hussein from power. He also cut off Secretary of State Colin Powell when he tried to discuss new sanctions strategies.[2] Thus, even prior to the terrorist attacks on New York and Washington, Baghdad was high on the foreign policy agenda of many top officials in the new administration, but initially it also had to compete with other top policy priorities, including enactment of a major tax cut.

The president's daily briefing on August 6, 2001, included a memo from Richard Clarke, counterterrorism adviser to the National Security Council, "Bin Laden Determined to Strike in U.S.," which began, "Clandestine, foreign government, and media reports indicate Bin Laden since 1997 has wanted to conduct terrorist attacks in the US." The memo went on to state, "We have not been able to corroborate some of the more sensational threat reporting, such as that from a [deleted] services in 1998 saying that Bin Laden wanted to hijack a US aircraft to gain a release of 'Blind Shayak' Umar Abd al-Rahman and other US-held extremists. Nevertheless, FBI information since that time indicates patterns of suspicious activity in this country consistent with preparations for hijackings or other types of attack, including recent surveillance of federal buildings in New York." The memo would appear to have validated the last-day briefings on major national security challenges by the outgoing Clinton administration, but it did not precipitate any extraordinary action by the administration, not even additional serious efforts to tighten airport security. Nor had policymakers been moved by an earlier memo, five days after the inauguration, from Clarke stating, "We *urgently* need a principals level review of the al Qida network." That memo included two attachments: "Strategy for Eliminating the Threat from the Jihadist Network of al-Qida: Status and Prospects" and "Pol-Mil Plan for al-Qida."[3]

Samuel Johnson once observed that "when a man knows he is to be hanged in a fortnight, it concentrates his mind wonderfully"; the September 11 terrorist attacks had a similar effect on the United States and its leaders. The immediate problems were dealing with the al Qaeda terrorist organization responsible for the 9/11 attacks and the Taliban regime in Afghanistan that had provided a home and base for al Qaeda. Even during the earliest discussions of a strategy for Afghanistan, owing to their conviction that Saddam Hussein had close ties to al Qaeda and had been involved in the 9/11 terrorist attacks, some top officials, including Cheney and Wolfowitz, proposed that Iraq should also targeted. Although the president agreed that al Qaeda and Afghanistan should take priority, he also asked Richard Clarke to conduct a thorough search for any evidence linking Saddam Hussein to the terrorist attacks. The events of 9/11 thus served to place Iraq in the crosshairs of administration policy targets. According to Wolfowitz, in a meeting on September 13 with the president, Rumsfeld, and others, the debate was not about *whether* but *when* to attack—whether to respond immediately or to concentrate on Afghanistan first.[4] The following day, Congress passed a "Joint Resolution to Authorize the Use of United States Armed Forces against Those Responsible for the Recent Attacks Launched against the United States." The votes authorizing the president to take military action against any nation, organization, or persons that had been involved in the 9/11 attacks were 420–1 in the House and 98–0 in the Senate.

The day after the 9/11 attacks, the United States spurned offers for military assistance from NATO defense ministers, who had invoked Article 5 of that treaty—a stipulation that an attack on one is an attack on all—for the first time since the alliance was formed in 1949. In making the unprecedented offer of assistance on such short notice, the NATO allies expended considerable political capital. Apparently acting on the belief that the costs of having to coordinate operations with allies outweighed the benefits of additional troops on the ground, Secretary of Defense Rumsfeld rebuffed NATO. As he put it, "The mission determines the coalition, the coalition does not determine the mission." Whether that was a sensible response from a narrow short-term military viewpoint is perhaps open to debate, but from a longer-term political perspective that rather brusque rejection came to haunt the United States in later years when Washington sought additional troops from allies to cope with a seriously deteriorating situation in Afghanistan. Despite the rebuff, Great Britain and Germany in fact deployed some forces to Afghanistan.

The American campaign against Afghanistan was a short-term military success. Congress passed a joint resolution backing tactical strikes in

Afghanistan on October 7. Operation Enduring Freedom, conducted by American Special Operations Forces and CIA personnel rather than conventional army and marine units, was initiated on October 7 and successfully overturned the Taliban regime in Kabul within five weeks. Taliban forces evacuated Kabul on November 12, but Osama bin Laden and many of his top al Qaeda lieutenants eluded capture, apparently finding a haven in the rugged terrain of the frontier region between Afghanistan and Pakistan. Shortly after the fall of Kabul, bin Laden appeared to have been located in Tora Bora, a complex of caves in the White Mountains of Afghanistan near the Khyber Pass. There are somewhat conflicting reports about how and why bin Laden escaped, with blame variously attributed to the Northern Alliance troops that joined the United States, United Kingdom, and Germany in the battle against the Taliban and al Qaeda, and the CIA. In any case, just as the British learned during their failed nineteenth-century foray into Afghanistan (1839–42) and the Soviets discovered after their invasion of that country in 1978, the fall of Kabul did not also ensure effective control of the entire country, as Taliban forces continued the fight in other provinces. The United Nations Security Council thereafter established the International Security Assistance Force (ISAF) in December, thus providing a significant international component to the continuing conflict in Afghanistan.

By two important standards, the initial phase of the Afghanistan campaign was a military success. The fall of Kabul drove the Taliban from power in the capital city, and this goal was achieved with very limited loss of American lives. The fear that American aircraft might be vulnerable to Taliban Stinger missiles, originally provided by the United States to anti-Soviet forces and which had wrought havoc with the Soviet invaders during their long (1978–89) but ultimately fruitless effort to control Afghanistan, proved to be misplaced as the United States did not lose any aircraft during the conflict.

With the apparent success of the Afghanistan campaign, the Iraq issue moved to the top of the administration's foreign policy agenda. Before the end of the year, for example, some top CIA experts on the region who had been dealing with Afghanistan-related issues were reassigned to focus on Iraq. According to Robert Grenier, former director of the CIA's counterintelligence center, throughout late 2002 and early 2003, "the best experienced, most qualified people who we had been using in Afghanistan shifted over to Iraq."[5] At the same time, Task Force Five, the 150 Special Operations Forces troops who were assigned to hunt down bin Laden, were moved to Iraq, while another 150 SOF troops were reduced to 30.

Secretary of Defense Rumsfeld wielded his immense influence within the administration to ensure that the United States would not become involved in nation-building activities in Afghanistan. According to Ryan Crocker, the first U.S. ambassador in Kabul after the war, the Pentagon view was, "Our job is done. Let's get out of here. We got rid of the evil and we should not get stuck." In contrast, Colin Powell wanted American troops to help ISAF expand its activities beyond the capital, a proposal that Rumsfeld shot down. Instead, the American strategy relied on Afghan warlords, whose 45,000 troops were on the CIA payroll. The effect of legitimating the warlords was to marginalize the Karzai government in Kabul. When President Bush, who hitherto had shown limited enthusiasm for nation-building, proposed a Marshall Plan for Afghanistan in a 2002 speech at the Virginia Military Institute (from which George Marshall graduated in 1901), the idea died for lack of support from Rumsfeld. Indeed, the defense secretary closed down the army's Peacekeeping Institute at Carlisle Barracks, its only nation-building training facility.[6] At a press conference in President Karzai's office in Kabul on May 1, 2003, Rumsfeld all but claimed a complete victory, asserting, "We clearly have moved from major combat activity to a period of stability and stabilization and reconstruction activities. The bulk of the country today is permissive, it's secure."[7]

In November 2001, the president directed Secretary of Defense Rumsfeld and General Tommy Franks, who was in charge of Central Command, to begin reviewing and developing a plan for war against Iraq. None of the other top leaders were informed of the president's order until December 28, when Franks briefed the National Security Council.[8]

The triumphalist mood generated by the successful military operation in Afghanistan was reflected in a column by an administration cheerleader and proponent of American unilateralism in a unipolar world. In a cheerful obituary for NATO, syndicated columnist Charles Krauthammer wrote, "The proximal cause of NATO's death was victory in Afghanistan—a swift and crushing U.S. victory that made clear America's military dominance and Europe's consequent military irrelevance."[9] The implications for any action against Iraq were clear: Allies might be nice if they don't get in the way too much, but they are hardly a necessity and certainly not to be taken seriously with respect to any important policy issues. Such sentiments also lay behind Secretary of Defense Rumsfeld's repeated prewar jibes directed at France, Germany, and other NATO allies—he described them as "old Europe," "chocolate makers," and "least helpful" countries in dealing with terrorism—as well as any other countries that failed to toe Washington's policy line on Iraq.

The most explicit public harbinger of American policy toward Iraq emerged from President Bush's 2002 State of the Union address in which he identified Iraq, along with Iran and North Korea, as an "axis of evil": "By seeking weapons of mass destruction, these regimes pose a grave and growing danger. They could provide these arms to terrorists, giving them the means to match their hatred. They could attack our allies or attempt to blackmail the United States."[10] His speech inaugurated a period of increasingly explicit signals that the issue of Iraq had moved to the very top of the administration's foreign policy agenda. Later that year, President Bush released the 2002 version of the National Security Strategy. Arguing that traditional theories of defense were no longer valid in light of threats arising from rogue regimes and terrorist organizations, the NSS essentially abandoned the twin pillars of Cold War defense policy—deterrence and containment—and replaced them with a forward-looking strategy that included preemptive strikes against hostile states and terrorist groups in any cases of *suspected threat,* as well as the need to maintain such a substantial military superiority that others would not seek to compete in that realm. Although the NSS used the term *preemptive,* in fact it proposed a policy of *preventive* war—the right to initiate a war for reasons of its own choosing. The right of self-defense has long been accepted in international law, and it is, in fact, embedded in Article 51 of the United Nations Charter, but in order to undertake preemptive use of military force, the threat must be massive, imminent, and permit no time for alternative responses.[11]

Second, the NSS asserted that the United States should expand development aid and actively promote democratic regime change, especially in the Middle East, to combat the threat of terrorism, and if necessary to do so unilaterally without the approval of the UN Security Council or other international bodies. It was also clear that *only* the United States had the right to act preemptively; the same privilege did not extend to Pakistan, India, China, or other countries that might come to perceive significant threats to *their* vital interests. Indeed, the United States warned other countries not to "use preemption as a pretext for aggression." The premise was that because American interests and global interests were identical, the United States was exempt from the rules and norms that it was prepared to enforce upon other countries. Nevertheless, India believed that Bush's new policy of preemption gave it the right to take unilateral action against Pakistan.[12]

Table 2.1, a chronology of some key events prior to and during the course of the Iraq War, provides a backdrop for the survey data presented in the next several sections of this chapter. Aside from identifying some major developments in the long conflict, it provides a very rough way of assessing how public perceptions and evaluations of the war reflected the course of events surrounding the war. The concluding chapter will revisit this issue in addressing the long-standing debate between those who depict public opinion as largely mindless and volatile owing to widespread ignorance and apathy about foreign affairs and others who adhere to the thesis that even a poorly informed public can, in the aggregate, respond with sensible judgments about public affairs—what one analyst has dubbed the "low information rationality" thesis.[13]

As noted in the introduction, the Iraq War gave rise to an unprecedented number of surveys by a large number of polling organizations. In order to avoid becoming captive to the sampling designs, question wording, or other features of any single survey, the results reported here draw upon responses to multiple polls whenever possible. Although some of the most frequently asked questions asked respondents to assess President Bush's policies and decisions on Iraq—for example, "Do you approve or disapprove of President Bush's handling of the Iraq War?"—these are deliberately excluded here in order to avoid, as much as possible, conflating views on the war and judgments about the president.[14]

DID THE UNITED STATES DO THE RIGHT THING IN IRAQ?

Following the invasion of Iraq in 2003, many polling organizations—including the Gallup Organization, the Program on International Policy Attitudes (PIPA), the Pew Research Center, CBS News/New York Times, ABC News/Washington Post, NBC/Wall Street Journal, CNN, and Newsweek—regularly asked the public about the propriety of the U.S. action, in each case using slightly different phrasing. One of the iron laws of survey research is that responses tend to be highly sensitive to wording of the questions; a corollary to that law is that when differently worded questions about an issue yield essentially similar responses, the results are more likely to be robust.

During the period between the September 11 attacks and the invasion of Iraq 18 months later, the public was regularly asked whether the United States should use force to effect a regime change in Baghdad. When the question of removing Saddam Hussein from power was posed as a "support" or "oppose" choice, the results were exceptionally consistent—every survey yielded a majority that would support the use of force to topple Saddam's government. As usual, variations in the precise wording of the questions affected the results, but only enough to change the size of the majority that favored removing Saddam Hussein, not the majority itself.

TABLE 2.1.   Chronology of Key Events concerning the Iraq War, 2001–10

January 31	2001	First cabinet meeting of Bush administration takes up issue of removing Saddam Hussein from power.
January 29	2002	President Bush's State of the Union Address identifies Iraq as part of the "axis of evil."
June 1	2002	President Bush's address at West Point justifies preemptive action against those who may harbor aggressive designs against the United States ("Bush doctrine").
August 26	2002	Vice President Dick Cheney tells VFW convention, "Simply stated, there is no doubt that Saddam Hussein now has WMDs."
September 4	2002	Bush administration begins campaign to gain congressional and allied support for the use of force against Iraq.
September 27	2002	Secretary of Defense Rumsfeld states that the U.S. has solid evidence of links between al-Qaeda and Iraq.
October 10–11	2002	By votes of 296–133 (House) and 77–23 (Senate), Congress backs the use of military force against Iraq.
November 8	2002	UN Security Council passes Resolution 1441 demanding that Iraq readmit UN inspectors to determine whether Iraq is in compliance with the 1991 agreements to dispose of WMDs.
February 5	2003	Secretary of State Colin Powell addresses UN Security Council, stating the U.S. is in possession of incontrovertible evidence that Iraq is in violation of the prohibition against WMDs.
February 25	2003	Army Chief of Staff Eric Shinseki tells Congress that "several hundred thousand troops" would be needed in postwar Iraq. Deputy Defense Secretary Paul Wolfowitz dismisses this estimate as "wildly off the mark" within days.
March 17	2003	U.S. withdraws Security Council Resolution 1442 approving the use of force against Iraq when it becomes clear that it will fail.
March 19	2003	U.S.-led invasion of Iraq begins, with support of troops from Great Britain.
March 30	2003	Defense Secretary Rumsfeld states on ABC *This Week,* "We know where Iraqi WMDs are."
April 9	2003	Baghdad falls to U.S. forces, but Saddam Hussein escapes.
April 23	2003	USAID administrator Andrew Nastios claims Iraq reconstruction will cost U.S. $1.7 billion.
May 1	2003	President Bush declares successful end of hostilities in Iraq ("Mission accomplished").
May 9	2003	Paul Wolfowitz: "We settled on [WMDs as the core reason to go to war because] everyone could agree."
July 2	2003	When asked about insurgents opposing U.S. occupation President Bush replies, "Bring them on."
July 11	2003	National Security Advisor Rice: If there were doubts about Iraq intelligence, they "were not communicated to the President."

(continues)

TABLE 2.1.—*Continued*

August 20	2003	UN headquarters in Baghdad bombed with heavy loss of life, includes Sergio Vierira de Mello, UN representative in Iraq.
September 3	2003	Secret report for the Joint Chiefs of Staff blames Iraq setbacks on flawed and rushed war-planning process.
September 9	2003	Colin Powell calls his February 5, 2003, speech to the UN "a blot, it was painful."
October 2	2003	David Kay, in a preliminary report to Congress, states that his inspection team failed to find WMDs in Iraq.
November 6	2003	President Bush declares that the spread of democracy to the Middle East is a vital American interest and that success in Iraq is a key part of achieving that goal.
December 9	2003	Paul Wolfowitz bars France, Germany, Canada, Mexico, Russia, and China from bids on Iraq reconstruction contracts.
December 13	2003	Saddam Hussein captured.
January 28	2004	Following his resignation, David Kay tells Congress, "We were almost all wrong" because there is no evidence that Iraq had stockpiled WMDs prior to U.S.-led invasion.
April 28 and 30	2004	*Sixty Minutes II* and *New Yorker* reveal photographic evidence of abuse of Iraqi prisoners at Abu Ghraib prison by American military personnel.
June 16	2004	9/11 Commission finds there is "no credible evidence that Iraq and al Qaeda cooperated on attacks against the U.S."
July 9	2004	Senate Intelligence Committee blames CIA and intelligence community for poor intelligence on Iraqi WMDs.
June 28	2004	U.S. hands over power to interim Iraqi government.
September 7	2004	Death toll of U.S. soldiers in Iraq reaches 1,000.
August 24	2004	Schlesinger Report blames all levels of command, up to the Pentagon, for "brutality and purposeless sadism" at Abu Ghraib prison.
September 16	2004	In response to an intelligence report warning of a civil war, the president states that the CIA is "just guessing."
September 30	2004	Report of the Iraq survey group, headed by Charles Duelfer, confirms Kay Report findings and states that Iraq's efforts to gain WMDs were aimed at Iran.
November	2004	U.S.-led counterinsurgency operation takes control of Fallujah, but most insurgency leaders escape.
November 2	2004	President Bush wins reelection.
December 20	2004	President Bush acknowledges that insurgents are having a significant effect but vows that planned January 2005 elections will be conducted as scheduled.
January 13	2005	Iraq survey group formally calls off its two searches for WMDs.

TABLE 2.1.—*Continued*

January 30	2005	Election turnout in Iraq is quite impressive—almost 60 percent—and exceeds that figure in Kurdish and Shiite areas.
March 31	2005	Silberman-Robb Commission concludes, "The intelligence community was dead wrong in almost all of its prewar judgments."
May 30	2005	Vice President Cheney declares insurgency is in "its last throes."
October 15	2005	Iraqis vote to ratify the draft constitution for an Islamic federal democracy with 79% support.
October 19	2005	Saddam Hussein goes on trial on charges of crimes against humanity.
October 26	2005	American military death toll in Iraq reaches 2,000.
November 15	2005	U.S. Senate votes 79–19 to demand regular reports from White House on progress toward phased withdrawal of U.S. troops.
November 18	2005	Representative John Murtha (D.PA) calls for troop withdrawal from Iraq.
November 30	2005	President Bush unveils "Plan for Victory" theme for Iraq. *National Strategy for Victory in Iraq* released by White House.
December 15	2005	The Iraqi people elect the first full-term government and parliament since the US-led invasion, with minimal violence.
December 18	2005	President Bush: "Much of the intelligence [on Iraq] turned out to be wrong."
January 20	2006	Shia-led United Iraqi Alliance emerges as the winner of December's parliamentary elections, although it failed to win an absolute majority.
February 2	2006	Defense Secretary Rumsfeld doubts "long war" in Iraq.
February 22	2006	Iraq's Golden Mosque in Samarra is badly damaged in a bomb attack that prompts a wave of sectarian violence.
February 28	2006	Report reveals that the administration never drew up a comprehensive plan for rebuilding Iraq.
March 19	2006	President Bush promises to "finish the mission" in "complete victory." Newly reelected president Talabani asks Shia compromise candidate Nuri al-Maliki to form a new government, breaking a four-month deadlock.
June 7	2006	Abu Masab al-Zarqawi, the al Qaeda leader in Iraq, is killed in an air strike.
June 20	2006	Iraqi national security adviser writes that U.S. troops should be out of Iraq by the end of 2008.
July	2006	3,438 Iraqi civilians died in July.
August 21	2006	President Bush acknowledges that Iraq had "nothing" to do with 9/11 and asserts, "We're not leaving [Iraq] so long as I'm the president."

(continues)

TABLE 2.1.—*Continued*

September 11	2006	Vice President Dick Cheney states that war critics aid terrorists; that U.S. would have gone to war even if it knew that Iraq lacked WMDs.
September 23	2006	National Intelligence Estimate: "Iraq has made the overall terrorism problem worse."
September 27	2006	71% of Iraqis want U.S. to withdraw within a year, according to a World Public Opinion survey.
October 12	2006	British Army chief states, "We must quit Iraq soon or risk catastrophic consequences."
November 5	2006	Saddam Hussein is sentenced to death by hanging.
November 7	2006	Republicans lose control of House and Senate. Iraq is the most important issue for many voters. Secretary Rumsfeld dismissed the following day.
November 9	2006	Iraqi health minister reports 150,000 Iraqi civilians have been killed in the war.
November 20	2006	Iraq and Syria restore diplomatic relations after a break of nearly a quarter century.
November 24	2006	Coordinated bombings kill 138 in Sadr City, a Shiite slum of Baghdad.
December 5	2006	Defense Secretary Gates acknowledges that U.S. is not winning the Iraq War.
December 6	2006	Iraq Study Group releases report that implicitly calls for a gradual pullback of the 15 American combat brigades stationed in Iraq and reaching out diplomatically to Iran and Syria.
December 30	2006	Saddam Hussein is executed by hanging.
January 2	2007	General George Casey warns against troop escalation in Iraq.
January 3	2007	U.S. military deaths in Iraq reach 3,000.
January 10	2007	President Bush announced his intention to send an additional 21,500 troops to Iraq, most of whom would be going to Baghdad.
January 11	2007	Republican senator Chuck Hagel calls the escalation of forces in Iraq "The most serious foreign policy blunder in this country since Vietnam."
January 15	2007	Barzan Ibrahim, Saddam Hussein's half-brother, and Awad Hamed al-Bandar, the former head of the Revolutionary Court, are executed by hanging.
January 17	2007	The UN releases a report that more than 34,000 civilians were killed in violence during 2006.
February 2	2007	National Intelligence Estimate on Iraq calls situation worse than a civil war.
February 3	2007	More than 130 people are killed by a bomb in Baghdad's Sadriya market.
February 16	2007	House of Representatives opposes Iraq escalation by a vote of 246–182.

TABLE 2.1.—*Continued*

February 17	2007	Senate vote of 56–34 to rebuke President Bush on the Iraq escalation falls short of a filibuster-proof majority.
March 2	2007	Pentagon adds 7,000 more troops to Iraq "surge."
March 14	2007	Pentagon acknowledges that Iraq is in a civil war.
March 29	2007	Senate passes war spending bill with a March 2008 withdrawal requirement.
April 6	2007	Pentagon report states that there was no Saddam Hussein–al Qaeda link.
April 25	2007	House and Senate pass Iraq military funding bills with time lines. House fails to override presidential veto.
May 9	2007	Majority of Iraq's parliament sign a petition calling for the U.S. to set a timetable for withdrawal.
July 8	2007	General Powell asserts, "I tried to avoid this war."
September 10–11	2007	General David Petraeus reports to Congress on the progress achieved by the U.S. troop "surge." When asked if Iraq War is making America safer, Petraeus replies, "Sir, I don't know actually."
March 23	2008	American military death toll in Iraq reaches 4,000.
April 9–11	2008	General Petraeus reports to Congress and is assured by President Bush that he will have all the troops and time needed for success in Iraq.
June 30	2008	*On Point II,* a 700-page study: "The U.S. Army says that while it was capable of toppling Saddam Hussein, it was not equipped to rebuild Iraq into a functioning country."
August 22	2008	U.S. says it will withdraw combat troops from Iraqi cities by June 2009, followed by removal of all combat troops by the end of 2011, if Iraq is stable and secure.
September 9	2008	Iraq withdraws plans to award Exxon-Mobil, Shell, Total, BP, and Chevron no-bid contracts to service Iraq's oil fields.
November 27	2008	Iraqi parliament passes Status of Forces (SOF) Agreement governing U.S. presence in Iraq through 2010 by 149–35.
January 31	2009	Iraq conducts peaceful provincial elections with a 51% turnout of eligible voters.
February 27	2009	President Obama states that most U.S. forces in Iraq will be withdrawn by the summer of 2010, leaving transitional forces that will depart by 2011.
June	2009	An uptick of violence makes June the deadliest month of 2009. Violence continues through the summer.
June 30	2009	In accordance with SOF Agreement of November 2008, U.S. military forces withdraw from Baghdad and other major cities.
December 6	2009	Iraqi government agrees on rules for the 2010 parliamentary elections, originally scheduled for January 16. Iraqis living in exile (mostly Sunnis) will gain additional representation.

(continues)

TABLE 2.1.—*Continued*

January 14	2010	Approximately 500 politicians disqualified by Iraq's Independent High Election Commission for illegal ties to Baath Party.
January 23	2010	Vice President Biden visits Iraq to encourage settlement of disputes that threaten elections scheduled for March 7.
January 23	2010	U.S. Marines begin pullout from Iraq, handing over duties to U.S. Army.
March 7	2010	Iraq's parliamentary election results in narrow victory for former interim prime minister Ayad Allawi's Iraqiya Party over incumbent prime minister Nuri al-Maliki's State of Law Party. Neither was close to a majority in the 325-seat parliament.
March–April	2010	Postelection bombings and charges of fraud by both al-Maliki and Allawi.
July 4–5	2010	Vice President Biden visits Baghdad but is unable to persuade Iraqi leaders to form a government.
August 2	2010	President Obama announces end of U.S. combat role and withdrawal of combat forces "on schedule."
August 31	2010	U.S. combat brigades withdraw from Iraq, leaving about 50,000 "non-combat troops" for training purposes.
November 2	2010	Two days after attacks by al Qaeda-linked groups on Christians killed 58, attacks on predominantly Shiite targets in Baghdad killed more than 100.
November 11	2010	Eight months after the March elections, a government is formed, keeping Nuri al-Maliki in office for a second term as Prime Minister.

When respondents were asked whether their support for military action was contingent on support from the UN Security Council, U.S. allies in NATO, or both, however, a somewhat more nuanced picture of public preferences appeared. Table 2.2 presents some evidence from Gallup and Pew surveys undertaken during the two years prior to the invasion as well as an earlier survey in 1992. The Gallup data indicate that the preference for action to effect a regime change in Baghdad dates back to the aftermath of the Gulf War (March 1992), and it also preceded the September 11 attacks (February 2001). Later surveys found majorities ranging between 59 percent and 74 percent in favor of military action versus Iraq. Six of the nine Pew surveys also asked advocates of military action whether their support was conditional on the support of major allies or whether they favored acting "even if allies won't join"; in none of these surveys did the "go it alone" option gain a majority. In the mid-March 2003 poll, just days before the invasion, more than a quarter of the 59 percent who favored military action conditioned their approval on the agreement of major allies to join the effort. None of the surveys asked whether the full support of Tony Blair's government in Britain qualified as sufficient assistance from major allies.

The Pew survey results were reinforced by responses to CBS/*New York Times* polls. Fourteen surveys undertaken between February 2002 and March 2003 revealed that majorities ranging from 64 to 74 percent expressed approval in response to a question about "the United States taking military action against Iraq to try and remove Saddam Hussein from power." Three polls during the month prior to the Iraq invasion also found support, ranging from 56 to 70 percent, for the proposition that "the U.S. should take into account the view

TABLE 2.2. Support for the Invasion of Iraq with or without Allies, 1992–2003 (percent responses)

	Mar. 13–16, 2003	Feb. 2003	Jan. 2003	Dec. 2002	Nov. 2002	Late Oct. 2002	Early Oct. 2002	Sept. 2002	Aug. 2002	June 2002	Nov. 2001	Feb. 2001	Mar. 1992
Would you favor or oppose taking military action in Iraq to end Saddam Hussein's rule? If favor, should we attack Iraq only if our major allies agree to join us, or attack Iraq even if allies do not want to join us?													
Favor	59	66	68	65	62	55	62	64	64	59	74	52	55
Even if allies won't join	38	38	26			27		33	30				
Only if allies agree	16	22	37			23		25	30				
Don't know/ refused	5	6	5			5		6	4				
Opposed	30	26	25	25	26	34	28	23	21	34	20	42	40
Don't know/ refused	11	8	7	10	12	11	10	13	15	7	6	6	5

Source: March 1992–June 2002: Gallup; August 2002–March 2003: Pew Research Center.

Gallup wording: "Would you favor or oppose sending American troops back to the Persian Gulf in order to remove Saddam Hussein from power in Iraq?"

When it comes to Iraq, do you think the United States should do what it thinks is right no matter what its allies think, or should the U.S. take into account the view of allies before taking action?

	Mar. 7–9, 2003	Mar. 4–5, 2003	Feb. 24–25, 2003
Do what it thinks is right	36	38	27
Take allies into account	60	56	70
Don't know/no answer	4	6	3

Source: CBS/*New York Times* surveys.

of allies before taking action" against Iraq. More broadly, these survey findings are consistent with the thesis that even among the majority of Americans who favor an active U.S. role in world affairs, "burden sharing" is more attractive than a solo leadership role.

The American-led war against Iraq started on March 19 with an airstrike at a farm where Saddam Hussein was believed to be hiding. The intelligence about his location turned out to be incorrect as he had not visited there since 1995. The land invasion began soon thereafter. Although some analysts had feared that Saddam Hussein might inflict heavy casualties on invading American and British forces by using chemical or other weapons of mass destruction, he did not employ any WMDs. Given his record of using chemical weapons during the Iran-Iraq War, Saddam's failure to do so in this instance might have been an early indication that he did not in fact possess such weapons.[15] The military operations were successful, culminating in the capture of Baghdad and the expulsion of the Baathist regime in less than three weeks. As had been the case in the Gulf War against Iraq twelve years earlier, American casualties were lower than many had feared. Public responses to the invasion were highly favorable, reaching a peak of 74 percent who described it as the "right thing" shortly after President Bush's declaration in early May that hostilities in Iraq had come to a successful end and that the mission of overthrowing the Baathist regime had been accomplished, even though Saddam Hussein had managed to avoid capture.[16] As summarized in figure 2.1, responses to two somewhat differently worded questions about whether the United States had done the "right thing" by invading Iraq in surveys by Pew, CBS/*New York Times*, and a more general question about support for the war (CNN) essentially followed a similar trajectory.

Judgments about the wisdom of American policy in Iraq declined somewhat during the remainder of 2003. Almost immediately after the fall of Baghdad, L. Paul Bremer III, chief of the Coalition Provisional Authority, disbanded the Iraqi army, thereby throwing several hundred thousand young men, many of them Sunnis, out of work. In addition, Bremer dismissed government employees who were members of the Baath party, even though many had joined only because party membership was a prerequisite for most government positions. The de-Baathification policy crippled the ability of the government to provide some of the most basic services. Some of the Iraqi insurgents who continued to resist the occupying American forces were almost certainly disgruntled, unemployed members of the former Iraqi military who took their military training and weapons with them.

Top American officials who had predicted prior to the war that the U.S. in-

FIG. 2.1. Assessments of the War in Iraq: Did the U.S. Do the Right Thing in Taking Military Action against Iraq? (2003–10)

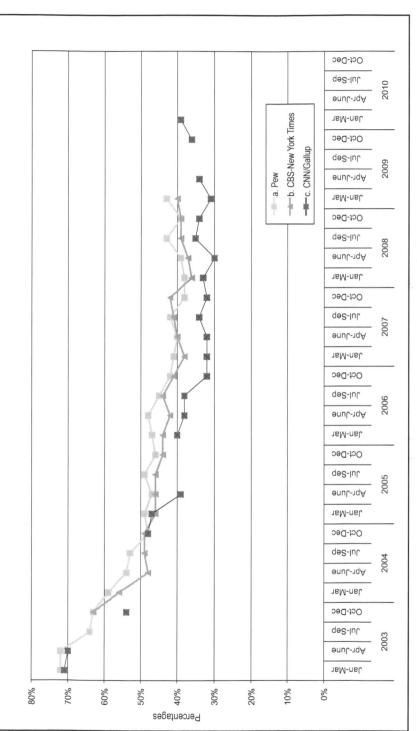

The questions were (a) "Do you think the U.S. made the right decision or the wrong decision in using military force against Iraq?" (% "right decision"); (b) "Looking back, do you think the U.S. did the right thing in taking military action against Iraq, or should the U.S. have stayed out?" (% "right thing"); (c) "Do you favor or oppose the U.S. war with Iraq?" (% favor).

vaders would be greeted as liberators were inclined to dismiss the importance of the developing insurgency. On June 18, Secretary of Defense Rumsfeld stated, "In those regions where pockets of dead enders are trying to reconstitute, General Franks and his team are routing them out." On the same day, his top deputy, Paul Wolfowitz, asserted, "I think these people are the last remnants of a dying cause."[17] Although those rosy assessments of the situation on the ground in Iraq proved to be somewhat less than prescient, as late as December 2003 supporters of the invasion generally outnumbered the naysayers by margins of about three-to-two or better. It is worth noting that the capture in mid-December of the hated Saddam Hussein in a "spider hole" near his hometown Tikrit was reflected almost immediately by an uptick of public approval for the Iraq invasion. For example, Pew and *Newsweek* surveys undertaken less than a week after Saddam's capture both revealed that "right thing" responses increased by 7 percent—to 67 and 62 percent, respectively—over the immediately preceding polls.

The Iraqi insurgency, which was especially active in the Sunni Triangle area of central Iraq that includes Baghdad and Fallujah, showed few signs of abating during the next three years. A record 147 American military personnel were killed or reported killed by insurgents in April 2004, a toll almost matched seven months later when U.S. forces retook the city of Fallujah. Favorable public judgments of the Iraq undertaking declined slowly rather than precipitously throughout 2004; they fell to just below 50 percent in some surveys, whereas others revealed slight majorities who judged that the United States had done the "right thing" when it used military force against Iraq.

Americans were not alone in expressing declining support for the war, as most publics abroad were even more critical. Great Britain was America's closest ally in the invasion of Iraq, but by a margin of 53 to 39 percent, British respondents to a 2005 Pew Research survey judged that London had made "the wrong decision" in using military forces against Iraq. Conversely, publics in countries that *refused* to join the U.S. invasion of Iraq asserted that their governments had made the "right decision" in staying out of the conflict, according to Pew surveys during 2003 through 2005. That was the case in NATO allies Canada (80 percent "right decision"), Germany (87 percent), France (92 percent), and Turkey (81 percent); in 12 other countries the "right decision" responses ranged from 63 percent in Pakistan to 96 percent in Brazil. There is also evidence that widespread opposition to American policy among leaders abroad, even during the months prior to the 2003 invasion, had an impact on American publics, especially Democrats and independents.[18]

By mid-2005, the number of respondents who approved of the military action in Iraq had fallen below 50 percent in all three surveys summarized in figure 2.1, and that figure fell further the following year. Although supporters of the war remained in the minority, a slight improvement in mid-2007 coincided with the president's announcement of a "surge" in the number of U.S. troops to be deployed in the Baghdad area and the appointment of the highly respected General David Petraeus as the top American officer in Iraq.

The highly unpopular defense secretary Rumsfeld left the Pentagon the day after the 2006 congressional elections that cost the Republicans their majorities in both the House and Senate. As Rumsfeld had been the architect and vocal defender of the invasion plan, his departure eased the way for the belated recognition that the Iraq invasion had been initiated with insufficient forces to deal with the post-Saddam situation. In his view, the capture of Baghdad in less than three weeks confirmed the wisdom of his strategy, and he seemed unwilling to confront any evidence questioning that plan. By 2006 a number of retired generals, including Paul Eaton, Gregory Newbold, John Batiste, Charles Swannack, Anthony Zinni, and John Riggs, went public with their critiques of Rumsfeld. Not only was Rumsfeld unpopular among the military officers with whom he had worked, but he also received mediocre and declining performance ratings from the general public. For example, three Fox News/Opinion Dynamics surveys found that the defense secretary's job rating, an unimpressive 44 percent in April 2005, fell to 40 percent in December and further to 35 percent in April 2006. Moreover, by a margin of 57 percent to 40 percent, the public thought it was appropriate for the retired generals to criticize Rumsfeld and to call for his resignation in public. The president was not amused. "I hear the voices and I read the front pages and I know the speculation. But I am the decider and I decide what is best. And what is best is for Don Rumsfeld to remain as Secretary of Defense."[19]

General Petraeus told Congress in mid-September 2007 that despite continuing political problems the security situation in Iraq had improved significantly since the "surge" and that it was premature to consider any major withdrawal of U.S. forces at that time.[20] Table 2.3 summarizes data on U.S. military casualties (deaths and seriously wounded) since the March 2003 invasion of Iraq. Although 2007 was the costliest year of the war for the American military, it also marked a turning point toward lower casualties.

By 2008–9 it was clear that the increased number of troops, combined with a major change in strategy that emphasized protecting Iraqi civilians rather than actively seeking out and fighting insurgents, was improving the situation in Iraq. In none of the surveys summarized in figure 2.1, however, did a majority of the American public express the view that the use of force against Iraq had been the "right thing." Despite evidence of declining violence in Iraq, most of those responding to Pew and CBS/*New York Times* surveys continued to express doubts on that score, and the level of support among those taking part in the CNN surveys remained well below 40 percent.

HOW WELL IS THE WAR GOING?

The American invasion of Iraq was based on two elements of "worst case" analysis—that Saddam Hussein possessed weapons of mass destruction and that, because he had had intimate ties to the al Qaeda terrorist organization that had carried out the September 11 attacks on New York and Washington, Saddam was also complicit in those attacks. The former belief was not wholly

TABLE 2.3. U.S. Military Deaths and Seriously Wounded in Iraq, 2003–10

Year	Deaths	Seriously Wounded
2003: March 19–June	206	750
July–December	290	1,666
2004: January–June	376	3,223
July–December	473	4,782
2005: January–June	420	2,959
July–December	426	2,985
2006: January–June	354	2,466
July–December	468	3,954
2007: January–June	576	3,852
July–December	328	2,256
2008: January–June	198	1,448
July–December	115	598
2009: January–June	101	
July–December	49	676[a]
2010: January–December	60	391
Totals	4,440	32,006

Source: Iraq Coalition Casualty Count, www.uscasualties.org; and Brookings Institution, *Iraq Index.* Slightly different counts appear in U.S. Casualties in Iraq, www.global.securities.org/militaries/Iraq_ca sualties.htm; and the Associated Press.

[a]Total for January–December 2009.

implausible, given Saddam's past record of using chemical weapons during the long Iraq-Iran war and his less than forthright conduct with United Nations inspectors who sought to determine whether Iraq was in full compliance with the post–Gulf War restrictions on WMDs and certain other types of weapons. But there is also evidence that top Bush administration officials were firmly wedded to that belief and were quite impervious in their decision-making processes to any signs that might call it into question, as these examples show.

"The starting point for all the agencies was recognition that Saddam was a threat. No one in any top-level interagency meeting disputed that Saddam had dangerous WMD programs and connections to terrorist groups."

"Those individuals, notably in the State Department and CIA, that did not fully support the plan to invade Iraq or raised questions that exposed weaknesses in the plan were seen as undermining the administration's ability to deal with the immediate threat."

"During this period [November 2001–March 2003], Rumsfeld and the Central Command commander at the time, General Tommy Franks, gave the president a dozen detailed briefings on the invasion plan. Every meeting was about *how* to go to war. There was no meeting to discuss *whether* to go to war. The president had never questioned its rightness and its rightness made it the only course."

"The whole atmosphere too often resembled a royal court, with Cheney and Rice in attendance, some upbeat stories, exaggerated good news, and good time had by all."[21]

The alleged ties between Baghdad and al Qaeda rested on much shakier foundations. While politics can indeed make strange bedfellows, nowhere more often than in the Middle East, collaboration between the Sunni-dominated secular regime in Baghdad and the fundamentalist terror organization led by Osama bin Laden should have been a hypothesis to be explored rather than a firm article of faith, especially as the basis on which to go to war. Although administration claims that Mohamed Atta, one of the 9/11 hijackers, had met with Iraqi officials in Prague could not be confirmed by American intelligence, Dick Cheney told audiences on *Sixty Minutes* (November 14, 2001) and *Meet the Press*

(December 9, 2001) that such a meeting had taken place. Later intelligence, based on telephone and other records, revealed that in fact Atta had been in the United States at the time of the alleged meeting.

In an attempt to buttress its case a few months after the invasion, the office of undersecretary of defense for policy Douglas J. Feith leaked a report about Saddam and Iraq to a reliable prowar administration supporter, the *Weekly Standard* magazine. An article by one of its staff writers, Stephen F. Hayes, used the report to assert that the case detailing cooperation between Saddam and Osama bin Laden was so compelling as to be "closed." While the timing of the Feith leak may have been a coincidence, it could not have come at a more fortuitous time for the administration because the other pillar justifying the Iraq invasion—Saddam's alleged weapons of mass destruction—was about to crumble in the face of reports from two teams of American inspectors headed by David Kay and Charles Duelfer who had been in Iraq searching fruitlessly for such weapons. Moreover, a developing insurgency cast serious doubts on the conviction that the invading American troops would be welcomed as liberators by most Iraqis.

The *Weekly Standard* article is not the end of the story on Saddam–al Qaeda ties, however. Numerous committees, including the 9/11 Commission, have explored the issue without finding definitive evidence of a Saddam–al Qaeda link. In 2006, President Bush twice denied that his administration had ever tied Saddam to the terrorist attacks: "Nobody ever suggested that the attacks of September 11th were ordered by Iraq." A report from Acting Inspector General Thomas F. Gimble also discounted Iraq's alleged ties to al Qaeda.

A 2007 report by the Joint Advanced Warfighting Program of the Institute for Defense Analyses, after a thorough analysis of some 600,000 Iraqi documents captured by the invasion, "found no 'smoking gun' (i.e. direct connection) between Saddam's Iraq and al Qaeda." As noted in chapter 1, Saddam had long made use of terrorism as an instrument of policy, and he cooperated with terrorist groups when doing so could help advance Iraq's long-term goals. For example, Iraq gave financial support to families of suicide bombers in Gaza and the West Bank. Yet the search through that massive collection of Iraqi documents failed to uncover compelling evidence of strong links to al Qaeda or the 9/11 terrorist attacks.[22]

Washington also acted on two elements of "best case" analysis, bordering on "strategic romanticism," the unshakable conviction that because one's ideological preferences and reality are identical, those preferences can effectively serve as the basis for identifying policy goals and allocating resources for pursuing them. The president and his top defense policy advisers were convinced that, because Saddam Hussein was undeniably a brutal tyrant, American forces would be greeted by Iraqis as liberators rather than conquerors. The two most passionate administration advocates for the invasion of Iraq left no doubt of their conviction about how the Iraqi people would view the invading American armed forces. Paul Wolfowitz told the Veterans of Foreign Wars conference shortly before the invasion, "Like the people of France in the 1940s, they [the people of Iraq] view us as their hoped-for liberator." Just a few days later, Vice President Cheney in response to a question about post-Saddam Iraq told *Meet the Press,* "Now I think things have gotten so bad inside Iraq, from the standpoint of the Iraqi people, my belief is we will, in fact, be greeted as liberators. The read we get on the people of Iraq is there is no question but what they want to get rid of Saddam Hussein and they will welcome as liberators the United States when we come to do that." Some other advocates of the war were even more optimistic, not only about its impact on Iraq but also about its wider regional consequences. A week before the invasion was launched, Senator John McCain (R-AZ) wrote in a *New York Times* opinion article, "Isn't it more likely that antipathy toward the United States in the Islamic world might diminish amid jubilant Iraqis celebrating the end of a regime that has few equals in its ruthlessness?"[23]

A related belief guiding American planning for the war was the firm conviction that the three main groups within Iraq—Shiites, Sunnis, and Kurds—would be willing to live at peace with each other and perhaps even to cooperate following the overthrow of the Baathist regime in Baghdad, thus ensuring a relatively peaceful transition toward establishing a stable post-Saddam civic order. That premise assumed that the 20 percent Sunni minority who had controlled most if not all of the levers of power during the decades of Baathist rule would willingly share power with the 60 percent Shiite majority, and that the latter would suppress any thoughts of revenge by overlooking decades of harsh treatment and second-class citizenship at the hands of the Sunnis. It also assumed that the Kurdish minority—who had been victims of chemical warfare during the 1980s, but who had also enjoyed a good deal of autonomy after the Gulf War had resulted in a "no-fly zone" that protected them from further attacks by Saddam's forces—would be willing to subordinate their goals of autonomy (and perhaps even of independence), and to share their substantial oil resources for the sake of stability and prosperity in a postwar Iraq. Paul Wolfowitz, a University of Chicago PhD in political science, expressed the administration's views in this respect, asserting that, unlike the situations in Bosnia or Kosovo after the disintegration of Yugoslavia, which had been marked by significant ethnic-religious violence, Iraq had been free of such conflict. He also stated that "Iraqis are by and large secular and they are overwhelmingly Shia."[24] That was a remarkable assumption by an official who had served in the elder President Bush's administration during and after the Gulf War. After the 1991 cease-fire ending that conflict, Saddam Hussein's regime attacked Kurds in northern Iraq and Shiites in the southern part of the country until a no-fly zone was established and enforced by the United States to prevent such violence by the Sunni-dominated Baghdad regime against the other two major sectarian groups. It is somewhat difficult to fathom how these rather dramatic events could have slipped from his mind—except perhaps as a strategically convenient form of amnesia—when Wolfowitz was publicly dismissing the possibility of sectarian violence in a post-Saddam Iraq as part of his persistent and single-minded efforts to promote an American invasion of that country. Had that optimistic vision proved valid, it would certainly have eased the burdens on American and British forces following the fall of Baghdad. Perhaps these examples illustrate the German philosopher Friedrich Nietzsche's dictum "Convictions are more dangerous enemies of truth than lies."

Rarely has any government had more substantial prior warnings than those provided to the Bush administration about its optimistic scenario for post-Saddam Iraq. Those with a historical bent might have pondered an article by Lt. Col. (retired) T. E. Lawrence—better known as Lawrence of Arabia—about the uprising facing the British occupiers of Mesopotamia (Iraq) in 1920.

> The people of England have been led in Mesopotamia into a trap from which it will be hard to escape with dignity and honor. They have been tricked into it by a steady withholding of information. The Baghdad communiqués are belated, insincere, incomplete. Things have been far worse than we have been told, our administration more bloody and inefficient than the public knows. It is a disgrace to our imperial record, and may soon be too inflamed for any ordinary cure. We are to-day not far from disaster. . . . Our government is worse than the old Turkish system. They kept fourteen thousand local conscripts embodied, and killed a yearly average of two hundred Arabs in maintaining peace. We keep ninety thousand men, with aeroplanes, armored cars, gunboats, and armored trains. We have killed about ten thousand Arabs in this rising this summer. We cannot hope to maintain such an average: it is a poor country, sparsely peopled; but Abd el Hamid would applaud his masters, if he saw us working. We are told the object of the rising was political, we are not told what the local people want.

It may be what the Cabinet has promised them. A Minister in the House of Lords said that we must have so many troops because the local people will not enlist. On Friday the Government announced the death of some local levies defending their British officers, and say that the services of these men have not yet been sufficiently recognized because they are too few (adding the characteristic Baghdad touch that they are men of bad character). There are seven thousand of them, just half the old Turkish force of occupation. Properly officered and distributed, they would relieve half our army there. Cromer controlled Egypt's six million people with five thousand British troops; Colonel Wilson fails to control Mesopotamia's three million people with ninety thousand troops.

We have not reached the limit of our military commitments. Four weeks ago the staff in Mesopotamia drew up a memorandum asking for four more divisions. I believe it was forwarded to the War Office, which has now sent three brigades from India. If the North-West Frontier cannot be further denuded, where is the balance to come from? Meanwhile, our unfortunate troops, Indian and British, under hard conditions of climate and supply, are policing an immense area, paying dearly every day in lives for the willfully wrong policy of the civil administration in Baghdad. General Dyer was relieved of his command in India for a much smaller error, but the responsibility in this case is not on the Army, which has acted only at the request of the civil authorities. The War Office has made every effort to reduce our forces, but the decisions of the Cabinet have been against them.

We say we are in Mesopotamia to develop it for the benefit of the world. . . . How long will we permit millions of pounds, thousands of Imperial troops, and tens of thousands of Arabs to be sacrificed on behalf of a colonial administration which can benefit nobody but its administrators?"

Lawrence was not alone in his critical assessment of the situation. Winston Churchill, who was in charge of Britain's Iraq policy, wrote Prime Minister Lloyd George in 1922, "At present we are paying eight million a year for the privilege of living on an ungrateful volcano, out of which we are in no circumstances to get anything worth having." A League of Nations report dated July 16, 1925, reinforced these fears: "Despite the good intentions of the statesmen of Iraq, whose political experience is necessarily small, it is to be feared that serious difficulties may arise out of the differences which in some cases exist in regard to political ideas between the Shiites of the South and Sunnites of the North, the racial differences between Arabs and Kurds, and the necessity of keeping the turbulent tribes under control."[25]

They might also have paid attention to warnings about dealing with Middle Eastern insurgencies from French president Jacques Chirac, who served as a young officer in the bloody but ultimately unsuccessful efforts to put down the Algerian rebellion against French rule. Or, looking much further back, they might have contemplated how invading "peacekeepers" from the world's greatest empire of the time were met in one of its colonies in 1776. The obvious rejoinder to these warnings is that 2003 was not the 1770s, 1920s, or 1950s, and, more important, even at the height of their imperial glory neither Britain nor France could claim the almost universally acknowledged status of the United States prior to the Iraq War—the world's only superpower.

There were many other warnings. Two of the more visible notes of caution during the months prior to the invasion of Iraq came from top-ranking officials who had served in the elder President Bush's administration during the Gulf War and thus had extensive firsthand experience and understanding of the challenges of dealing with Saddam Hussein as well as of the uncertainties that would follow his overthrow: Brent Scowcroft and James Baker. The former national security adviser and former secretary of state published opinion articles in major national newspapers that warned about the possible adverse consequences of invading Iraq to topple the Saddam Hussein regime. This was not the first time that Scowcroft and Baker had challenged those who advocated military action to overturn the Saddam Hussein regime in Iraq. In response to the letter-writing campaign by Paul Wolfowitz and others demanding action against Iraq, both had written opinion articles in major national newspapers in 1998 supporting the strategy of containment as an effective policy for dealing with the Iraqi dictator. In their later efforts during the months prior to the invasion, they were joined by another important figure in the elder President Bush's administration: Lawrence Eagleburger.

Their views are also of special interest because of the extraordinarily close ties that they had established with the Bush family. Scowcroft had been the senior President Bush's closest adviser—so close that they wrote a joint memoir of their policy-making during the latter's presidency—and Baker had not only served as secretary of state in the elder Bush's administration, but he had also spearheaded his son's successful campaign to have the Supreme Court declare him the winner of the highly controversial 2000 presidential election. Eagleburger served as secretary of state in the closing months of the elder Bush's administration. According to Scowcroft, "there is scant evidence to tie Saddam to terrorist organizations, and even less to the September 11 attacks. Indeed Saddam's goals have little in common with the terrorists who threaten us, and there is little incentive for him to make common cause with them." Consequently, an attack on Iraq "would turn the whole region into a cauldron and destroy the War on Terror," and it would probably serve as a recruiting incentive for terrorist organizations. As a member of the Foreign Intelligence Advisory Board (FIAB), Scowcroft had access to whatever information was available on Iraq and its policies.

Baker's thesis was equally prescient. "If we are to change the regime in Iraq, we will have to occupy the country militarily. The costs of doing so politically, economically and in terms of casualties, could be great. They will be lessened if the president brings together an international coalition behind the effort. *Doing so would also help in achieving the continuing support of the American people, a necessary prerequisite for any successful foreign policy.*" These warnings fell on deaf ears among administration policymakers. Some of the president's aides referred sneeringly referred to Scowcroft as "Neville," an obvious effort to link him to the appeasing British prime minister of the late 1930s, and there is strong reason to believe that Scowcroft's article led to his later dismissal from the FIAB by the president who, upon reading the article, stated that "Scowcroft has become a pain in the ass in his old age."[26]

A study organized by the Council on Foreign Relations and headed by James R. Schlesinger and Thomas Pickering, who had served Republican presidents Nixon, Ford, and George H. W. Bush in high-ranking positions, concluded that reconstructing postwar Iraq would be far more expensive and require more troops than rosy administration estimates.[27] A 1,249-page State Department study involving scores of experts on Iraq offered ample evidence about potential difficulties that should have caused at least some second thoughts among top administration officials, but it was largely disregarded by Pentagon and White House officials who were responsible for planning and executing the invasion of Iraq. Indeed, Secretary of Defense Rumsfeld told retired lieutenant general Jay Garner, who had been selected to oversee postwar reconstruction in Iraq, to ignore the *Future of Iraq Project* report. This was but one example of Rumsfeld's continuing and largely successful efforts to marginalize the State Department and Colin Powell.[28] Reports from the National Intelligence Council to the president two months before the invasion warned that it could ignite factional violence and an anti-American insurgency and that a U.S.-led occupation could "increase popular sympathy for terrorist objectives." Similar prewar warnings emerged from the CIA, Defense Intelligence Agency, and the Army and National Guard Intelligence Center.

A study undertaken by the American Academy of Arts and Sciences also provided ample warnings about the costs and consequences of a war with Iraq, along with a depiction of policy alternatives. If a largely academic study could easily be dismissed by the administration policymakers, they might have considered a War College report, *Reconstructing Iraq: Challenges and Missions for Military Forces in a Post-Conflict Scenario*, which warned: "Long term gratitude is unlikely and suspicion U.S. motives will increase as the occupation continues. A force initially viewed as liberators can rapidly be relegated to the status of invaders should an unwelcome occupation continue for a prolonged time. Occupation problems may be especially acute if the United States must implement the bulk of the occupation itself rather than turn these duties over to a postwar international force."[29]

In an electrifying appearance before the Senate Armed Services Committee, in response to a question from Senator Carl Levin (D-MI) about military requirements for dealing with the postwar situation in Iraq, Army Chief of Staff Eric Shinseki replied, "I would say that what's been mobilized to this point, something on the order of several hundred thousand soldiers, are probably, you know, a figure that would be required. We're talking about post-hostilities control over a piece of geography that's fairly significant, with the kinds of ethnic tensions that could lead to other problems. It takes significant ground forces presence to maintain a safe and secure environment to ensure that people are fed, that water is distributed, all the normal responsibilities that go along with administering a situation like this." His assessment was not a casual "seat-of-the-pants" estimate. It was based on war games conducted by Central Command in 1999—Operation Desert Crossing—which concluded that 300,000 troops would be required, and on an Iraq War contingency plan—OPLAN 1003-90—that called for 500,000 troops.[30]

Shinseki was promptly and publicly ridiculed by top Defense Department officials Paul Wolfowitz and Donald Rumsfeld. Two days after Shinseki's testimony, Wolfowitz told the House Budget Committee, "There has been a good deal of comment—some of it quite outlandish—about what our postwar requirements might be in Iraq. Some of the higher end predictions that we have been hearing recently, such as the notion that it will take several hundred thousand U.S. troops to provide stability in post-Saddam Iraq, are wildly off the mark. . . . It is hard to conceive that it would take more forces to provide stability in post-Saddam Iraq than it would take to conduct the war and to secure the surrender of Saddam's security forces and his army—hard to imagine." He later added, "I can't imagine anyone here wanting to spend another $30 billion to be there for another 12 years." Not only did Wolfowitz assert that Shinseki's number were wildly off the mark because there were no reasons to expect postwar ethnic or sectarian violence in Iraq, but he also disputed an estimated $95 billion for costs of the war as much too high because Iraq's oil resources would cover most of the reconstruction costs. Shortly after Lawrence Lindsey, director of the National Economic Council, stated that the war would cost 100 to 200 billion dollars, he was dismissed.[31]

If that had not been a sufficiently clear message to military officers that any deviation from the administration's game plan would not be warmly received, Shinseki was subjected to further humiliation at his retirement ceremony a few months later, when neither President Bush nor Secretary of Defense Rumsfeld could spare the time to say a few words of thanks for his 38 years of military service. Paul Wolfowitz had asked to attend but Shinseki declined to invite him. In his memoirs, Rumsfeld makes the dubious assertion that no one in the military presented the case for additional troops at an important pre-invasion meeting in the Pentagon. But the defense secretary had already ruled out a post-Saddam nation-building role for the United States and he had effectively marginalized General Shinseki—who knew from his experience in Bosnia that the postwar military needs will exceed those of combat operations—by making it clear that Shinseki would not serve a second term on the Joint Chiefs. Army Secretary Thomas White, who refused to reprimand Shinseki for his testimony and had regarded the invasion of Iraq as peripheral to defeating al Qaeda, was forced to resign in April. Marine Lt. Gen. Gregory Newbold, Director of Operations (J-3) for the Joint Chiefs, who had briefed the Pentagon on the Iraq contingency plan and had privately opposed the invasion of Iraq, discreetly retired in 2002, but in 2006 made his views known as part of the "revolt of the generals."

Finally, in a private meeting with the president on August 5, 2002, Secretary of State Powell expressed his concerns about the impending invasion of Iraq. After taking down Saddam, he said, "You will become the government until you get a new government. You are going to be the proud owner of 25 million people. You will own all their hopes, aspirations, and problems. You will own it all. It's going to suck all the oxygen out of everything." Because the Iraqis had never experienced democracy, "You need to understand that this is not going to be a walk in the woods. It's nice to say that we can do it unilaterally, except you can't." Powell had earlier dismissed a plan by Iraqi exile Ahmed Chalabi to support opposition groups as a way of overthrowing the Saddam Hussein regime as "one of the most absurd, strategically unsound proposals he had ever heard," and he warned the president, "This is not as easy as it is being presented." Powell's warnings carried little weight with the president, however, compared to the optimistic post-Saddam scenarios depicted by Cheney, Rumsfeld, Wolfowitz, and other ardent proponents of the invasion. After the invasion, Cheney had a celebratory dinner with some aides and friends. "Colin always had major reservations about what we were trying to do, Cheney told the group as they toasted Bush and laughed at Powell."[32]

In short, the administration was quite impervious to warnings about the war and its aftermath. Thomas Ricks summarized the point well: "What is remarkable is that again and again during the crucial months before the invasion such warnings from experts weren't heeded—or even welcomed."

In contrast, even highly dubious intelligence *was* warmly received. The example of "Curveball" is illustrative. That was the code name assigned to Rafid Ahmed Alwan, an Iraqi citizen who defected in 1999 and eventually arrived in Germany. He claimed to be a chemical engineer with impressive academic credentials who had worked in an Iraqi plant that manufactured mobile chemical weapons. German intelligence authorities did not allow American intelligence to interview Curveball, but after many reports on him they warned the United States about the doubtful authenticity of his claims. However, his assertions seemed to reinforce the thesis that Iraq was in violation of post–Gulf War prohibitions against the acquisition of WMDs, and thus they were welcomed by the administration. Curveball's claims played an important role in Colin Powell's infamous February 5, 2003, address to the United Nations in which he laid out the "evidence" that Iraq was in possession of WMDs. Curveball admitted in 2011 that he had lied about the WMDs: "I had the chance to fabricate something to topple the regime. I and my sons are proud of that and we are proud that we were the reason to give Iraq the margin of democracy."[33]

These warnings notwithstanding, shortly after U.S. forces had predictably routed the poorly equipped and poorly led Iraqi armed forces, large majorities of 70 percent or more in several polls judged that the military effort was going well, but the onset of the insurgency during the months following the capture of Baghdad coincided with growing public skepticism on that score. As revealed in figure 2.2, although the questions posed by the Pew, Gallup, and CBS News/*New York Times* surveys were quite similar, they initially yielded some sharply different responses about how well the war was going. For example, in November 2003, about two-thirds of Pew respondents judged that the U.S. efforts were going well, but fewer than 40 percent of those polled by CBS/*New York Times* responded similarly.

The capture of Saddam Hussein on December 13, 2003, gave rise to increased optimism about the success of the Iraq undertaking, but that proved to

FIG. 2.2. Assessments of the War in Iraq: Is the War Going Well? (2003–9)

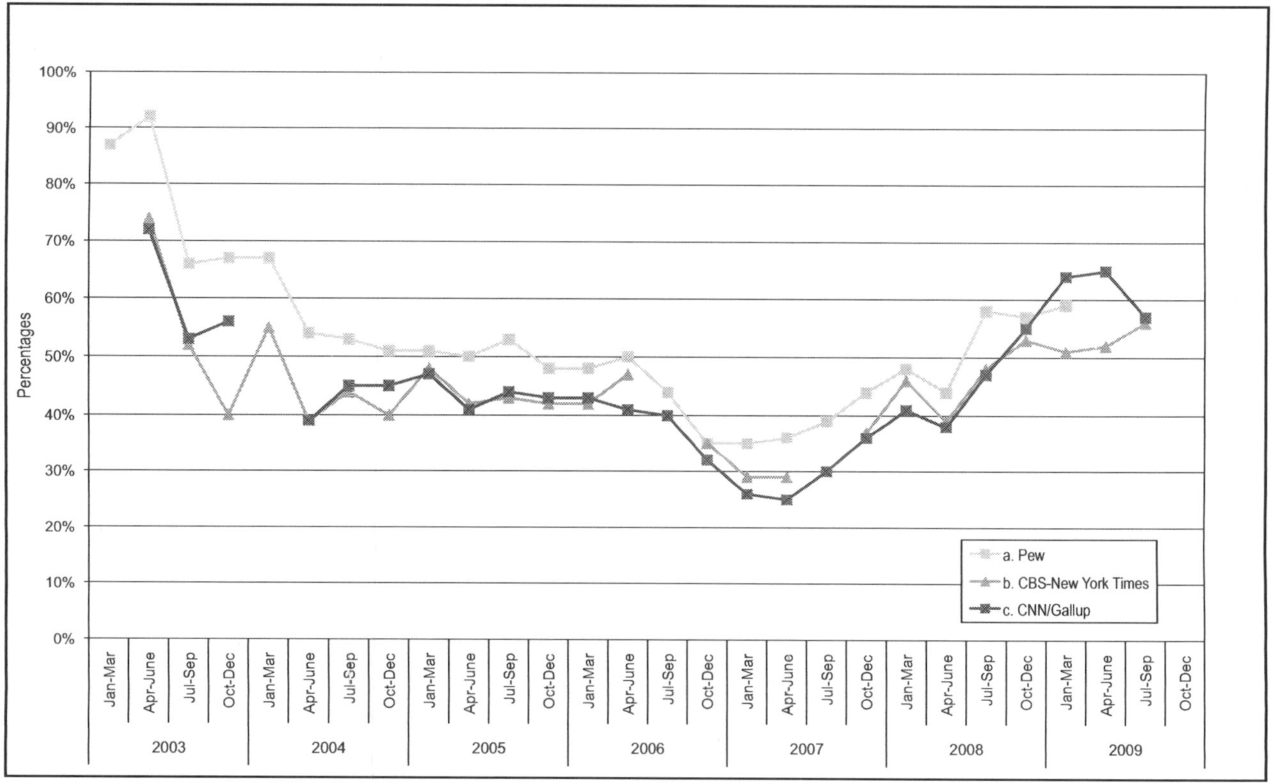

The questions were (a) "How well is the U.S. military effort in Iraq going: very well, fairly well, not very well, or not well at all?" (% "very well" plus "fairly well"); (b) "In general, how would you say things are going for the U.S. in Iraq: very well, moderately well, moderately badly, or very badly? (% "very well" plus "moderately well"); (c) "How would you say things are going for the U.S. in its effort to bring stability and order to Iraq? Would you say things are going very well, somewhat well, somewhat badly, or very badly? (% "very well" plus "somewhat well").

be rather short-lived. After repeated failures to locate the alleged Iraqi weapons of mass destruction that had served as the *casus belli,* and a continuing insurgency that revealed how poorly Washington had planned for a post-Saddam regime in Baghdad, favorable assessments of the war began to erode. By mid-2005, respondents in two of the three surveys summarized in figure 2.2 were less than optimistic, and in the third (Pew Research Center) survey only a very slight majority expressed the view that the war effort was going well. Vice President Cheney told *Larry King Live* in mid-2005 that the situation in Iraq had improved, and that the fighting would end before the end of the Bush administration.[34] Apparently many Americans were paying more attention to evidence of increasing sectarian violence and rising military and civilian casualties than to optimistic prognoses from administration officials, including the architects of the blueprint for the war effort.

It was in this context that the Bush administration launched its "Victory in Iraq" public relations campaign in November 2005 to counter the charge from congressional critics, including from the traditionally "hawkish" and Pentagon-friendly Representative John Murtha (D-PA), who claimed, "American forces had united a disparate array of insurgents in a seemingly endless cycle of violence that was impeding Iraq's progress toward stability and self-governance." Consequently, Murtha urged a withdrawal of the 153,000 U.S. troops within six months. The "Victory in Iraq" campaign was aimed at countering the criticism that the United States did not have a coherent strategy for the conflict, and to persuade the public that in fact the war effort would be successful.[35] Apparently operating on the noncontroversial premises that Americans share the almost universal preference for victory rather than defeat, and that the human costs of war—casualties—would be easier to bear if they led to victory, the president launched the effort with a major speech at the U.S. Naval Academy in Annapolis at the end of November in which he declared that the United States had in place an effective strategy and that "our mission in Iraq is to win the war. Our troops will return home when that mission is complete."[36]

The *National Strategy for Victory in Iraq* document, written by the National Security Council and released by the White House, was not universally applauded, however. Richard Haass, who had worked for the elder Bush administration as senior director of the National Security Council on the Gulf War and other issues concerning Iraq and as principal adviser to Secretary of State Colin Powell from 2001 to 2003, was less than impressed. "It was impossible to read the text and not conclude it was wholly divorced from Iraqi reality. It was so bad that after receiving an advance copy from a friend at the NSC

I wrote him back asking if someone had stolen his email account and was circulating bogus material."[37]

There was a brief uptick in favorable assessments of the war effort at the end of 2005, but the president's pledge of victory only temporarily persuaded large segments of the public to overlook events on the ground. To be sure, there was some good news. Impressive numbers of Iraqi voters had approved a new constitution and elected a parliament, but despite American training efforts, Iraqi security forces on balance proved to be less than competent and reliable. Moreover, the election served to confirm the isolation of the Sunnis and may have contributed to the sectarian violence, which continued unabated. The question of whether the insurgency had morphed into a "civil war" depended on one's definition of that term. Public appraisals of the U.S. effort in Iraq continued to decline through much of 2006, and the slight improvement in 2007 still found that fewer than half of those taking part in the three polls responded that things were going "very well" or "fairly well." By midyear the optimists were clearly a declining minority. A July CBS/*New York Times* survey revealed that only 25 percent of respondents judged that the war was going well, and for the first time fewer than half of Republicans rendered a favorable assessment.

A long-awaited report, written by the White House staff and based on appraisals by General Petraeus, concluded that despite some disappointing political developments, the 2007 "surge" of American forces—the deployment of an additional 21,500 troops, mostly to the Baghdad area—had sufficiently improved the military situation, especially in Anbar Province, to justify maintaining most of the 160,000 troops in Iraq. The administration's strategy was to change the yardstick of progress. Two reports issued just prior to General Petraeus's appearance before Congress—the National Intelligence Estimate and a report from the Government Accountability Office—provided pessimistic assessments of progress and future prospects for Iraq. A draft of the latter report found that Iraq had fallen short on 13 of 18 benchmarks of progress, but it was later revised to present a somewhat rosier picture.[38]

Although the first half of 2007 saw U.S. casualties reach a peak, there was significant improvement during the fall and winter (table 2.3). At the same time public appraisals of "how things are going" in Iraq improved. The apparent success of the American military "surge" in dampening violence in late 2007 and early 2008 clearly had an impact on public appraisals, as all three polling organizations cited in figure 2.2 reported increases of about 10 percent in favorable judgments about the war effort, although these figures failed to reach 50 percent. The further reduction of violence and casualties in 2008 was also reflected in public appraisals, as those who judged the war effort to be going well slightly outnumbered those who disagreed on that score. By 2009 most of those taking part in surveys judged that the war in Iraq was "going well," reaching a peak of 71 percent in a CBS/New York Times survey in late April. However, there was an uptick of sectarian violence in Iraq starting at about that time; a mid-June survey by the same organization revealed a rather sharp drop, to 62 percent, of respondents who judged that the war was going well. Subsequent surveys in early and late July found that "very well" and "somewhat well" responses had declined to 58 and 56 percent respectively. A June 2010 Gallup survey revealed that favorable judgments had fallen still further, to 52 percent.

Yet even in the light of the somewhat more favorable appraisals of the situation on the ground in Iraq—compared to the dark days of 2006–7—those harboring doubts about whether the United States had done the "right thing" in using force against Iraq continued to outnumber those who expressed approval of the invasion (fig. 2.1). Is this an example of public irrationality in the face of evidence that the situation in Iraq was improving? An alternative and more convincing explanation is that the public was in fact paying attention to developments in Iraq, while still holding the view that the undertaking had not been worth its heavy costs in blood and treasure. This would appear to be a reasonable response, especially as the reasons for going to war—Iraq's alleged weapons of mass destruction and ties to al Qaeda—had long since been discredited.

HAS THE WAR MADE THE UNITED STATES SAFER?

One of the continuing themes in the Bush administration's policy pronouncements is that Iraq represented the front lines in the "global war on terrorism" (GWOT).[39] Since the somber days following the September 11 terrorist attacks President Bush and most of his top advisers had repeatedly asserted that the Saddam Hussein regime in Baghdad presented an imminent threat to American security because of its weapons of mass destruction and its intimate links to terrorist organizations, including Osama bin Laden's al Qaeda. In the absence of compelling evidence either proving or disproving the validity of Washington's claims, during the months immediately following the fall of Baghdad, solid if not overwhelming majorities among respondents to surveys by ABC News/Washington Post, Pew, and CNN/USA Today/Gallup agreed that the United States was indeed safer as a consequence of the successful Iraq invasion (fig. 2.3).

Failure to uncover WMDs in Iraq after the fall of Baghdad, despite the best

FIG. 2.3. Assessments of the War in Iraq: Has the War Made the U.S. Safer? (2003–7)

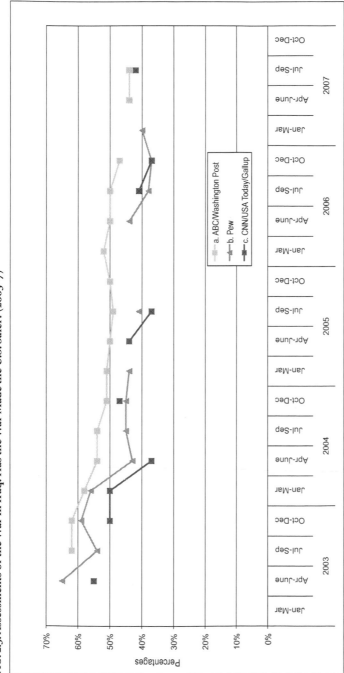

The questions were (a) "Do you think the war in Iraq has or has not contributed to the long-term security of the United States?" (% "has"); (b) "Do you think the war in Iraq has helped the war on terrorism, or has it hurt the war on terrorism?" (% "helped"); (c) "Do you think the war in Iraq has made the U.S. safer or less safe from terrorism?" (% "safer").

efforts of expert inspection groups headed by Americans David Kay and Charles A. Duelfer, may have contributed to growing doubts about whether the United States was indeed safer as a result of the war in Iraq. Kay, who had supported the invasion, told the Senate on January 28, 2004, "Let me begin by saying we were almost all wrong [about Iraq's WMDs], and I include myself." In a later interview, he stated, "There were continuing clandestine activities [in Iraq], but increasingly driven more by corruption than driven by purposeful directed weapons programs." According to the Duelfer Report, "Saddam Hussein ordered his arsenal of chemical and biological weapons destroyed in 1991 and 1992 and halted nuclear weapons developments, all in hopes of lifting crippling economic sanctions."[40]

Compelling evidence about the rather improbable ties between Saddam Hussein's secular Sunni-dominated regime in Iraq and such hard-core fundamentalist terrorist groups as al Qaeda also eluded Bush administration officials, although Vice President Dick Cheney continued to claim that he was in possession of such information.[41] Al Qaeda leader Osama bin Laden had not hesitated to criticize Saddam for ruling as a secular "socialist." Although he urged resistance to any American attack on Iraq, bin Laden also asserted, "Socialists are infidels wherever they are."[42] Barring some unlikely new revelations about WMDs and ties to al Qaeda, the evidence in figure 2.3 suggests that increasingly skeptical public appraisals of triumphant claims about the consequences of the war for American security are likely to persist. A Pew poll in early 2007 found that fewer than 40 percent of respondents believed at that time that "the war in Iraq had helped the war on terrorism." In response to a question by Senator John Warner (R-VA) whether his proposed strategy for Iraq would make the United States safer, General Petraeus replied, "Sir, I don't know actually."[43] This ambivalence was also reflected in the survey data, most of which revealed that the public was almost evenly divided on the question. Three 2006–7 ABC News/*Washington Post* surveys found that positive responses ranged from 44 to 46 percent. The passage of time only seemed to increase public skepticism about the effects of the war in Iraq. Just days before the withdrawal of American combat brigades in August 2010, only 25 percent of respondents in a CBS survey stated that military action in Iraq had made the United States "more safe," whereas a majority of 55 percent replied that "it hasn't made any difference."

By 2008 the three polling organizations had largely stopped posing the question with the wording described in figure 2.3. However, in eight surveys between 2007 and 2009 the ABC News/*Washington Post* poll began posing a somewhat related query: "Do you think the United States must win the war in Iraq in order for the broader war on terrorism to be a success, or do you think the war on terrorism can be a success without the United States winning the war in Iraq?" Respondents who believed that there was in fact a link between success in the wars in Iraq and against terrorism ranged between 31 and 45 percent. In the most recent survey in February 2009, respondents were closely divided between those who believed that the United States must win the war in Iraq (44 percent) and those who denied such a link between the two conflicts (50 percent).

Despite lack of conclusive evidence about prewar ties between Saddam Hussein and Osama bin Laden, some al Qaeda elements—"al Qaeda in Mesopotamia"—in fact contributed to the violence that has engulfed parts of Iraq since the American occupation. However, that organization did not exist prior to the U.S. invasion. Moreover, available evidence indicates that most of its members are Iraqis rather than outsiders. U.S. administration officials have repeatedly asserted that failure to defeat terrorist groups in Iraq will encourage them to attack the United States, a thesis that apparently has not gained a great deal of traction among Americans. In the meanwhile, military efforts against al Qaeda were not wholly successful until May 2011 when Navy SEAL and CIA units raided bin Laden's compound in Pakistan and killed him. Prewar warnings by Brent Scowcroft and others that an invasion of Iraq might serve to strengthen rather than weaken terrorist organizations have apparently proven correct. According to the 2006 National Intelligence Estimate entitled *Trends in Global Terrorism: Implications for the U.S.,* "The Iraq conflict has become a 'cause celebre' for jihadists, breeding a deep resentment of U.S. involvement in the Muslim world and cultivating supporters for the global jihadist movement." The 2007 NIE on the topic also warned that al Qaeda was "exponentially stronger than before."[44]

WAS THE WAR WORTH IT?

One of the most frequent polling items asked respondents about the bottom line: Was the Iraq War worth it or was it a mistake? The CBS/*New York Times* poll asked, "Do you think the result of the war with Iraq was worth the loss of American life and other costs of attacking Iraq"; the Gallup Organization asked, "Did or did not the U.S. make a mistake in sending troops to Iraq"; and ABC News/*Washington Post* also posed a similar question. The results of these surveys are summarized in figure 2.4.

In the immediate aftermath of the capture of Baghdad and the ouster of the Baathist regime, about 70 percent of the respondents to the Gallup and

FIG. 2.4. Assessments of the War in Iraq: Was the Situation in Iraq Worth Going to War? (2003–9)

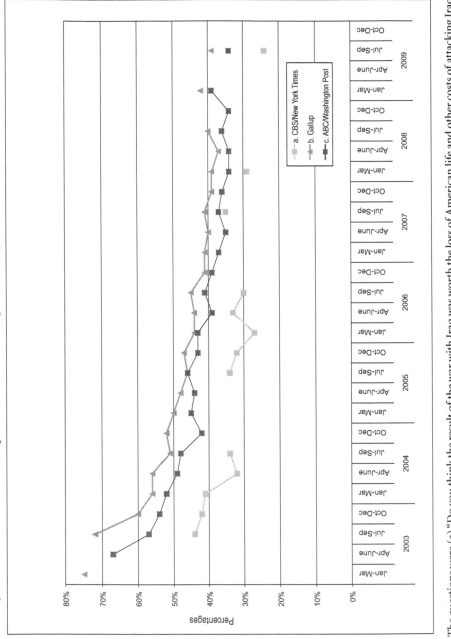

The questions were (a) "Do you think the result of the war with Iraq was worth the loss of American life and other costs of attacking Iraq, or not worth it?" (% "worth it") (2007 wording: "removing Saddam from power" rather than "results of the war with Iraq"); (b) "In view of developments since we first sent troops to Iraq, do you think the United States made a mistake in sending troops to Iraq, or not?" (% "no, not a mistake"); (c) "All in all, considering the costs to the United States versus the benefits to the United States, do you think the war with Iraq was worth fighting or not?" (% "worth fighting").

ABC/*Washington Post* surveys deemed the invasion to have been worth the costs. The speed with which the American forces overwhelmed those of Iraq, combined with relatively light U.S. casualties—138 military personnel were killed during the course of the invasion—no doubt contributed to this judgment. Any fears that Iraq would unleash WMDs against the invading forces turned out to be unwarranted. Those taking part in the CBS/*New York Times* surveys offered less favorable responses, almost surely because the question asked them to consider not only the military *outcome* but also the human and other *costs* of the war. This provides further evidence that question wording can be important. With the passage of time, however, those differences were largely reduced as respondents in all three of the surveys summarized in figure 2.4 began to express increasingly negative conclusions about the war.

Although President Bush recognized that the fall of Baghdad did not bring a complete end to low-level skirmishes, he seemed to welcome the opportunity to rout the remaining insurgents—"My answer is bring them on," he famously asserted on July 1, 2003—but the months that followed brought growing evidence that the U.S. military faced more than a few "dead enders."[45] The impact on public judgments about the war was felt almost immediately as those answering the "was worth it" question in the affirmative fell below 60 percent, except for a brief upward blip following the capture of Saddam Hussein in December 2003. Members of the public who believed that the Iraq invasion was worth it constituted a gradually shrinking majority throughout the first half of 2004, and they were reduced further to a minority in many polls undertaken during the second half of the year. The overall pattern of responses during the next several years confirms that the American public was deeply divided in its verdict about whether the Iraq invasion was "worth it" or, conversely, "a mistake." Despite significant abatement of violence and a decline in American military casualties as a result of the "surge" of U.S. troops in mid-2007, in none of the polls summarized in figure 2.4 did majorities respond with favorable judgment on the war. Those expressing the view that the war in Iraq was "worth it" continued to be a distinct minority through mid-2009 as those taking the opposite position, that it was "not worth it," constituted about three-fifths of those taking part in these surveys.

HOW LONG SHOULD U.S. TROOPS STAY IN IRAQ?

The invasion of Iraq has been described by Thomas Ricks, a journalist with extensive military expertise based on his many years of covering the Pentagon and frequent trips to Iraq, as "perhaps the worst battle plan in American history." The entire invasion force of 145,000 troops included 20,000 from Great Britain.[46] Washington's decision to undertake the Iraq invasion with relatively modest troop levels was based in part on an accurate assessment of Iraq's inferior military capabilities and leadership, but even more importantly it also reflected Secretary of Defense Rumsfeld's determination to transform the American military from its Cold War configuration into a light, mobile force that he believed would be better capable of dealing with twenty-first-century threats. Shortly after the invasion of Afghanistan but before the attack on Iraq, he wrote, "The future of war lay not with massive armies and protracted trench warfare, but in small, high quality, mobile shock forces, supported by airpower and capable of pulling 'lightning strikes' against the enemy." Stated differently, he wanted to drive a stake through the (Colin) "Powell doctrine" that should interventions abroad be necessary, they should have public and congressional support, entail massive forces, and have a clear exit plan.[47] Iraq and the earlier invasion of Afghanistan would provide a test case of Rumsfeld's long-range goals for the Pentagon. As noted earlier, General Shinseki was immediately and publicly rebuked for his estimate that "several hundred thousand" military personnel would be required to secure post-Saddam Iraq. Questions about appropriate troop levels and the duration of their deployment took on greater urgency in light of the sectarian violence in Iraq that, as of early 2011, had resulted in the deaths of more than 4,400 American military personnel—more than 30 times the deaths incurred in the 2003 invasion.

The Pew Research Center and ABC/*Washington Post* surveys have periodically asked respondents to judge whether American troops should remain in Iraq until order has been restored there or whether they should be brought home. CBS News has also posed a related question about increasing, maintaining, reducing, or removing U.S. troops from Iraq. The results from these three polling organizations are summarized in figure 2.5.

Embedded within the issue of troop reduction or withdrawal are estimates of the consequences of the various course of action.

- If American troops remain in Iraq, does their presence constitute a provocation to Iraqis who might be motivated to employ terrorist tactics against them?
- If American troops remain in Iraq, does that reduce the incentive for Iraqi military and police units to work together and to take an increasingly active and effective role in securing their own country?

Fig. 2.5. Assessments of the War in Iraq: Keeping Troops in Iraq (2003–8)

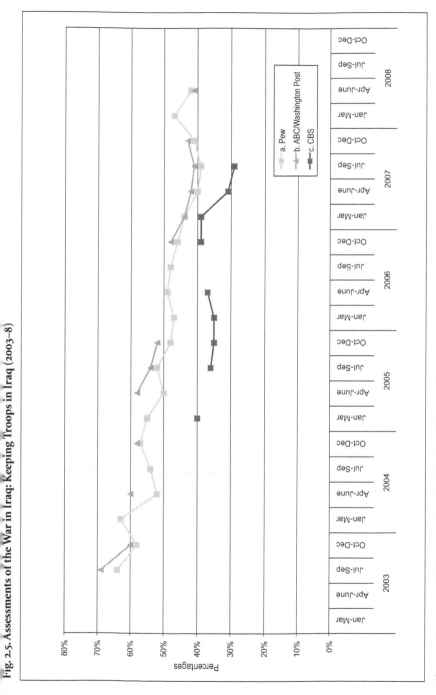

The questions were (a) "Do you think the U.S. should keep military troops in Iraq until the situation has stabilized, or do you think the U.S. should bring its troops home as soon as possible?" (% keep troops); (b) "Do you think the United States should keep its military forces in Iraq until civil order is restored there, even if that means continued U.S. military casualties, or do you think the United States should withdraw its forces in Iraq in order to avoid further U.S. military casualties, even if that means civil order is not restored there?" (% "stay"); (c) "From what you have seen or heard about the situation in Iraq, what should the United States do now? Should the U.S. increase the number of U.S. troops in Iraq, keep the same number of U.S. troops in Iraq, decrease the number of U.S. troops in Iraq, or remove all its troops from Iraq?" (% "increase" plus "keep same").

- If American troops are reduced or withdrawn, will that give rise to even greater levels of violence in Iraq by removing the last effective barrier to a full-scale civil war among sectarian factions there? Will it encourage intervention by Iraq's neighbors on behalf of one or another of its sectarian groups? Will it encourage terrorist groups to view the United States as a "paper tiger" and, thus, an inviting target for future attacks?
- Does the so-called Pottery Barn rule—because the United States "broke" Iraq, it now "owns" it—impose an obligation to maintain or perhaps even increase its forces there until the country is stable and secure?

As late as mid-2005 many respondents opposed withdrawal or reduction of U.S. forces. At the time of the administration's "Victory in Iraq" public relations campaign there were official estimates that by the summer of 2006 U.S. forces could be reduced to 138,000 and that a further drawdown to the 100,000 level was possible by the end of the year. In light of growing rather than diminishing insurgent violence and continuing disappointment in the performance of Iraqi military and police units, those estimates proved to be far too optimistic. At the same time, public support for maintaining or increasing troop levels eroded rather steadily.

In January 2007 the president announced a "surge" in U.S. forces, with the deployment of 21,500 additional military personnel, largely to the Baghdad area. As revealed in figure 2.5, that policy change did stem and partially reverse declining support for keeping American forces in Iraq, but none of the surveys revealed majorities favoring the retention of military forces there. A supplemental funding bill for the war led the newly elected Democratic Congress to engage in a debate on a timeline for reducing or withdrawing the American military presence in Iraq. After employing only the second veto during his six years in office on a special appropriations bill for the wars in Iraq and Afghanistan that included benchmarks and a timeline, President Bush prevailed when an override effort in the House of Representatives fell far short of the required two-thirds votes, and it received support from only 52 senators, including 4 Republicans. A subsequent vote on the appropriations bill without a withdrawal timeline passed in both houses of Congress. A mid-July vote following an all-night debate on the issue in the Senate revealed that proponents of a phased withdrawal fell well short of a filibuster-proof majority of 60 votes. At about the same time, surveys by Pew and CBS News/*New York Times* revealed continuing erosion of support for keeping troops in Iraq. By mid-July 2007, the latter poll found that 61 percent of respondents favored funding

American troops with a timetable for withdrawal, 28 percent supported full funding without a timetable, and 8 percent preferred to block all funding.

The apparent success of the 2007 troop surge in reducing sectarian violence and American military casualties resulted in a somewhat greater public willingness to maintain troops in Iraq until the situation there has stabilized.[48] For example, 47 percent of those taking part in a February 2008 Pew survey expressed support for that course of action, but that figure declined slightly in subsequent surveys. Somewhat differently worded questions in several other 2008 surveys revealed consistent but not overwhelming support for plans to reduce or withdraw U.S. forces according to a timetable rather than waiting for the situation in Iraq to become stable.

The issue of reduction or withdrawal of American forces from Iraq became more than a hypothetical question in 2008. Long negotiations between Washington and Baghdad led to an "Agreement between the United States of America and the Republic of Iraq on the Withdrawal of the United States Forces from Iraq and Organization of Their Activities during Their Temporary Presence in Iraq." The detailed agreement consisting of 31 articles was signed by Iraqi Foreign Minister Hoshiyar Zebari and U.S. Ambassador Ryan Crocker on November 17. It was then ratified by the Iraqi Parliament on November 27, 2008, and by Iraq's Presidential Council the following month. On the U.S. side it was deemed an executive agreement rather than a treaty that would require approval by a two-thirds majority of the Senate. Indeed, the extended negotiations with Iraq were conducted behind closed doors without any consultation with members of Congress. In essence, the agreement called for the withdrawal of U.S. combat forces from Iraqi cities by June 30, 2009, and the withdrawal of all U.S. forces from the country by the end of 2011. If the Iraqi prime minister determined that the country was insufficiently stable by that time, the agreement included the possibility for further negotiations.[49]

During the same period, the U.S. presidential election pitted Senator Barack Obama (D-IL) a longtime opponent of the war, against his Senate colleague, John McCain (R-AZ). McCain had been a firm supporter of the war effort from the outset and, unlike Obama, had supported the 2007 "surge" of U.S. forces. During the campaign Obama pledged to withdraw from Iraq within sixteen months after taking office. In his first major speech as president on the issue in February 2009, Obama outlined his plan for a phased withdrawal by September 2010, a bit later than his original 16-month timetable, and it would also leave a residual force of 35,000 to 50,000 in Iraq for training purposes and for dealing with possible terrorist threats.[50] In short, the Obama plan was only modestly different than the U.S.-Iraq withdrawal agreement negotiated during the waning months of the Bush administration.

In keeping with the general trend toward a somewhat reduced focus on the war in Iraq by polling organizations, there have been fewer assessments of the Obama administration's policies during the months since he was inaugurated, but the limited evidence points toward strong public support for the administration's withdrawal plan. An AP-Gfk survey asked respondents, "Do you approve, disapprove, or neither approve nor disapprove of Barack Obama's decision to end the combat role of U.S. troops and remove most but not all U.S. troops from Iraq by August 31, 2010?" Those expressing their support for the plan easily outnumbered the opponents by a margin of 74 percent to 21 percent. Although their questions about the Obama withdrawal plan were somewhat differently worded, surveys conducted by *Newsweek* and the Pew Research Center yielded almost identical results, with approval ratings of 73 percent and 76 percent, respectively. Finally, CNN posed a question that also included a reference to the troops who would remain in Iraq: "Barack Obama has announced that he will remove most U.S. troops from Iraq by August of next year but keep 35,000 to 50,000 troops in that country longer than that. Do you favor or oppose this plan?" Surveys in March and April 2009 revealed that 70 percent and 69 percent, respectively, supported the plan, as did 62 percent and 64 percent in surveys conducted in January and May 2010. When asked about the pace of withdrawal, "about right" judgments ranged between 46 percent and 55 percent, with the remainder about evenly split between "too slow" and "too fast" responses. There is, however, widespread skepticism on the implementation of the withdrawal plan. The Gallup poll asked, "Just your best guess, do you think all U.S. forces will or will not be out of Iraq (by the end of 2011)?" Only 27 percent agreed that they will be out. A similar sense of skepticism emerged from a CNN/OR survey just days after the pullout of combat brigades. Fifty-three percent stated that it was unlikely that the remaining troops would be withdrawn by the end of 2011, only 29 percent felt that the remaining troops would not be involved in combat, and 66 percent doubted that "the Iraqi government will be able to maintain order in Iraq once U.S. troops are removed from that country."[51]

Although Iraq experienced a significant uptick of sectarian violence starting in May 2009 and continuing through early 2011, Iraqi prime minister Nuri al-Maliki was adamant about sticking to the withdrawal schedule that his government negotiated with the Bush administration in 2008, and the movement of U.S. troops out of urban areas in fact took place as scheduled on June 30, 2009. Even in the face of increasing violence following the U.S. withdrawal from cities, the prime minister insisted that his government forces could cope effectively with the situation. He told the *Wall Street Journal* at the end of 2010: "The last American soldier will leave Iraq. . . . This agreement is not subject to extension, not subject to alteration. It is sealed."[52]

AFGHANISTAN

During the opening weeks of his presidency, Obama also approved a plan to send an additional 21,000 U.S. troops to Afghanistan in an effort to deal with the seriously deteriorating military situation there. Although the two primary goals of American and allied forces in Afghanistan—elimination of the Taliban as a force in the life of the country and the capture of Osama bin Laden and his top al Qaeda henchmen—had proved elusive in more than nine years of combat, public support for the war has consistently exceeded that of the Iraq War. No doubt the well-established links between the Taliban regime in Kabul, al Qaeda, and the September 11 terrorist attacks have provided an important degree of legitimacy to the October 2001 invasion and the ensuing military operations in Afghanistan. Nevertheless, as indicated in table 2.4, support for the war has declined since the heady days following the swift and successful capture of Kabul with very limited American casualties. Two surveys in 2008 revealed moderately strong support—55 percent and 56 percent—for a "plan to reduce the number of U.S. combat troops in Iraq and increase the number of U.S. combat troops in Afghanistan," and the Obama plan to send additional troops to Afghanistan also received support by a margin of better than two-to-one in an April 2009 *Newsweek* survey. That level of support fell during the summer; an IPSOS/McClatchy poll at the end of August revealed that those opposing deployment of additional troops outnumbered supporters by a margin of 56 to 35 percent. The comparable figures from a CNN/OR survey in mid-October were 59 and 39 percent.[53]

On his first trip to Europe President Obama had hoped to gain additional commitments of troops for Afghanistan, especially for deployment to the provinces where fighting has been the heaviest, but his quest proved only partially successful, although in late January 2010 the German government pledged to add 850 troops to their current contingent of 4,300. Given the brusque rejection of NATO offers of military assistance by Pentagon officials Donald Rumsfeld and Paul Wolfowitz in the days immediately following the September 11 attacks, the lack of enthusiasm for additional military deployments into an area of increasing violence is hardly a surprise. The inability of European countries to

TABLE 2.4. Assessments of the War in Afghanistan, 2001–11 (percent responses)

Thinking now about U.S. military action in Afghanistan that began in October 2001: Do you think the United States made a mistake in sending military forces to Afghanistan, or not?

	Mistake	Not a Mistake
November 8–11, 2001	9	89
January 7–9, 2002	6	93
July 19–21, 2004	25	72
August 3–5, 2007	25	70
July 25–27, 2008	28	68
August 21–23, 2008	34	63
January 20–February 1, 2009	30	66
March 14–15, 2009	42	52
July 10–12, 2009	36	61
August 31–September 2, 2009	37	61
November 20–22, 2009	36	60
July 8–11, 2010	38	58
July 27–August 1, 2010	43	52
November 19–21, 2010	39	58

All in all, considering the cost to the United States versus the benefits to the United States, do you think the war in Afghanistan was worth fighting, or not?

	Worth Fighting	Not Worth Fighting
February 22–25, 2007	56	41
July 10–13, 2008	51	45
December 11–14, 2008	55	39
February 19–22, 2009	50	47
March 26–29, 2009	56	41
July 15–18, 2009	51	45
August 13–17, 2009	47	51
September 10–12, 2009	46	51
October 15–18, 2009	47	49
November 12–15, 2009	44	52
December 10–13, 2009	52	44
April 22–25, 2010	45	52
June 3–6, 2010	44	53
April 22–25, 2010	45	52
June 3–6, 2010	44	53
July 7–11, 2010	43	53
December 9–12, 2010	34	60

Do you favor or oppose the U.S. war in Afghanistan?

	Favor	Oppose
September 22–24, 2006	50	48
January 19–21, 2007	44	52

TABLE 2.4.— *Continued*

July 27–29, 2008	46	52
December 1–2, 2008	52	46
February 18–19, 2009	47	52
April 3–5, 2009	53	46
May 14–17, 2009	50	48
July 31–August 2, 2009	41	54
August 28–31, 2009	42	57
September 11–13, 2009	39	58
October 30–November 1, 2009	40	58
November 13–15, 2009	45	52
December 2–3, 2009	46	51
December 16–20, 2009	43	55
January 22–24, 2010	47	52
March 19–21, 2010	48	49
May 21–25, 2010	42	56
August 6–10, 2010	37	62
September 1–2, 2010	41	57
October 5–7, 2010	37	58
December 17–19, 2010	35	63
January 21–23, 2011	40	58

What is your impression of how the war in Afghanistan is going for the United States right now: very well, somewhat well, somewhat badly, or very badly?

	Very Well	Somewhat Well	Somewhat Badly	Very Badly
March 20–24, 2003	30	46	11	3
August 15–18, 2008	3	25	40	18
September 21–14, 2008	2	29	32	23
December 4–7, 2008	2	25	44	18
March 12–26, 2009	3	30	36	21
April 1–5, 2009	3	33	37	15
April 22–26, 2009	1	37	40	13
June 12–26, 2009	2	28	40	15
July 9–12, 2009	2	34	40	15
July 24–28, 2009	3	30	39	18
August 27–31, 2009	2	35	34	18
September 19–23, 2009	3	32	38	15
November 13–16, 2009	4	19	42	27
December 4–8, 2009	1	29	43	17
May 20–24, 2010	2	38	37	12
July 7–9, 2010	2	29	41	21
July 27–August 1, 2010	1	33	42	20
November 19–21, 2010	3	42	38	16

Source: USA Today/Gallup polls, 2001–10; ABC News/*Washington Post* polls, 2007–10; CNN/Opinion Research Corp. polls 2006–11; and CBS News/*New York Times* polls, 2003–10. "Unsure" responses omitted.

evade the global financial crisis that originated in the collapsed housing bubble in the United States no doubt added to their reluctance to accommodate Obama by increasing their commitments to an already unpopular undertaking. A 2009 World Public Opinion survey found that 89 percent of Germans said they have confidence in Obama to "do the right thing in world affairs." Although 78 percent expressed the view that it would be "very bad" if the Taliban were to regain power in Afghanistan, only 42 percent believed that "the NATO mission in Afghanistan should be continued," and only 37 percent approved of Obama's decision to increase the number of U.S. troops in Afghanistan. In addition, 68 percent of the German respondents stated that the economic policies of the United States contributed "a lot" to the downturn in Germany's economy.

A larger-scale survey by the Pew Research Center revealed comparable results. When asked about increased deployment of NATO forces to Afghanistan, the level of agreement ranged between 42 percent among Canadian respondents to a very meager 14 percent in Turkey. A question about keeping or removing troops from Afghanistan revealed a somewhat greater degree of support in France (50 percent keep, 49 percent remove) and Germany (48 percent, 47 percent), with almost even divisions in Great Britain (46 percent, 48 percent) and Spain (44 percent, 46 percent). Respondents in Canada (43 percent, 50 percent), Poland (30 percent, 57 percent), and Turkey (15 percent, 63 percent) were the least supportive.[54]

If events in Iraq are any guide to public reactions, over any extended period the level of support for U.S. policies is likely to reflect events on the ground. A convergence of two major events during the summer of 2009 combined to raise increasing doubts not only about American policy but also about the entire Afghanistan undertaking: increasing American casualties and the Afghan presidential elections in July. According to a September 2009 Gallup survey, by a margin of 61 percent to 35 percent, respondent judged that the war in Afghanistan was "going badly" rather than well; the comparable figures only a month earlier had been 54 percent and 43 percent, and, as shown in table 2.4, CBS/New York Times surveys found that since mid-2008, the public has rather steadily judged that the situation there was going badly, although there was an uptick in appraisals that it was going "well" to 45 percent in November 2010. However, in July 2010, fewer than one respondent in three had told an NBC News/Wall Street Journal survey that the conflict was going well, and only 23 percent were confident that the war in Afghanistan "will come to a successful conclusion."

American troop deaths (317) in Afghanistan during 2009 exceeded those of any year since the 2001 invasion and were more than twice those of the previous highest year—155 in 2008—with especially sharp increases during the summer months. In light of the worsening situation in Afghanistan—according to General David Petraeus attacks against U.S. forces in June 2009 reached a level not seen since the Taliban were driven out of Kabul in December 2001—the newly appointed General Stanley McChrystal was given extraordinary latitude to pursue a new strategy there. In important respects the strategy followed the postsurge template in Iraq by placing primary emphasis on protecting the Afghan population rather than seeking out and attacking Taliban forces.[55]

At the end of August, McChrystal sent a memo, "Commander's Initial Assessment," to Secretary of Defense Gates that requested additional troops. He wrote, "Failure to provide adequate resources also risks a longer conflict, greater casualties, higher overall costs and, ultimately, a critical loss of political support. Any of these, in turn, are likely to result in mission failure." Shortly thereafter, McChrystal's 66-page memo was leaked—whether by an opponent or supporter of the troop request is not clear—to Bob Woodward of the *Washington Post*. McChrystal's request triggered off a spirited debate, not only about the appropriate level of U.S. forces in Afghanistan but also about the entire war effort. Public reactions to that request revealed considerable ambivalence. An ABC News/*Washington Post* survey posed this question: "U.S. military commanders have requested approximately 40,000 more U.S. troops for Afghanistan. Do you think Obama should or should not order these additional forces for Afghanistan?" Responses were almost evenly split between "should" (47 percent) and "should not" (49 percent). A *USA Today*/Gallup poll found a very similar division between those in favor (48 percent) and opposed (45 percent).[56]

Aside from growing American casualties and the possibility of further troop deployments, the 2009 presidential election in Afghanistan, pitting President Karzai against a large field of other candidates, drew renewed attention to charges of incompetence and corruption in the Kabul government. Karzai was initially declared the winner with more than the 50 percent required to avoid a runoff vote. However, after many of his votes were thrown out as fraudulent by international inspectors, a runoff election was scheduled for November 7. Just prior to that vote, Karzai's main competitor, Abdullah Abdullah, withdrew, charging that it would be impossible to conduct a fair election. Karzai was subsequently sworn in for a second term as president. The revelation that Karzai's half brother had been on the CIA payroll while also deeply involved in the lucrative drug trade did little to enhance confidence in the Kabul regime. Transparency International rated Afghanistan as the second most corrupt country in the world, topped only by Somalia in that category.

The election raised important questions in some minds about possible parallels between the wars in Afghanistan and Vietnam. During the first week of September, several widely read columnists, representing virtually the whole political spectrum, raised significant questions about the entire American effort in Afghanistan. For example, the reliably conservative George Will, in a column entitled "Time to Get Out of Afghanistan," described the Karzai government as "inept, corrupt, and predatory." Consequently, he proposed a strategy of deploying American forces offshore, "using intelligence, drones, cruise missiles, airstrikes, and small, potent Special Forces units, concentrating the military operations on the 1,500-mile border with Pakistan." In mid-2010 he called the American undertaking in Afghanistan "a fool's errand." Fellow conservative William Kristol took strong exception, accusing Will of "urging retreat and accepting defeat." Will was not alone in suggesting a basic reconsideration of American policy. Bob Herbert, Thomas Friedman, Nicholas Kristof, and Doyle McManus not only focused on the incompetence and corruption in Kabul but also described some disturbing, if not exactly perfect parallels to the conflict in Vietnam. Fuller length critiques and recommendations for a drawdown from Afghanistan appeared in an article by Richard Haass, who served in the administrations of both presidents Bush, and in a book by a former Reagan administration official, Bing West.[57]

In a major speech to the nation on December 1, President Obama announced that, in response to General McChrystal's request, he would deploy an additional 30,000 U.S. troops to Afghanistan, while reaffirming his commitment to the war effort. He also stated that withdrawal of U.S. forces would begin in 18 months—that is, by mid-2011. A few days later, Obama also used his Nobel Peace Prize speech to underscore his beliefs that the war in Afghanistan was both in the country's national interest and sustained by "just war" reasoning.[58] The initial public response to Obama's decision was moderately favorable, as revealed by CNN/Opinion Research polls in early December (62 percent in favor), mid-December (69 percent in favor), and late January (61 percent in favor). However, longer-term support is not likely to survive unless there are some clear signs that the situation in Afghanistan is improving.

A joint operation by American and Afghan forces to oust the Taliban from the city of Marja, launched in mid-February 2010, was the first major test of American policy. After the military assault, an effective government was to be installed in Marja in the hopes that it would gain sufficient support among the population to prevent a return of the Taliban. According to General Petraeus, this was the "initial salvo" in a military campaign that could last 12 to 18 months.[59] The military operation proved to be effective in driving out the Taliban, many of whom appear to have fled Pakistan, but it was much less successful in establishing an administration capable of providing basic needs. Moreover, during the operation a misfired missile landed on a civilian home, with significant loss of life. General McChrystal immediately offered an apology aimed at assuaging the anger of civilians, whose support is crucial for the long-term success of the operation.

Military efforts to rout the Taliban and the almost inevitable civilian casualties that arise from such operations were only one facet of the serious problems that the United States and its allies encountered in Afghanistan. Political difficulties arising from relations with Afghan president Karzai were at least as significant. Karzai asserted the right to name all members of the body supervising upcoming elections. Given the strong evidence of widespread malfeasance in the 2009 presidential elections that resulted in a second term for Karzai, national security adviser James Jones and others in the administration publicly called for serious efforts by Karzai to clean up the corruption in Kabul and postponed his planned visit to the United States. The Afghan president responded to American criticism by inviting Mahmoud Ahmadinejad to Kabul, where, predictably, the Iranian president delivered a blistering critique of the United States. Karzai followed up with a similar denunciation of Western powers, alleging that they sought control of Afghanistan to establish permanent military bases there, and he even threatened to join the Taliban. The Afghan president also asserted that Peter Galbraith, who served for three months as the UN secretary general's deputy representative for Afghanistan and uncovered electoral fraud, was in fact responsible for any deficiencies in the 2009 election in his country.

President Obama traveled to Afghanistan in March 2010 to deliver personally the message that Karzai must take seriously demands that he clean up his government, but evidence that the message had the desired effect is hardly conclusive at this writing. Indeed, in late August Karzai fired the top Afghan official in charge of investigating and indicting those suspected of corruption. In suggesting that he might join the Taliban, Karzai appeared to be playing a game of chicken, knowing that the United States and its allies were unlikely to invoke the ultimate threat—to pull their forces out of Afghanistan—because he believed that, at least in 2010, they had too much at stake to carry out the threat.

Moreover, he probably calculated—correctly—that whatever his deficiencies, the United States and its allies could find no credible alternative Afghan leader to whom they might switch their support. By mid-April 2010, the tone of rhetoric in Washington and Kabul improved somewhat, but that hardly indicated a permanent meeting of the minds on how to deal with the conflict in Afghanistan.

In late June, General McChrystal and some of his officers expressed their dissatisfaction—bordering on contempt—for the leadership in Washington, including vice president Biden ("bite who?"), the president ("intimidated"), and national security adviser Jones ("a clown"). They did so knowing that they were in the presence of a reporter from *Rolling Stone* magazine.[60] Publication of the story led to an offer of resignation from General McChrystal—quickly accepted by the president—and his replacement by the highly regarded General David Petraeus. As Petraeus had "written the book" on counterinsurgency warfare and had experienced some success in Iraq, there were widespread expectations that McChrystal's departure would not further damage the already difficult campaign in Afghanistan. Before the end of September, NATO casualties had increased to 529, the highest level in the conflict, and American troop deaths in 2010 reached a record total of 500. After an American operation in March 2011 resulted in the deaths of 9 Afghan boys, General Petraeus apologized. President Karzai refused to accept the apology, a response that no doubt played well among his domestic constituents.

CONCLUSION

The data summarized in figures 2.1 through 2.5 indicate quite clearly that public opinion on Iraq has followed events on the ground rather faithfully. There is little evidence that public reactions have been, as depicted by Walter Lippmann and other critics of the American public, largely random and out of synch with reality. Since the Gulf War precipitated by Iraq's invasion of Kuwait in August 1990, Saddam Hussein had been the enemy that almost all Americans could love to hate. Public approval for using force to effect a regime change in Iraq was consistently conditioned on doing so with support from the UN or NATO, but the rapid victory, culminating in the capture of Baghdad and the ouster of the Baath regime in April 2003, elicited strong public approval. Saddam Hussein had no friends in this country who would lament the end of his bloody regime. For a short time, the quick military victory that cost fewer American lives than some had feared seemed to confirm the optimistic script written by the president and other advocates of the invasion.

The erosion of that support and a growing sense that the American effort was not going well were closely linked with events in Iraq and with the level of American casualties. Once again the public responses, in the aggregate, seemed to be reasonable reactions to developments in Iraq. Even when improvements in the situation in Iraq led to somewhat more optimistic judgments about how well the war was going (fig. 2.2), substantial majorities of Americans continued to reject the proposition that the United States had done "the right thing" in using force against Iraq (fig. 2.1), and they continued to believe that doing so was "a mistake" (fig. 2.4). By that time, it had become quite clear that the stated reasons for the invasion—Iraq's alleged possession of WMDs and its putative ties to the terrorists responsible for the September 11 terrorist attacks—had been discredited.

The subsequently developed rationale that the war would bring democracy to Iraq, and perhaps to the entire Middle East region, never appears to have gained much traction among the public. Given America's limited successes in promoting democracy in the region—Israel was the one exception to a rather dismal record on that score—public skepticism was also a reasonable response. Indeed, when CNN/Operations Research surveys undertaken in 2006, 2007, and 2008 asked whether "the United States' action in Iraq is morally justified or not," fewer than half the respondents agreed that it was. In the most recent poll (March 2008), those stating that the American action is "morally justified" (45 percent) were outnumbered by respondents who disagreed (52 percent).

The aggregated figures summarized in this chapter fail, however, to describe in full detail how Americans appraised the Iraq War. Bush administration efforts to rally public support for the war effort, to be discussed more fully in chapter 5, have been far more successful with members of the president's own party than with Democrats or independents, giving rise to partisan gaps of unprecedented proportions.

CHAPTER 3

Partisanship

The dictum that "politics stops at the water's edge" is often attributed to Senator Arthur Vandenberg (R-MI), one of the pillars of post–World War II American foreign policy. His thesis was that if foreign policy is to be credible, other countries must be persuaded that the United States is not divided by partisan differences that might lead to policy changes as the result of the next election, and that in fact, Americans of all political persuasions stand united when dealing with external threats and opportunities. This has been a favorite slogan of countless orators on the hustings as well as presidents and other administration officials who seek to stifle criticism of their policies from members of the opposing political party. Whether it is an accurate description of the American foreign policy process over any extended period is open to question as it would be hard to deny that partisan differences have colored debates on issues as diverse as responses to the wars arising from the French Revolution, the tariff issue at various times during the nineteenth and early twentieth centuries, and the question of American participation in the League of Nations following World War I.

Even in times of crisis or war, when Benjamin Franklin's advice that "unless we hang together we shall surely hang separately" might seem most germane to the question, history reveals that strong criticism of foreign policy, often rooted in partisanship, is not uncommon. For example, in the early days of the Republic, even a leader of George Washington's towering stature could not wholly contain the differences between proponents of leaning toward France or Great Britain during his second presidential term. The partisan differences engulfed two of the most brilliant members of his cabinet. Secretary of the Treasury Alexander Hamilton and most Federalists supported the British, especially after the French Revolution took a more radical turn with the Reign of Terror that included the execution of Louis XVI and his wife, Marie Antoinette. In contrast, Secretary of State Thomas Jefferson and many Democratic-Republicans were much more sympathetic to France and its revolution. After France declared war on Great Britain in February 1793, Washington, fearing that the young country would be dragged into a European war, issued a proclamation of neutrality: "Whereas it appears that a state of war exists between Austria, Prussia, Sardinia, Great Britain and the United Netherlands, on the one part, and France on the other, the duty and interests of the United States require that with sincerity and good faith adopt and pursue a conduct friendly and impartial toward the Belligerent Powers." Rather than ending the partisan bickering, the Neutrality Proclamation gave rise to a flurry of pamphlets between the Federalist Hamilton (writing as "Pacificus") in support of neutrality, and Democratic-Republican James Madison (writing as "Helvidius") who asserted that supporters of the Neutrality Proclamation were secret monarchists. Other examples abound. The War of 1812, the Mexican War, the darkening world situation during the late 1930s, and the later stages of the conflicts in Korea and Vietnam were marked by bitter debates that, more often than not, fell along rather than across partisan lines.

In contrast, deliberate efforts by the Franklin Roosevelt administration to develop a bipartisan coalition in support of American policies during the months immediately preceding World War II and throughout the war were generally successful. His coalition brought together internationalists in the two parties, and thus it sought to replace partisan loyalties by shared ideological bonds on foreign policy issues. The Pearl Harbor attack united Americans who, until that day, had been deeply divided on the country's proper international position in the war that had engulfed Europe and Asia. Although the question of whether to give priority to defeating Japan or Germany was somewhat divisive, it was not primarily a partisan issue. An agreement between Secretary of State Cordell Hull and the leading adviser to Republican nominee Thomas E. Dewey, John Foster Dulles, largely defused the question of American participation in a postwar international organization during the 1944 presidential campaign. That effort played an important role in Senate approval the following year of the United Nations Treaty by an overwhelming vote of 89 to 2.

Senator Vandenberg, a leading isolationist during the 1930s, had started his noted diary with the assertion that the Pearl Harbor attack "ended isolationism for any realist."[1] When the Republicans gained control of the Congress for the first time in 16 years as a result of the 1946 midterm elections, he assumed the chairmanship of the Senate Foreign Relations Committee. In that position he established an effective working relationship with the Democratic Truman administration, and thus he played a key role in some of the most important foreign policy initiatives of the period, including aid to Greece and Turkey (the Truman Doctrine), the Marshall Plan to assist the postwar reconstruction of Europe, the Berlin airlift to circumvent the Soviet blockade of that divided city, and, later, in the creation of the North Atlantic Treaty Organization (NATO). Each of these striking departures from traditional American foreign policies had rather solid political support from both sides of the aisle.

The 1952 presidential election played a crucial role in bipartisan support for key elements of a liberal internationalist foreign policy. General Dwight D. Eisenhower gained the Republican nomination, defeating Senator Robert A. Taft (R-OH)—the son of a president, "Mr. Republican" in the eyes of many conservative members of his party, and a leading critic of expanding American commitments abroad—in a tumultuous convention. That nomination and Eisenhower's landslide victory in the general election that fall were important steps in sustaining foreign policy bipartisanship, as his policies were broadly in line with those established by the Roosevelt and Truman administrations, including support for the North Atlantic Treaty Organization (which Eisenhower had headed as Supreme Allied Commander prior to assuming the presidency), the United Nations, and many other international organizations; foreign aid, trade liberalization; and the like. Eisenhower found more consistent support from Congress during the last six years of his two terms in office, when Democrats controlled both houses, than during his first two years when senators of his own party—including William Knowland (R-CA), John Bricker (R-OH), and Joseph McCarthy (R-WI)—were often a major source of presidential heartburn. In contrast, Democratic Senate leader Lyndon Johnson (D-TX) and House Speaker Sam Rayburn (D-TX) generally worked better with Eisenhower.

There were, to be sure, often bitter partisan debates arising from President Truman's decision to fire the insubordinate General Douglas MacArthur in the midst of the Korean War in 1951; the bogus issue of "who lost China" after communists came to power there in 1949; charges of treason by Senator Joseph McCarthy against such establishment figures as Secretary of State Dean Acheson and General George C. Marshall; election-year dustups over the Suez crisis (1956); charges of a "missile gap" and inadequate policies on Cuba (1960); and who was better able to maintain effective control of nuclear weapons (1964). But on many issues, especially those relating to security in Europe, leaders of the two major political parties were generally in agreement on the basic defense strategies of containment and deterrence, if not necessarily on how best to implement them.

There is ample evidence that members of the general public often take their cues from policy debates, as conveyed by the media, at the leadership level. When there is a broad bipartisan agreement among Democratic and Republic opinion leaders, that is likely to be reflected in surveys of the general public.[2] The agreement at the leadership level no doubt contributed to the fact that among the general public, Republicans and Democrats differed little on many important foreign policy issues. Table 3.1 provides a brief overview of how Republicans and Democrats among the general public appraised such important and diverse foreign policy issues as the Truman Doctrine, formation of a military alliance with European countries (NATO), the level of defense spending, deployment of U.S. troops to Europe and Indo-China, trade with the Soviet Union, and foreign aid. Typically, differences between Republicans and Democrats responding to these Gallup polls were small and within the margin of error of such surveys.

One of the most interesting of these concerned possible American military intervention in the spring of 1954 to support the failing French campaign to maintain control of Indo-China. The Eisenhower administration was internally divided on the issue, with Secretary of State John Foster Dulles and Vice President Richard Nixon favoring such action, but President Eisenhower had doubts. The president sent one of his World War II colleagues, General Matthew Ridgway, to Indo-China to assess the situation and to recommend a course of action. As Eisenhower had expected, Ridgway opposed sending U.S. troops into another land war in Asia; the Korean War had only recently ended in July 1953 with an armistice, but without a peace treaty. Eisenhower accepted that recommendation. By margins of better than four-to-one, both Republicans and Democrats agreed with the president and opposed the deployment of American troops to Indo-China.

For more than a decade following World War II, then, whatever differences divided the American public on foreign policy issues rarely fell along lines defined by partisan loyalties. Writing in the 1970s, Barry Hughes concluded that "the evidence points overwhelmingly to insignificant party differences in the general population" on most foreign policy issues.[3] Indeed, prior to the Viet-

TABLE 3.1. Partisanship on Selected Foreign Policy Issues, 1946–63 (percent responses)

Date	Issue[a]	Responses	Republicans	Democrats	Independents	Partisan Gap[b]
Feb. 1946	U.S. role in world affairs	Active	72	72	NR	0
		Stay out	23	22	NR	
March 1947	Aid to Greece (Truman Doctrine)	Approve	56	56	NR	0
		Disapprove	31	32	NR	
April 1948	Should U.S. and European Marshall Plan nations join a permanent military alliance?	Yes	66	68	57	−2
		No	22	16	29	
July 1948	Evaluation of U.S. policy toward the U.S.S.R.	Too soft	73	70	NR	3
		Too tough	3	4	NR	
		About right	14	14		
Feb. 1950	Defense budget	Too much	16	12	18	4
		Too little	22	25	24	
		About right	46	46	40	
July 1950	Send military supplies to Chiang Kai–shek government on Taiwan?	Should	48	50	NR	−2
		Should not	39	32	NR	
July 1951	Send U.S. troops to Europe or keep them home to defend America?	Europe	53	61	49	−8
		At home	39	30	38	
May 1954	Send U.S. troops to Indo–China?	Approve	18	22	17	−4
		Disapprove	76	70	72	
June 1955	Should the U.S. and Russia work out a trade agreement?	Should	55	57	54	−2
		Should not	33	27	29	
Dec. 1956	Approve foreign aid to stop Communism	Yes	59	58	58	1
		No	28	28	28	
Jan. 1963	Foreign aid	For	54	59	61	−5
		Against	35	28	28	

Source: Gallup Organization surveys.

[a]Statement of issue rather than exact question wording.

[b]Partisan gap: % Republican responses minus % Democrat responses.

NR = Not reported.

nam War the distribution of attitudes among supporters of the two major parties was sufficiently similar that the self-identified independents often stood on one side of the Democrats and Republicans rather than between them.

Bipartisan consensus on foreign policy did not survive the disastrous war in Vietnam. One of the early harbingers of change in this respect was the nomination of Senator Barry Goldwater (R-AZ) as the Republican candidate for president in 1964. Although escalation of the American commitment to Vietnam had yet to begin in earnest and the most divisive events of the war such as the Tet offensive were still some years in the future, Goldwater had been quite open in his criticism of the policies he attributed to the "liberal eastern establishment" that, in his view, had come to dominate and stifle debate within both political parties. His campaign slogan was "a choice, not an echo," and his book, *The Conscience of a Conservative,* became something of a bible for conservatives, especially on a broad range of domestic issues.[4] Although incumbent president Lyndon Johnson rolled to an overwhelming victory in the general election, the losing Goldwater campaign played a significant role in laying the groundwork within the GOP for policies that later, especially during the Reagan years, challenged some key tenets of the postwar bipartisan consensus on liberal internationalist foreign and defense policies.

Although the long Vietnam War spanned both Democratic (Kennedy, Johnson) and Republican (Nixon, Ford) administrations, it ultimately divided the country along largely partisan lines. After Gerald Ford assumed the presidency in the wake of Richard Nixon's resignation, he was asked at a press conference about the lessons to be learned from the war. His reply was that the lessons were "obvious" and that because Americans largely agreed on the substance of those lessons, they might serve as the basis for a post-Vietnam foreign policy consensus. In fact, quite the opposite was the case. Whether the question was about the wisdom of the U.S. intervention in Vietnam, the sources of the American defeat, or the lessons to be applied to the future conduct of foreign affairs, the public was deeply divided largely along partisan lines. In this they reflected the divisions among the country's opinion leaders. Indeed, the very concept of bipartisanship came under increased attack from several quarters. By 1981, a leading Republican senator publicly called for a renewal of bipartisanship in foreign affairs, but he was defeated in his next election in large part because of opposition by a staunchly conservative senator who preferred to cleanse the party of moderates.[5]

In the face of growing partisan discord, several administrations sought to create a post-Vietnam foreign policy consensus, but they fell short of that goal for a variety of reasons. The Nixon-Kissinger administration attempted to do so through a policy of détente with the Soviet Union and opening relations with China as part of an ambitious post-Vietnam plan to create a multipolar international structure, but those moves provoked some domestic criticism as an amoral exercise in realpolitik. The policy ultimately fell victim to Nixon's resignation in August 1974 to avert the certainty of impeachment by the House of Representatives and conviction by the Senate over his role in the Watergate crimes. Although Kissinger stayed on in the Ford administration, he and his policies were the targets of some hard-line Democrats such as Senator "Scoop" Jackson (D-WA), as well as vocal critics within the Republican Party, including California governor Ronald Reagan and his supporters. Ford won the Republican presidential nomination after a heated challenge from Reagan, but he lost the 1976 election to Jimmy Carter.

Efforts by the Carter administration to achieve the same goal through an emphasis on human rights as a bedrock of American policy—to create "a foreign policy that the American people could be proud of"—also failed for both domestic (high inflation) and external reasons (the oil embargo, the Iran hostage crisis, and the Soviet invasion of Afghanistan). Carter made an effort to drive home the point that coping with excessive reliance on imported oil would involve some sacrifices—he called a major conservation effort "the moral equivalent of war"—but that message yielded far more derision than support.[6] Ronald Reagan easily defeated Carter's bid for reelection in 1980.

The Reagan administration initially sought to forge a consensus around a more confrontational stance toward the Soviet Union, which Reagan called "an evil empire." In a stunning turnaround during his second term, Reagan sought bipartisan consensus on an unprecedented level of cooperation between Washington and Moscow on several issues, grounded in the relationship he developed with Soviet president Mikhail Gorbachev.[7] However, the Iran-Contra episode, wherein the United States secretly shipped arms to Iran—to a government that had held American diplomats in Tehran hostage for 444 days—and secretly used the proceeds to fund the Contra rebels in Nicaragua in the face of a direct congressional prohibition for such assistance, cast a dark shadow on the closing months of the Reagan administration, and as a consequence his approval ratings plunged.

Following the demolition of the Berlin Wall, the disintegration of the Soviet Union, and increasing signs of independence by Eastern European members of the Warsaw Pact, President George H. W. Bush proclaimed the goal of establishing a "new world order." The 1990–91 Gulf War that successfully drove Iraqi invaders out of Kuwait gave rise to bipartisan agreement on U.S. actions for a short period of time, as well as to record levels of public approval for the president immediately following the conflict. However, that support began to erode within months.[8] The president's reelection bid in 1992 floundered on a number of domestic economic issues; for example, he earned the enmity of many Republicans for raising taxes despite a campaign pledge not to do so. Democratic presidential nominee and election victor Bill Clinton campaigned on the slogan, "It's the economy, stupid," and independent candidate Ross Perot also attacked Bush's economic policies.

Bill Clinton sought to gain bipartisan support for promotion of a "democratic peace" through expansion of democracy abroad. When he used force abroad, as in air strikes against Iraq and Sudan, he found himself accused by Republicans of employing "wag the dog" tactics to divert attention from domestic problems. Some of Clinton's problems were self-inflicted, notably from the Monica Lewinsky affair and Clinton's subsequent impeachment, but there is also ample evidence that the American public does not rate the goal of promoting democracy abroad very highly, especially if doing so involves the use of military force. The latter point will be revisited in more detail in chapter 4.

Three perceptive observers of American foreign policy, one of whom later served as national security adviser to President Clinton, asserted in 1984, "For two decades the making of American foreign policy has been growing far more political—or more precisely, far more ideological and partisan."[9] That explanation for the inability of both Democratic and Republican presidents to sustain a bipartisan consensus in the wake of the Vietnam War is reflected in public opinion surveys. In contrast to the results presented in table 3.1, responses to some Gallup surveys during the post-Vietnam era encompassing the Carter, Reagan, Bush, and Clinton administrations reveal that the American public was sharply divided along party lines on a broad range of important foreign and defense issues, including a trial balloon proposal to withdraw troops from South Korea, the deployment of U.S. Marines to Lebanon, the appropriate size of the defense budget, policies toward Nicaragua, sanctions on South Africa for its system of apartheid, aid to the former Soviet Union, immigration policy, deployment of troops to parts of the former Yugoslavia, creation of an antimissile defense system, and policy toward Cuba (table 3.2). Indeed, except for responses to the immigration question, the differences between Republicans and Democrats consistently reached double digits, ranging from 11 to 39 percent.

And, in contrast to opinions expressed during the pre-Vietnam decades (table 3.1), the views of independents generally fell between the consistently wide gaps between the opinion of Democrats and Republicans.

THE WAR IN IRAQ

President George W. Bush, having described himself as "a uniter, not a divider" during the 2000 election campaign, promised to end the acrimonious post-Vietnam partisan divisions in Washington. Although there is occasional evidence that the general public does not always take its cues from political leaders, success in becoming a "uniter" would very likely have been reflected in diminution of the sharp divisions at the level of public opinion.[10] As noted earlier, the presidential nomination and landslide election of Republican Dwight D. Eisenhower in 1952 played a significant role in engendering public support, including from many Republicans, for the multilateral internationalist policies of his two Democratic predecessors in the White House.

The heinous nature of the September 11 terrorist attacks brought Democrats and Republicans together for a short time. In the wake of those attacks, President Bush enjoyed widespread support among members of both political parties, and his own job performance ratings reflected a dramatic "rally-round-the-flag" upward spike.[11] Bipartisan support also carried over to the military operations in Afghanistan to hunt down Osama bin Laden and his fellow terrorists and to overturn the Taliban regime that had provided a home and base of operations for al Qaeda. The fact that both houses of Congress had given such overwhelming bipartisan support for the invasion of Afghanistan—the votes were 420–1 in the House and 98–0 in the Senate—no doubt contributed to the overwhelming public support for that campaign. A USA Today/Gallup survey in November 2001 found that 89 percent of the public asserted that the United States had *not* made a mistake in sending military forces to Afghanistan, and one month later support for that military operation reached 93 percent.[12]

Even before the September 11 terrorist attacks, top leaders in the Bush administration had focused on regime change in Iraq as a high-priority foreign policy goal. During the decade following the Gulf War, surveys consistently revealed strong support for ousting Saddam Hussein, as reflected in the overwhelming congressional vote in the "Liberation of Iraq" resolution in 1998. But as noted earlier, support for achieving that end through the use of American armed forces was generally conditioned on gaining the support of NATO allies, the United Nations, or both.

TABLE 3.2. Partisanship on Selected Foreign Policy Issues, 1977–2000 (percent responses)

Date	Issue[a]	Responses	Republicans	Democrats	Independents	Partisan Gap[b]
June 1977	Withdrawal of U.S. troops from South Korea	Favor Oppose	32	47	36	−15
March 1982	Defense budget	Too much Too little About right	18 27 46	43 16 32	39 18 36	−25
October 1983	Mistake to send Marines to Lebanon?	Yes, mistake No	36 53	61 29	50 36	−25
January 1985	Defense budget	Too much Too little About right	29 15 49	60 7 27	49 10 35	−31
May 1985	Trade embargo against Nicaragua	Approve Disapprove	65 16	26 58	45 38	39
March 1986	Should U.S. provide aid to Contras in Nicaragua?	Should Should not	44 44	29 60	34 51	15
July 1991	Removal of economic sanctions against South Africa	Approve Disapprove	56 22	35 39	45 31	21
April 1992	Join other nations in providing aid to former Soviet Union?	Favor Oppose	64 33	46 50	50 45	18
July 1993	Keep immigration at present level, increase, or decrease?	Present level Increase Decrease	26 4 69	33 7 59	23 9 65	−7
Dec. 1995	Presence of U.S. troops in Bosnia	Approve Disapprove	30 67	57 37	36 58	−27
June 1999	Presence of U.S. troops in Kosovo peacekeeping force	Favor Oppose	57 15	73 12	65 14	−16
July 2000	Build a missile defense system?	Favor Oppose	63 NR	51 NR	47 NR	12
October 2000	Reestablish diplomatic relations with Cuba	Favor Oppose	50 NR	61 NR	54 NR	−11

Source: Gallup Organization surveys.
[a]Statement of issue rather than exact question wording.
[b]Partisan gap: % Republican responses minus % Democrat responses.
NR = Not reported.

The administration's campaign to gain approval for its Iraq policies included an October 2002 congressional resolution authorizing the use of force against the Saddam Hussein regime, which gained the support of many Democrats in the House (81) and Senate (29). The United Nations Security Council also unanimously approved Resolution 1441 in November demanding that UN inspectors be allowed to return to Iraq to determine whether the Baghdad regime was in full compliance with post–Gulf War prohibitions against the acquisition of weapons of mass destruction and certain other classes of weapons.

The quick military victory in Iraq and ouster of the Saddam Hussein regime gained widespread public approval, as summarized in figure 2.1, but subsequent events on the ground, including a growing insurgency that gave the lie to the optimistic premise that American troops would be viewed as liberators, soon eroded the post–September 11 bipartisanship. Indeed, U.S. policies in Iraq created partisan differences—perhaps more accurately described as chasms—unprecedented in the history of polling on American foreign policy. Those differences spanned a broad spectrum of views about the war, including values, facts, and prescriptions.

A number of polling organizations asked respondents some variant of questions about whether the United States had done the "right thing" in going to war against Iraq. Table 3.3 summarizes responses to questions posed by seven

TABLE 3.3. Partisanship and Assessments of the War in Iraq, 2004–10: Values

Survey	Date	Responses by				
		All	Reps.	Dems.	Indeps.	Partisan Gap[a]
Did the U.S. do the right thing to go to war against Iraq? *(% yes, the right thing)*						
Time Magazine	May 2004	48	75	29	48	46
CBS/*New York Times*	July 2004	45	78	22	42	56
CBS/*New York Times*	October 2004	52	89	21	47	68
CBS/*New York Times*	June 2005	45	78	22	40	56
Newsweek	September 2005	46	85	18	46	67
Pew	October 2005	44	76	22	42	54
CBS/*New York Times*	April 2008	34	68	13	32	55
CBS	March 2009	40	79	17	39	62
Pew	September 2010	41	68	28	36	40
Did the U.S. make a mistake in sending troops to Iraq, or not? *(% no, not a mistake)*						
Gallup	January 2005	47	83	22	36	61
Gallup	October 2005	45	79	19	39	60
Gallup	December 2005	50	80	25	48	55

TABLE 3.3.— *Continued*

Gallup	January 2006	46	84	21	36	63
Gallup	March 2009	47	81	17	50	64
Gallup	July 2010	46	75	26	43	49

Do you favor the war with Iraq? (% favor)

Gallup	March 2005	47	81	15	40	66
Gallup	June 2005	39	70	17	32	53

Was the situation in Iraq worth going to war over? (% yes, worth it)

LA Times	July 2004	44	80	18	42	62
Gallup	January 2005	46	82	16	35	66
Gallup	April 2005	45	79	17	36	62

Do you think the results of the war in Iraq were worth the loss of American life and other costs of attacking Iraq, or not worth it? (% yes, worth it)

CBS/New York Times	July 2004	34	69	13	26	56
CBS/New York Times	October 2005	32	62	8	30	54
CBS/New York Times	November 2005	31	65	11	29	54
CBS	August 2010	20	36	11	18	25

Looking back, do you think the United States did the right thing in taking military action against Iraq, or should the U.S. have stayed out? (% right thing)

CBS	August 2010	37	63	21	33	42

If, before the war, U.S. intelligence had concluded that Iraq did not have weapons of mass destruction and was not providing substantial support to al Qaeda, should the U.S. have gone to Iraq for other reasons? (% should have)

World Public Opinion	October 2004	21	36	9	20	29
	March 2006	27	43	11	29	32

Should the U.S. have permanent military bases in Iraq (% should)

World Public Opinion	October 2004	30	39	22	33	17
	March 2006	27	39	17	27	22

Which is the more important war for the United States: The war in Iraq or the war in Afghanistan? (% Iraq)

Gallup	July 2008	38	47	31	38	16

[a]Partisan gap: % Republican responses minus % Democrat responses.

polling organizations spanning the period between May 2004 (one year after President Bush declared the successful end of hostilities in Iraq) and mid-2010 (shortly before the withdrawal of U.S. combat brigades from Iraq, in accordance with the Bush–al Maliki agreement of late 2008). If respondents are classified by partisan self-identification, the result can only be described as stunning. Because the data are drawn from responses to somewhat differently worded questions and from several polling organizations, they cannot easily be dismissed as idiosyncrasies or flaws arising from sampling problems or other significant deficiencies that might be associated with any single survey.

The overall responses from those taking part in these surveys reflected a less than enthusiastic assessment of the use of force against Iraq, even after the "surge" of U.S. forces in mid-2007 significantly reduced the death toll among civilians and American military personnel. At no point after an October 2004 CBS/*New York Times* survey did a majority of respondents offer a favorable judgment on U.S. policy. Even by 2009, after a year of progress in reducing the levels of violence in Iraq, the "right thing" option was selected by only two in five respondents. But those overall figures fail completely to reveal the depths of partisan cleavages on the war. In eighteen of the twenty-five questions about the invasion of Iraq, 70 percent or more of the Republican respondents asserted that they favored the war, that the United States had done the "right thing" in using force against Iraq, and that the results were "worth it." In contrast, the level of approval among Democrats was less than 25 percent in all but three surveys. Consequently, the partisan gap averaged more than 54 percent. Even when the question included the phrase "the loss of American life and other costs" of the war, resulting in somewhat reduced overall "worth it" responses, the partisan gap remained well over 50 percent.

Two additional questions asked respondents whether the United States should have gone to war even if U.S. intelligence found that Iraq did not possess weapons of mass destruction, and whether the United States should maintain permanent bases in Iraq. Although neither proposition gained support from a majority of those taking part in the World Public Opinion polls, the responses nevertheless revealed quite substantial partisan gaps.

A second cluster of questions asked respondents about the "facts" surrounding developments in Iraq, as they understood them. The results of fourteen questions, posed a total of thirty-eight times by six polling organizations, are presented in table 3.4. They address clusters of items focused on how well the U.S. effort in Iraq is going with respect to such goals as defeating the insurgents, reducing civilian casualties, establishing a secure and democratic Iraq, and preventing a civil war. Two other items asked respondents about the veracity of American claims about Iraqi weapons of mass destruction and Saddam Hussein's connection to the September 11 terrorist attacks.

The overall judgments about the American undertaking in Iraq hardly provide a brilliant scorecard for the various ways of measuring success. They do, however, reflect some postsurge improvements in reaching such goals as defeating the Iraqi insurgents, preventing a civil war, and reducing civilian casualties. A series of four Pew Research Center surveys between February 2007 and

TABLE 3.4. Partisanship and Assessments of the War in Iraq, 2004-10: Facts

Survey	Date	Responses by				
		All	Reps.	Dems.	Indeps.	Partisan Gap[a]
	How well is the U.S. effort in Iraq going? (% very well or somewhat well)					
CBS/*New York Times*	July 2004	43	71	25	40	46
Gallup	January 2005	40	68	18	33	50
CBS/*New York Times*	June 2005	40	69	20	36	49
Gallup	August 2005	43	72	19	38	53
Pew	October 2005	44	74	24	40	50
Pew	October 2006	35	58	18	26	40
CBS/*New York Times*	July 2007	25	49	8	22	41
Pew	June 2008	44	84	27	40	57
Pew	September 2008	58	71	40	57	31
Gallup	June 2009	59	76	46	55	30
Gallup	June 2010	52	60	44	50	16
Gallup	August 2010	50	60	44	50	16
	Who do you think is currently winning Iraq —the U.S. and its allies, the insurgents in Iraq, or neither side? (% U.S. and its allies)					
Gallup	February 2006	31	58	12	25	46
Gallup	October 2006	19	51	3	13	48
	All in all, is the U.S. making progress or losing ground in its effort to establish security and democracy in Iraq? (% making progress)					
Newsweek	October 2006	29	65	10	23	55
	When the U.S. and Britain claimed that Iraq had weapons of mass destruction, was it because they themselves were misinformed by bad intelligence, or was it because they lied to provide a reason for invading Iraq? (% misinformed)					
Pew	November 2005	41	69	20	39	49

(continues)

TABLE 3.4.—*Continued*

Survey	Date	Responses by				
		All	Reps.	Dems.	Indeps.	Partisan Gap[a]
	Do you think the Bush Administration deliberately misled the American public about whether Iraq had weapons of mass destruction, or not? (% no, did not)					
CNN/*USA Today*, Gallup	January 2006	46	84	14	39	70
	Were Saddam Hussein and the September 11 terrorists working together in the months before the war in Iraq? (% yes, working together)					
CBS/*New York Times*	October 2005	39	61	28	35	33
	Was Saddam Hussein personally involved in the September 11, 2001, terrorist attacks? (% yes, involved)					
CBS/*New York Times*	October 2005	33	44	25	32	19
CBS/*New York Times*	September 2007	33	40	27	32	13
	The U.S. is making progress defeating the insurgents. (% agree)					
Pew	February 2007	30	53	18	29	35
	September 2007	37	67	16	31	51
	November 2007	43	66	29	39	37
	February 2008	49	80	36	44	44
	The U.S. is making progress preventing civil war. (% agree)					
Pew	February 2007	18	34	10	18	24
	September 2007	26	49	14	20	35
	November 2007	32	52	20	27	32
	February 2008	35	53	26	33	27
PIPA[b]	*Do you think the U.S. presence is currently a stabilizing force or is it provoking more conflict than it is preventing? (% stabilizing force)*					
	October 2004	46	75	19	50	56
	March 2006	43	75	19	37	56
	February 2008	35	68	14	30	54
Pew	*Does America's safety from terrorism depend on our success in Iraq? (% yes)*					
	January 2007	37	62	23	35	39

TABLE 3.4.—*Continued*

Survey	Date	All	Reps.	Dems.	Indeps.	Partisan Gap[a]
				Responses by		
	The U.S. is making progress reducing civilian casualties. (% agree)					
Pew	February 2007	20	32	13	16	19
	September 2007	37	59	28	33	31
	November 2007	43	60	28	42	32
	February 2008	46	65	33	52	32
	All in all, do you think the situation in Iraq is getting better for the United States, staying the same, or getting worse for the United States? (% getting better)					
Gallup	October 2007	16	34	3	16	31
	Regardless of whether you think taking military action in Iraq was the right thing to do, would you say the U.S. has succeeded in accomplishing its objectives in Iraq, or has it not succeeded? (% succeeded)					
CBS	August 2010	41	57	36	34	21

[a]Partisan gap: % Republican responses minus % Democrat responses.
[b]Program on International Policy Attitudes.

February 2008 revealed steadily increasing public optimism about "making progress" toward reaching each of these American goals, but in none of them did as many as half of the respondents express a favorable judgment.

When respondents are classified according to party identification, the results again reveal wide partisan gaps. Whereas Republicans consistently judged that the situation in Iraq was going well on most measures of success, Democrats were far less optimistic, although in each case their assessments on progress increased during the 2007–8 period. Finally, when asked whether the United States had achieved its objectives in Iraq, only two respondents in five answered in the affirmative, but Republicans were far more likely (57 percent) than Democrats (36 percent) to judge the Iraq undertaking a success. As a result, their responses gave rise to partisan gaps on the order of 40 percent or more on eighteen questions, and in no case did their differences fall below double digits.

Two polling organizations also posed questions about whether the Bush administration had deliberately misled the public concerning charges that Iraq possessed weapons of mass destruction. Forty-six percent of the respondents believed that they had indeed been misinformed on that issue, but the almost even division of opinion once more masked the very substantial partisan differences. Republicans overwhelmingly (84 percent) rejected the charge that the administration had *deliberately* misled the public, whereas few (14 percent) Democrats did so.

When asked about whether Saddam Hussein had been involved in the September 11 terrorist attack, fewer than half of the respondents agreed that the Iraqi dictator was indeed guilty, but far more (44 percent) Republicans than Democrats (25 percent) expressed that view in 2005. Interestingly, although President Bush acknowledged in August 2006 that Saddam had nothing to do with September 11, his statement barely affected public responses to that question. CBS/*New York Times* surveys in 2005 and 2007 revealed that in each case one-third of the public responded affirmatively when asked, "Was Saddam Hussein personally involved in the September 11, 2001 terrorist attacks?"

At first glance, the results presented in table 3.4 might make one wonder whether Republicans and Democrats were in fact describing the same war. The huge partisan differences on assessments of events in Iraq can probably be explained at least in part by cognitive dissonance theory. Those who believed that the United States had done the "right thing" in using force against Iraq—that is, a very strong majority of Republican respondents—(table 3.3) were most likely to view events on the ground as pointing toward success, thereby sustaining and reinforcing their policy preferences on the issue. Conversely, far fewer Democrats supported the war, and in light of that it is hardly surprising that they were more likely to assess events there, including the post-Saddam insurgency, in a much less optimistic light.

A third cluster of survey items focused on prescriptions for policies that the United States should pursue: How long should American forces remain in Iraq? Under what conditions should they be withdrawn? Should there be a timetable for withdrawal, or should troops remain in Iraq until certain goals have been achieved? The Gallup Organization, CBS/*New York Times,* and three other polling organizations posed several such questions in their surveys, mostly since 2007. Following President Bush's announcement in January 2007 that he would send additional troops to Iraq, the issue of a possible timetable for withdrawal came up several times in Congress, and soon thereafter it entered into the debates surrounding the 2008 elections.

As revealed in table 3.5, various proposals about the conditions and possible timetables for withdrawal of American forces from Iraq generally received at least moderate support from a majority of respondents. A CBS/*New York Times* survey in late 2005 found that the public was almost evenly divided between keeping troops in Iraq until a "stable democracy" has been established there and withdrawing as soon as possible. But later polls in 2007 and 2008, several of them taken in the context of the debate surrounding the deployment of additional U.S. forces as part of the "surge" strategy, yielded increasing support for military withdrawal in accordance with various timetables. Those who favored some kind of plan for bringing American forces out of Iraq generally outnumbered respondents who opposed such plans by margins of about two-to-one. After General David Petraeus had been appointed to oversee the new postsurge strategy in Iraq he became a highly visible and articulate voice for the administration's policy, including during several televised appearances before Congress. Consequently, several Gallup surveys asked for judgments about General Petraeus. Finally, as American combat brigades were preparing to withdraw from Iraq in August 2010, a Gallup poll asked respondents whether American troops should remain there if Iraqi forces fail to maintain security.

As had been the case with the other clusters of questions, when respondents are classified according to their stated party preferences, the results revealed consistently sharp partisan differences. Eighteen of the nineteen items in table 3.5 gave rise to gaps between Republicans and Democrats exceeding 30 percent, and on seven of them the differences were 50 percent or more. The latter consistently provided stronger support for the various withdrawal proposals. The question about keeping American troops in Iraq beyond 2011 if Iraqi forces fail gained the support of only 43 percent of respondents, but the gap between Republicans (65 percent agreed that they should remain in those circumstances) and Democrats (26 percent) was nevertheless quite substantial. In addition, following the pattern found on previous clusters of questions, in each case the responses of self-described independents fell between those of Republicans and Democrats.

In summary, the finding presented in tables 3.3 through 3.5 fit a highly consistent pattern of partisan differences. Republicans were stronger supporters of using force against Iraq and the post-Saddam policies of the administration, they were much more likely to interpret events on the ground in an optimistic light, and they were also less likely to favor any of the various proposals for withdrawal of U.S. forces. These partisan differences were reinforced by media exposure. The print and electronic media generally painted rather different pictures of events surrounding the war in Iraq and, not surprisingly, members of the public tended to rely on sources that sustained their predilections.[13]

TABLE 3.5. Partisanship and Assessments of the War in Iraq, 2004–10: Prescriptions

Survey	Date	Responses by				
		All	Reps.	Dems.	Indeps.	Partisan Gap[a]

Should the United States stay in Iraq as long as it takes to make sure Iraq is a stable democracy, even if it takes a long time, or should U.S. troops leave Iraq as soon as possible, even if Iraq is not completely stable? (% stay)

Survey	Date	All	Reps.	Dems.	Indeps.	Partisan Gap
CBS/*New York*	October 2005	36	61	24	29	37
Times	November 2005	43	68	30	39	38

Do you support or oppose the legislation passed this week by the U.S. Senate calling for the withdrawal of U.S. troops from Iraq by March 2008? (% support)

Survey	Date	All	Reps.	Dems.	Indeps.	Partisan Gap
Newsweek	March 2007	57	28	81	58	−53

Do you think the U.S. should keep military troops in Iraq until the situation has stabilized, or do you think the U.S. should bring its troops home as soon as possible? (% keep troops in Iraq)

Survey	Date	All	Reps.	Dems.	Indeps.	Partisan Gap
Pew	February 2007	40	71	23	40	48
	April 2007	41	72	21	41	51
	June 2007	39	71	22	39	49
	October 2007	42	68	23	43	45
	December 2007	40	69	21	39	48
	February 2008	47	81	27	49	54

Do you think the U.S. should or should not set a timetable for the withdrawal of U.S. troops from Iraq that would have MOST U.S. troops out by September 2008? (% should)

Survey	Date	All	Reps.	Dems.	Indeps.	Partisan Gap
CBS	March 2007	59	36	77	59	−41

If you had to choose, which do you think is better for the U.S., to keep a significant number of troops in Iraq until the situation there gets better, even if that takes many years, or to set a timetable for removing troops from Iraq and to stick to that timetable regardless of what is going on in Iraq? (% keep troops in Iraq)

Survey	Date	All	Reps.	Dems.	Indeps.	Partisan Gap
Gallup/*USA Today*	February 2008	35	65	15	32	50

Regardless of how you intend to vote, which would you prefer the next president do about the war in Iraq? Would you prefer the next president to try to end the war in Iraq within the next year or two, no matter what, or continue to fight the war in Iraq as long as they felt it was necessary? (% continue)

Survey	Date	All	Reps.	Dems.	Indeps.	Partisan Gap
CBS/*New York Times*	April 2008	34	68	10	31	58

TABLE 3.5.—*Continued*

Survey	Date	Responses by				
		All	Reps.	Dems.	Indeps.	Partisan Gap[a]
	In your opinion, should the United States withdraw troops from Iraq right away, or should the U.S. begin bringing troops home within the next year, or should troops stay in Iraq as long as it takes to win the war? (% stay)					
LA Times/ Bloomberg	January 2008	31	61	8	26	53
	Opinions of General David Petraeus (% favorable)					
Gallup	August 2008	47	67	33	95	34
	September 7–8, 2008	52	73	41	49	32
	September 14–16, 2008	61	83	43	59	40
	How much longer should U.S. troops remain in Iraq? (% less than two years)					
Pew	November 2009	65	53	77	65	−24
	U.S. should withdraw from Iraq by 2011 regardless, or U.S. should keep troops in Iraq beyond 2011 if Iraqi forces fail. (% keep troops beyond 2011)					
Gallup	August 2010	43	65	26	NR	39

[a]Partisan gap: % Republican responses minus % Democrat responses.

CONCLUSION

Bipartisanship is not the natural state of affairs in the conduct of American foreign affairs, and, in any case, agreement across party lines does not provide any assurance that the resulting policies will effectively serve vital national interests. In August 1964, after only one day of debate, Congress passed the "Gulf of Tonkin Resolution," unanimously (416–0) in the House and with only 2 dissenting votes in the Senate. That vote was an important step in authorizing the Johnson administration to escalate the American effort in Vietnam, and it was later cited by the successor Nixon administration as justifying its actions in that disastrous war. The bipartisan Cold War consensus that had, by and large, served the country well on security issues in Europe stifled serious debate about whether and how events in Vietnam were linked to core national interests.[14]

That said, the country is not inevitably doomed to experience corrosive bickering, rooted in partisanship rather than in serious assessments of vital interests, that may threaten the quality of its external relations. Presidents may demand cooperation across party lines, but the "my way or the highway" approach will rarely be successful for more than a brief period. After the September 11 terrorist attacks, President Bush told foreign governments that "you are with us or you are with the terrorists," and in the immediate aftermath of those attacks, most Americans in fact supported the invasion of Afghanistan to hunt down al Qaeda terrorists and the Taliban government that had provided Osama bin Laden and his colleagues with a haven. But as shown above, agreement across partisan lines did not survive beyond the early months of the war in Iraq as it became increasingly clear that the overthrow of the Saddam Hussein regime, while widely welcomed by most Americans of both political parties, was only the first act in a drama that came increasingly to resemble a tragedy rather than a feel-good story in which the valiant heroes rescue the fair maiden and dispatch the black hats in short order.

Not the least barrier to bipartisanship were efforts by some members of the Bush administration and its cheerleaders in the media that equated any questions about the conduct of the Iraq campaign with giving aid and comfort to the enemy in time of war—that is, treason. For example, the *Wall Street Journal* accused the *New York Times* of having "as a major goal not winning the war on terror but obstructing it," and Vice President Dick Cheney warned that if the electorate makes the wrong choice in 2004—sending John Kerry to the White House—"then the danger is that we'll get hit [by terrorists] again, and we'll be hit in a way that will be devastating from the standpoint of the United States."[15] In a similar vein, the president attacked Democratic critics who questioned his prewar use of intelligence in a 2005 Veterans Day speech as "deeply irresponsible," and he charged that "these baseless attacks send the wrong signal to our troops and to an enemy that is questioning American's will."[16]

In much the same spirit, top White House aide Karl Rove compared the conservative and liberal approaches to terrorism in a speech to the New York Conservative Party. Although the divisive 2004 presidential election had come and gone, and, given the difficulties in Iraq, it might have been time for efforts at reconciliation and efforts to work more cooperatively with the other party, Rove chose a rather different path.

> Conservatives saw the savagery of 9/11 and the attacks and prepared for war; liberals saw the savagery of the 9/11 attacks and wanted to prepare an indictment and offer therapy and understanding for our attackers. In the wake of 9/11, con-

servatives believed it was time to unleash the might and power of the United States military against the Taliban; in the wake of 9/11, liberals believed it was time to submit a petition. . . . Conservatives saw what happened to us on 9/11 and said: We will defeat our enemies. Liberals saw what happened to us and said: We must understand our enemies.[17]

Although Rove's defenders stated that he had compared ideologies rather than parties, when he identified the targets of attack, they were such Democrats as Senator Richard Durbin (D-IL) and party chairman Howard Dean. The fact that virtually all Democrats—and liberals—supported the October 2001 invasion of Afghanistan to rout the Taliban and to capture or kill al Qaeda leaders apparently was deemed irrelevant by Rove.

The presidential power of appointment provides an important tool that may be used to mitigate the impact of partisanship by laying one foundation for a bridge to the opposition party. In selecting the American delegation to the Versailles Peace Conference following World War I, Democratic president Woodrow Wilson could have included any of several distinguished Republicans who were on record as favoring the creation of an international organization as part of the peace settlement. It would have been especially prudent to do so in light of the 1918 congressional elections that gave the GOP control of the Senate. Even if bitter personal animosities had ruled out including Henry Cabot Lodge (R-MA), who chaired the Senate Foreign Relations Committee, former president William Howard Taft, a supporter of a postwar international organization, might have been appointed. Or, with an eye toward the crucial role of the Senate in the treaty ratification process, Wilson might have selected a leading Republican senator other than Lodge. By failing to include a prominent Republican on the delegation, Wilson went a long way toward framing the question of American membership in the League of Nations as a partisan issue, thereby materially reducing the chances that the Versailles Treaty would gain approval by the Republican-dominated Senate.[18]

Some of Wilson's successors have demonstrated greater political acumen. After the collapse of the French army in 1940, anticipating that the United States would ultimately be drawn into World War II, Franklin Roosevelt fired his isolationist secretaries of navy and war, both Democrats, and replaced them with Frank Knox (the Republican vice-presidential candidate in 1936) and Henry Stimson (among the most distinguished Republican foreign policy officials of the twentieth century, who had served as secretary of war and secretary of state in the cabinets of presidents William Howard Taft and Herbert Hoover).

When faced with the very complex challenge of negotiating a peace treaty with all the countries that had been at war with Japan and then guiding the treaty through the U.S. Senate, Harry Truman turned to Republican stalwart John Foster Dulles, who would soon thereafter serve as President Eisenhower's secretary of state. In addition to his stature within the GOP, Dulles had served briefly in the Senate. Thus, his appointment was an important step in reducing the likelihood that the treaty would fail owing to partisan differences.

And, after winning a very close election in 1960, John F. Kennedy appointed Republicans Douglas Dillon and Robert McNamara to head the Treasury and Defense Departments. These appointments certainly did not ensure Republican support for all administration foreign and defense policies, but they represented significant steps in eliciting bipartisan cooperation on some important issues during World War II and the ensuing Cold War. During the most dangerous Cold War confrontation, the Cuban missile crisis, the presence of distinguished Republicans on the "Ex Com"—the Executive Committee of the National Security Council—defused any credible charges that President Kennedy had conjured up an international crisis to rally public support for Democrats in the upcoming 1962 congressional elections.

During his 2000 campaign for the presidency, George W. Bush pledged that if elected he would defuse partisan bickering in Washington. However, he made little use of his power of appointment for achieving that goal. His original cabinet included only one Democrat, former congressman Norman Mineta (D-CA) as head of the Transportation Department. After the hijackings of four commercial aircraft by the September 11 attackers, Mineta played an important role in efforts to secure the American transportation system, but he had little if any impact on foreign policy. He left the administration in 2006.

The personnel changes following the president's successful 2004 reelection campaign provided another significant opportunity toward trying to bridge the widening partisan chasms that had arisen in the wake of the chaotic situation in Iraq. Because of his immense stature and widespread popularity, Secretary of State Colin Powell was the official who might have worked most effectively with the opposition party, but he was fired within days of the president's reelection. Powell was one of several top-ranking officials who had lost favor in an administration that exhibited little tolerance for those who might be perceived as less than fully and enthusiastically committed to every detail of policy strategies and tactics, among them, Lawrence Lindsey, Paul O'Neill, Thomas White, and General Eric Shinseki.

Openings at the United Nations and the World Bank provided President

Bush with an opportunity for minor gestures toward bipartisanship, especially as neither of these organizations played a central role in the administration's foreign policy calculations. Instead of grasping at the chance to demonstrate that during his second term he would in fact try to work more effectively with the Democrats on foreign and defense policy, the president appointed two of the most partisan and outspokenly ideological officials of his first administration—Paul Wolfowitz and John R. Bolton—to serve as president of the World Bank and as U.S. ambassador to the United Nations. Ironically, neither appointment worked out well for the administration. Wolfowitz was forced to resign after it was revealed that he had made special arrangements for his mistress, Shaha Ali Riza, to be transferred from the World Bank, with a $60,000 annual raise, to the State Department where she would report to Liz Cheney, daughter of the vice president. Bolton had repeatedly been on record as attacking the United Nations and even deploring its very existence. His appointment seemed as appropriate as naming an avowed Holocaust denier to be U.S. ambassador to Israel. The Republican-controlled Senate Foreign Relations Committee refused to approve the Bolton nomination. Thus he served only briefly as an interim appointee, and the administration did not make a second effort to nominate him for a full term as UN ambassador.

President Barack Obama has apparently seen the advantages of reaching out to the opposition party for important foreign and defense policy appointments. Robert Gates, who had served as defense secretary during the last two years of the Bush administration, was asked to stay on in a position made all the more important by the wars in Iraq and Afghanistan that Obama inherited from his predecessor. Stuart Levey, undersecretary of the Treasury for Terrorism and Financial Intelligence in the Bush administration, was also retained. His position is especially important as he will play a key role in any financial sanctions on Iran arising from its nuclear program. Obama appointed retired marine corps general James Jones to be his national security adviser. General Jones had served in a number of important positions prior to his retirement in 2007, and thus he too was a carryover appointment from the Bush administration.[19] In another gesture toward bipartisanship, President Obama has shown rather limited enthusiasm for investigations of a wide range of possible misdeeds by members of the Bush administration, citing the need to "move forward rather than look back." In his speech announcing the withdrawal of American combat brigades from Iraq, President Obama pointed out that he opposed the Iraq invasion, but he also graciously praised his predecessor as a patriot who had always supported the American troops.

In still other efforts toward trying to build some bridges across the partisan divide by reaching out to Republicans, Obama appointed Utah governor Jon M. Huntsman Jr., a member of the GOP in a solidly Republican state, as American ambassador to China. Huntsman had served in the elder President Bush's administration as ambassador to Singapore and had also been a deputy U.S. trade representative in the George W. Bush administration. Huntsman, who had served his Mormon mission to China, is fluent in Mandarin, and he and his wife have adopted a child from China. In the light of China's increasingly important global role—not the least as the major financier of America's gigantic trade and budget deficits—as well as its regional position as the neighbor and ally of an increasingly bellicose North Korea, this is an ambassadorial position of immense importance. Obama followed that with the appointment of John M. McHugh, a senior Republican on the House Armed Services Committee, to be secretary of the army, another important appointment because of the two wars that he inherited from his predecessor and the certainty that his administration will face contentious budget debates on funding several very costly and highly controversial weapons systems.

In an appointment that bridges domestic and foreign affairs, Obama also reappointed Federal Reserve chairman Paul Bernanke for a second term. Finally, although the Department of Transportation and National Endowment for the Humanities have little if any impact on foreign and defense policy issues, the president appointed former congressmen Ray LaHood (R-IL) and Jim Leach (R-IA) to head those agencies.

There is, of course, no certainty that Obama's appointments will begin to bridge the unprecedented partisan chasms of the past decade. To the extent that former vice president Dick Cheney has become the most prominent spokesperson for the GOP on foreign and defense policy, the initial indications of restoring some degree of bipartisan cooperation are not especially promising. Nor will the appointment of these Republicans to important positions ensure foreign policy successes, especially in the most difficult and riskiest undertaking of the Obama administration: the increased commitment of troops and other resources to bring peace and stability to Afghanistan. Conspicuous setbacks in either Iraq or Afghanistan—both countries were experiencing increased levels of violence in 2009 and 2010—are certain to give rise to controversies and disagreements between Republicans and Democrats, but the presence of Gates and Jones in the inner circles of the administration may at least serve to reduce partisan passions.

CHAPTER 4

The War in Iraq: A Spillover to Other Opinions on Foreign Policy?

Franklin D. Roosevelt was the first American president to make use of the "new science" of public opinion polling as a tool in policy-making. He had witnessed how a young upstart pollster, George Gallup, had correctly called Roosevelt's landslide victory over Republican nominee Alf Landon in the 1936 presidential election, whereas the established *Literary Digest* poll had confidently predicted that the Kansas governor would oust FDR from the White House. The *Literary Digest* used a very large but unrepresentative sample—for example, auto registration lists during the Depression—while Gallup effectively relied on a much smaller but more representative sample of the electorate.

With financial support from a pharmaceutical company heir, Gerald Lambert, Roosevelt hired Hadley Cantril of Princeton University to conduct private polls for him throughout World War II. FDR was especially interested in tracking public attitudes on America's proper international role and, more specifically, the level of public support for joining a postwar general international organization. As a member of the Woodrow Wilson administration during World War I he had witnessed firsthand the process that led to the rejection of the Treaty of Versailles within which the League of Nations Covenant was embedded.

Interest in the postwar state of American public opinion on foreign affairs was also reflected in the frequency with which Gallup and other polling organizations asked respondents general questions about the United States taking an "active role" or "staying out" of world affairs, and more specific ones about support or opposition to American membership in a general international organization. These surveys seemed to indicate that substantial majorities among the general public in fact rejected a return to isolationism. A survey undertaken by the Office of Public Opinion Research a month after the Pearl Harbor attack revealed that, by a margin of 71 to 24 percent, Americans preferred taking "an active role" in world affairs after the war. The same question was posed nine times between February 1942 and November 1946, a period that encompassed a series of early defeats in the Pacific theater; the Allied invasions of North Africa, Sicily, Italy, and Normandy; the defeat of Nazi Germany; the atomic bomb attacks that led to Japan's surrender; and the first signs that the wartime cooperation among the victorious Allies would not extend into the postwar period. Responses to each of these surveys indicated, by margins ranging between three- and four-to-one, that the public rejected an American retreat from active participation in international affairs.

Public opinion polls also revealed very strong support for joining a general international organization. As noted earlier, Roosevelt avoided Woodrow Wilson's errors on the League of Nations issue by actively working for the support of top Republican leaders on the United Nations Treaty. The success of these efforts was reflected in strong public approval for American membership that transcended party lines.

While these surveys should have provided the president with some assurance that the public seemed unprepared to replay the post–World War I scenario with respect to international affairs, his fears on this score persisted. They were amplified by a memorandum that his private pollster, Hadley Cantril, gave Roosevelt just before he left for the Yalta Conference with Churchill and Stalin early in 1945.

> Although the overwhelming majority of the American people now favor a strong international organization necessarily dominated by the big powers, it is unrealistic to assume that Americans are internationally-minded. Their policy is rather one of expediency, which, at the moment takes the form of internationalism. The present internationalism rests on a rather unstable foundation: it is recent, it is not rooted in any broad or long-range conception of self-interest, it has little intellectual basis.[1]

That advice reinforced Roosevelt's judgment. He said privately, "Anybody who thinks that isolationism is dead in this country is crazy. As soon as this war is over, it may well be stronger than ever."[2]

The pessimism about public opinion expressed by Cantril and Roosevelt turned out to be misplaced. The question about America's proper role in world affairs was posed repeatedly during the decades following the Pearl Harbor attack. It was included in more than 50 surveys encompassing World War II; the onset of the nuclear age; two long and costly wars in Asia and a victorious one in the Persian Gulf region; crises in the Caribbean, the Taiwan Straits, Berlin, and the Middle East; several periods of warming relations between Moscow and Washington; the end of the Cold War and the disintegration of the USSR; controversial interventions in Panama, Somalia, Haiti, Bosnia, Kosovo, and elsewhere; and the months following the September 11 attacks. Despite the almost unprecedented international turbulence of this period and some variations in the precise wording of the questions, at no time did fewer than 53 percent of the public express a preference for "an active role" in world affairs. Indeed, the results were so stable that the question was not posed between November 1956 and January 1965, apparently because survey organizations assumed that public preferences about the American stance toward world affairs had been settled in favor of an active role and thus it was no longer worth further probes (fig. 4.1).

The "active role–stay out" questions reappeared in Gallup surveys in 1965, shortly after the United States had started to escalate its commitment in Vietnam, but well before that conflict had engendered the bitter domestic debates that came to dominate the presidential elections in 1968 and 1972. In the first of those campaigns the Vietnam issue essentially drove Lyndon Johnson out of the White House only four years after his landslide victory over Barry Goldwater. Johnson barely won the New Hampshire Democratic primary against Senator Eugene McCarthy (D-MN), a vocal antiwar critic, and as a consequence he withdrew from the race for the Democratic nomination. The 1972 election pitted incumbent Richard Nixon against George McGovern. McGovern had made "come home, America" one of his major campaign themes, but the election results indicated that, despite growing opposition to the Vietnam War, the country was not ready to follow that path as a general guide to foreign affairs. McGovern was not alone in questioning the country's internationalist foreign policy stance, but even as public disenchantment with the Vietnam War increased, it did not result in a wholesale repudiation of an "active role" in world affairs; those favoring the "stay out of world affairs" option never reached 40 percent, much less a majority.[3] The lowest level of public support for international engagement—53 percent—occurred in 1982, during the first Reagan administration, when it appeared that Cold War II would replace the détente policies of the Nixon, Ford, and Carter administrations.

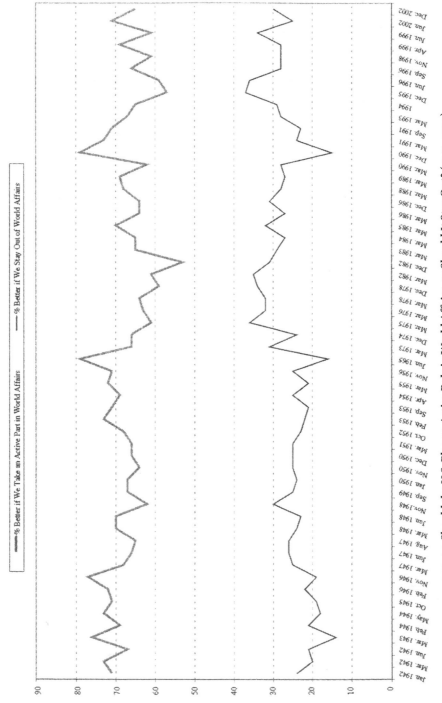

FIG. 4.1. Should the U.S. Play an Active Role in World Affairs, or Should It Stay Out? (1942–2002)

The disintegration of the Soviet Union in 1991 and end of more than four decades of Cold War tensions was the next major international turning point that might well have given rise to rethinking the country's global role. As noted, the distinguished historian Arthur M. Schlesinger Jr. believed that he had discerned precisely that trend—the end of what he called "the magnificent dream" of the liberal internationalism that had come to characterize American policy since World War II—because the sources and sustenance for those policies were to be found in the Soviet threat. He forecast the resurrection of isolationist sentiments among both opinion leaders and the general public under a new guise—American unilateralism.

Schlesinger's analysis seemed highly plausible in the light of realist theories that identify the international environment as the primary source of foreign policy. Kenneth Waltz, a leading theorist of the realist school who had forecast that neither the United States nor the Soviet Union could back off from their competition in a bipolar system, subsequently predicted that the disintegration of the USSR would result in major changes, such as the disappearance of the North Atlantic Treaty Organization, which had been created to contain the Soviet Union in Europe. In his words, "NATO's days are not numbered, but its years are."[4] American public opinion did not, however, conform to that prognosis. Less than two years after disintegration of the Soviet Union, Pew Research Center surveys started posing a question that offered a wider range of response options than "active role" or "stay out." Those taking part in the Pew surveys were asked, "What kind of leadership role should the United States play in the world?" Choices offered to respondents ranged from "be the single world leader" to "shouldn't play any leadership role," and included three possible kinds of "shared leadership role."[5]

The findings from ten surveys conducted between September 1993 and November 2009, summarized in table 4.1, offer striking evidence that public opinion on this aspect of American foreign policy remained exceptionally stable. Each survey revealed support from no fewer than 70 percent for a "shared leadership role" and, conversely, limited interest in either playing no international leadership role or in being the single world leader. Even the terrible events of September 11, the most devastating attack on American soil since the Japanese strike at Pearl Harbor almost six decades earlier that brought the United States into World War II, did not fundamentally alter public preferences on this country's position in the global system. Virtually the only discernible changes between the early September and October 2001 Pew surveys that bracketed the 9/11 terrorist attacks were increased preferences for a shared leadership role and a somewhat greater willingness to be the "most active leading nation." However, each of the subsequent surveys (2003–9) revealed diminishing support for the "most active" role.

Another example of the importance of question wording emerges from the 2009 Pew survey on items relating to unilateralism versus multilateralism. Forty-four percent of respondents agreed with the statement, "Since the U.S. is the most powerful nation in the world, we should go our way in international matters, not worrying too much about whether other countries agree with us or not." Yet by an overwhelming 78 percent to 14 percent margin they also agreed, "In deciding on its foreign policies, the U.S. should take into account the views of its major allies," and a smaller majority supported the proposition, "The U.S. should cooperate fully with the United Nations."

Additional evidence on this issue emerges from questions posed in surveys conducted by the Gallup Organization since 2001. Respondents were offered four options ranging from "the leading role" to "no role at all." The results, summarized in table 4.2, once again reveal the overall stability of public views on the question while also largely confirming those of the Pew surveys. Majorities ranging from 50 percent to 58 percent—the differences are close to the margin of error for such surveys—favored "a major role but not the leading role" for the United States. The period following the 9/11 terrorist attacks did witness a modest increase to 26 percent in those preferring "the leading role," but that

TABLE 4.1.   America's Role in the World, 1993–2009 (in percentages)

					Early					
What kind of leadership role should the United States play in the world?										
	Sept. 1993	Oct. 1993	June 1995	Sept. 1997	Sept. 2001	Oct. 2001	June 2003	July 2004	Oct. 2005	Nov. 2009
Be the single world leader	10	9	13	12	13	12	13	11	12	14
A shared leadership role	81	78	74	73	75	79	76	74	74	70
Most active leading nation	27	23	25	22	25	33	30	27	25	19
About as active as other leading nations	52	53	47	50	49	45	44	44	47	48
Don't know/refused	2	2	2	1	1	1	2	3	2	2
Shouldn't play any leadership role	7	9	9	11	8	3	7	9	10	11
Don't know/refused	2	4	4	4	4	6	4	6	4	6

Source: Pew Research Center, *America's New International Point of View,* Washington, DC, December 2001; and *America's Place in the World,* Washington, DC, 2009.

change did not persist. The "minor role" and "no role at all" response options, even when combined, were favored by only a small minority of respondents.

For present purposes the most important question is how the war in Iraq may have changed public views of the country's international role, especially given the growing disenchantment with that conflict. The February 2004–7 surveys revealed a slight erosion of "leading role" preferences and a concomitant increase in those favoring a "minor role," but the dominant pattern of responses revealed in the top half of table 4.2 is one of exceptional stability. Neither the shock of September 11 attacks nor the increasingly unpopular Iraq War significantly changed a persisting preference for international engagement, perhaps best characterized by the term *burden sharing* that, in turn, implies multilateralism, cooperation, consultation, and coordination with others. The dictum that "9/11 changed everything" was frequently asserted, but it was decidedly not the case with respect to public preference on America's international role.

The same Gallup polls posed a related question: "How satisfied are you with the United States' position in the world today?" In the first study after the 9/11 attacks and the American invasion of Afghanistan, more than seven in ten respondents expressed satisfaction with the U.S. global position. A sharp decline in satisfaction just prior to the invasion of Iraq in March 2003 was reversed the following month after American forces routed the Iraqi army and captured Baghdad in less than three weeks with relatively modest casualties. From that high point, when two-thirds of those taking part in the Gallup surveys stated that they were satisfied, there was a steady decline in that judgment. Even after the "surge" of American military forces and a change in strategy to emphasize protecting the civilian population rather than seeking out and attacking insurgents had significantly reduced violence and American casualties in Iraq, more than two-thirds of those taking part in the 2008 Gallup survey expressed their dissatisfaction with the American position. The two most recent Gallup polls revealed some improvement in this respect, but those who are dissatisfied still constituted a clear majority.

Taken together, the results in table 4.2 indicate that, despite manifest dissatisfaction that can almost certainly be traced to the increasingly unpopular Iraq War, the American public is not prepared for a wholesale retreat from active global engagement. At the same time, there seems to be limited enthusiasm for the role espoused by those who have argued that, as the world's only superpower, the United States best serves its interests—and those of the world—by pursuing its goals, unilaterally if necessary, without constraints from abroad.[6]

TABLE 4.2. America's Role in the World, 2001–11 (in percentages)

Next we would like you to think about the role the U.S. should play in trying to solve international problems. Do you think the U.S. should take . . .

	The Leading Role	A Major Role but not the Leading Role	A Minor Role	No Role at All
February 2001	16	57	21	4
February 2002	26	52	16	4
February 2003	26	53	16	3
February 2004	21	53	21	4
February 2005	19	53	21	5
February 2006	19	55	20	4
February 2007	15	58	21	4
February 2008	19	56	19	5
February 2009	23	52	17	6
February 2010	19	52	22	6
February 2011	16	50	25	7

How satisfied are you with the United States' position in the world today?

	Satisfied	Dissatisfied
July 1962	49	45
August 1965	43	48
September 1966	44	46
May 2000	65	33
February 2001	67	30
February 2002	71	27
February 2003[a]	53	46
March 2003	69	29
April 2003	67	30
February 2004	47	51
February 2005	48	51
February 2006	43	54
February 2007	37	61
February 2008	30	68
February 2009	32	66
February 2010	35	63

Source: Gallup Organization surveys. "No opinion" and "unsure" responses excluded.
[a]Average of two surveys in February 2003.

Thus, there is little evidence to sustain Arthur Schlesinger's fears that in the post–Cold War era the American public would espouse a unilateralist foreign policy.

The Gallup surveys also posed another question with implications for the country's international role: "How does the United States rate in the eyes of the world?" Americans have generally believed that this country is highly regarded by most people abroad. America's role in World War II, its enlightened policies in dealing with Germany and Japan after that conflict, its leading role in helping to create the United Nations and other major international institutions, and its foreign aid programs, highlighted by the Marshall Plan, Point Four, and the Peace Corps, have in fact provided substantial grounds for those who believe that the United States has generally played a constructive role in world affairs during recent decades. In rebuttal, critics can point to the disastrous Vietnam War as well as American interventions to overthrow popularly elected governments in Iran, Guatemala, Chile, and elsewhere. Nevertheless, in thinking about how their country is assessed abroad, Americans have usually judged that the glass is substantially more than half full.

However, in a lecture entitled "Challenges the Next President Will Face" a few days before the 2008 election, Brent Scowcroft, national security adviser to Republican presidents Gerald Ford and George H. W. Bush, told a Harvard Kennedy School audience that repairing America's reputation abroad is a top priority: "We've always had the benefit of the doubt. We don't have that anymore." Results of the Gallup polls undertaken since the turn of the century confirm Scowcroft's diagnosis and strongly suggest that the Iraq War had had a significant impact upon what Americans believe about how the United States rates in the eyes of the world (table 4.3). Prior to 9/11 more than 70 percent of respondents expressed the view that this country is viewed either "very" or "somewhat" favorably abroad. The first poll after the terrorist attacks, which brought forth widespread expressions of sympathy and support from many quarters abroad, found that almost four out of five expressed that judgment. Subsequent Gallup surveys overlapped with the run-up to the Iraq invasion, the successful defeat of Iraqi forces, followed by the bloody insurgency that began not long after the overthrow of the Baath regime in Baghdad. The overall pattern of responses reflects growing recognition by Americans that this country is not on balance favorably seen "in the eyes of the world." In the surveys between 2005 and 2009, those who believed that the United States is viewed "favorably" were outstripped by those who selected the "unfavorably" response option. There was some improvement in the 2010 and 2011 Gallup polls, both of which found that the "favorably" response options slightly outnumbered the "unfavorably" ones.[7] The reduced level of violence arising from the introduction of additional U.S. forces into Iraq in 2007 did not materially change that pattern. It is worth noting, however, that the growing recognition of disapproval by leaders and publics abroad has not given rise to widespread demands for a drastically reduced involvement with the global system. To be sure, some vocal pundits and administration cheerleaders dismissed criticism from abroad as either irrelevant or as a further reason for the United States to pursue its goals unilaterally, but as shown in tables 4.1 and 4.2, that view is not widely shared by Americans.[8]

Additional evidence on this point emerges from a series of eight Pew Research Center surveys conducted between 1984 and 2009, the results of which are summarized in the bottom part of table 4.3. Whereas in 1984 just over one-third of respondents stated that the United States is "less respected by other countries these days," that figure had almost doubled by 2008. Moreover, there was a growing tendency of those who believed that the United States is less respected to view that as "a major problem." Once again the data strongly suggest a public recognition that most other countries did not support American policy in Iraq.

THREATS TO VITAL AMERICAN INTERESTS

Each of the surveys conducted by the Chicago Council included a cluster of items that asked respondents to assess various threats to vital American interests during the 1998–2008 decade. With a few exceptions public threat assessments have remained quite stable over the course of a period that encompassed the 9/11 terrorist attacks, the invasion of Iraq, and the onset and growth of sectarian violence in that country (table 4.4). Not surprisingly, international terrorism led the rankings in four of the five Chicago Council surveys. Even before the 9/11 terrorist attacks the public was clearly sensitive to the threat as 84 percent rated it as "critical." Interestingly, that assessment far outstripped the judgment of opinion leaders (61 percent), including experts on foreign affairs, to whom that question was posed at the same time. The related national security issues of proliferation of nuclear and other weapons of mass destruction steadily ranked among the most critical perceived threats. Disruption of energy supplies—the top-ranked threat in 2008—and the movement of large numbers of immigrants into the United States were also highly ranked. The war in Iraq

TABLE 4.3. How the United States Is Rated Abroad, 1984–2011 (in percentages)

How does the United States rate in the eyes of the world?

	Favorably		Unfavorably	
	Very	Somewhat	Somewhat	Very
May 2000	20	53	22	4
February 2001	18	57	20	4
February 2002	20	59	17	3
March 2002	20	46	26	5
February 2003[a]	9	47	34	9
April 2003	12	49	28	9
February 2004	10	44	34	11
February 2005	7	41	39	12
February 2006	7	41	37	13
February 2007	5	40	38	16
February 2008	6	37	41	14
February 2009	4	41	40	13
February 2010	7	44	38	9
February 2011	6	44	37	12

Source: Gallup Organization surveys. "No opinion" and "unsure" responses excluded.
[a]Average of two surveys in February 2003.

Compared with the past, would you say the U.S. is more respected by other countries these days, less respected by other countries, or is it as respected as it has been in the past? If less, this is a major, minor, or not a problem?

	More	Less	If Less, What Kind of Problem			As Respected
			Major	Minor	Not Problem	
January 1984	27	36	—	—	—	29
May 1987	19	55	—	—	—	23
July 2004	10	67	43	19	4	20
October 2005	9	66	43	18	4	21
August 2007	7	65	48	14	2	23
May 2008	7	71	56	11	3	18
September 2008	8	70	48	21		22
November 2009	21	56	38	14	4	20

Source: Pew Research Center, *More See America's Loss of Global Respect as Major Problem,* June 16, 2008; and Pew Research Center, *America's Place in the World,* Washington, DC, 2009.

TABLE 4.4.   Threats to Vital U.S. Interests, 1998–2008 Chicago Council on Foreign Relations Surveys (percent "critical" assessments)

	1998	2002	2004	2006	2008	Change, 1998–2008
International terrorism	84	91	81	74	70	−14
Chemical and biological weapons	76	86	70	—	—	—
The possibility of unfriendly countries becoming nuclear powers	75	85	66	69	67	−8
AIDS, the Ebola virus, and other potential epidemics[a]	72	68	55	49	—	—
Large numbers of immigrants and refugees coming into the U.S.	55	60	51	51	51	−4
Military conflict between Israel and its Arab neighbors	—	67	43	—	—	—
Islamic fundamentalism	38	61	38	43	42	+4
Global warming	43	46	37	46	44	+1
Economic competition from low-wage countries	40	31	35	32	38	−2
The development of China as a world power	57	56	40	36	40	−17
World population growth	—	44	30	—	—	—
Tension between India and Pakistan	—	54	27	17	—	—
Economic competition from Europe	24	13	20	—	—	—
Disruption in energy supply	—	—	—	59	72	—
A confrontation between mainland China and Taiwan	—	—	—	18	19	—
Instability and conflict on the Korean peninsula	—	—	—	38	—	—
Islamic extremism	—	—	—	—	60	—
Violent Islamic groups in Pakistan and Afghanistan	—	—	—	—	55	—
Climate change	—	—	—	—	39	—
Instability and violence in countries with weak governments	—	—	—	—	26	—

[a]2006: "avian flu" replaced "Ebola virus."
Source: Chicago Council on Foreign Relations (CCFR), *Global Views 2004: American Public Opinion and Foreign Policy: Topline Data from U.S. Public Survey; U.S. Leaders Survey* (Chicago: CCFR, 2004); CCFR, *Global Views 2006* (Chicago: CCFR, 2006); and Chicago Council on Global Affairs, *Global Views 2008* (Chicago: CCGA, 2008).
— = No data.

thus appears to have had very limited impact by changing perceptions of critical threats.

Some potential threats to vital American interests were judged to be less critical in the most recent Chicago Council study. These included potential international epidemics, the growing power of China, and tensions between India and Pakistan, nuclear-armed Asian neighbors who have gone to war three times since achieving independence after World War II. These changes reflect the absence of recent threats of pandemics such as SARS and of crises in relations between Washington and Beijing, as well as a few signs that India and Pakistan may be moving, albeit fitfully, toward resolving some of the issues that have roiled relations between them during the past six decades.

Seven Pew Research Center surveys during approximately the same period (1999–2009) also asked those taking part to assess "threats to the well-being of the United States" (table 4.5). Although the Pew studies included only ten items, not all of which appeared on each survey, and the wording of the question and response options differed from those of the Chicago Council surveys, the results are rather similar. Terrorism, as represented by the question on Islamic extremist groups, and nuclear proliferation—specifically the programs in Iran and North Korea—once again topped the list of perceived threats. A new item—the growing strength of the Taliban in Afghanistan—was also seen as a major threat in the 2009 survey. In one significant respect the two surveys differed. Whereas those taking part in the Chicago Council study judged that the development of China as a world power represented a declining threat, the views of Pew respondents changed little over the course of the seven surveys. Whereas the earlier surveys asked respondents to assess "growing authoritarianism in Russia," the two most recent of the Pew studies included an item on tensions between Russia and its neighbors. The more malign view of Russia no doubt reflected the brief war between Russia and Georgia in August 2008.

The Gallup Organization posed a somewhat similar question in a February 2010 survey, asking respondents to assess seven international threats, with "critical threat" as the top response option. The results did not vary sharply from those in tables 4.4 and 4.5. "International terrorism" was judged to be a critical threat by 81 percent of respondents, followed by "the military power of Iran" (61 percent), "the military power of North Korea" (61 percent), "the conflict between Israel and the Palestinians" (47 percent), "the military power of China" (46 percent), "the conflict between India and Pakistan" (32 percent), and "the military power of Russia" (23 percent).

On balance, then, Americans continue to perceive substantial international threats to vital national interests, but their views in this respect have tended to be quite stable. That may help to explain the remarkably stable opinions, as depicted in tables 4.1 and 4.2, about the country's proper role in the world. Thus, there are few indications that growing disenchantment with the Iraq War has spilled over into an important aspect of how the public appraises the global environment.

GOALS FOR AMERICAN FOREIGN POLICY

Since their inception in 1974, surveys undertaken by the Chicago Council on Foreign Relations (now the Chicago Council on Global Affairs) have asked the public to assess the importance of a wide range of possible goals for American foreign policy. This cluster of items has been especially useful because, unlike the "active role–stay out" question, it provides respondents with the opportu-

TABLE 4.5.   Threats to the Well-being of the United States: Pew Research Center Surveys, 1999–2009 (percent "major threat")

	July 1999	May 2001	Oct. 2005	Feb. 2006	May 2008	Sept. 2008	Jan. 2009	June 2009	Nov. 2009
China's emergence as a world power	53	51	52	47	50	48	46	52	53
Growing tension between Russia and its neighbors	—	—	—	—	—	44	37	—	38
Growing authoritarianism in Russia	40	27	23	22	24	—	—	—	—
North Korea's nuclear program	—	—	66	60	55	55	53	72	69
Iran's nuclear program	—	—	61	65	62	60	65	69	72
Political instability in Pakistan	—	—	—	—	41	43	47	50	49
Islamic extremist groups like al Qaeda	—	—	—	—	72	72	77	78	76
International financial instability	—	—	—	—	—	—	—	—	61
Global climate change	—	—	—	—	—	—	—	—	44
The Taliban's growing strength in Afghanistan	—	—	—	—	—	—	—	—	70

Source: Pew Research Center Surveys; a report released September 24, 2008, includes results of the earlier surveys. Pew Research Center, *America's Place in the World,* Washington, DC, 2009.
— = No data.

nity to be selective about the more specific undertakings subsumed under an "active role." The 1998 study preceded the September 11 terrorist attacks, the 2002 survey took place less than a year after those tragic events, and the three most recent ones encompassed the invasion of Iraq, the overthrow of the Baathist regime, the capture and execution of Saddam Hussein, an increasingly violent insurgency pitting Sunnis against Shiites, as well as attacks against American occupation forces and Iraqis perceived to be collaborating with the United States, and the somewhat less violent environment in Iraq at the time of the 2008 survey.

Responses to the 1998 and 2002 studies provide a baseline against which to assess the three surveys that were undertaken after the invasion of Iraq. The results summarized in table 4.6 give rise to several generalizations, the most striking of which is the relative stability of foreign policy goal assessments over the decade covered by the Chicago Council surveys. Not surprisingly, coping with terrorism and nuclear proliferation have steadily ranked among the goals with the highest "very important" ratings. Maintenance of American military superiority was also seen as important, but one of the possible purposes of such capabilities—protecting weaker nations against aggression, as the United States is committed to doing in the NATO and several other security treaties—has declined rather sharply, with fewer than one-fourth of the respondents giving it the top rating in the three post-Iraq invasion surveys.

As in past Chicago Council studies, goals addressing American economic interests, including job protection, energy security, and immigration control, have consistently drawn many top ratings from the public. The 2008 survey was undertaken before the full extent of the international economic crisis arising from the collapse of the U.S. housing bubble and irresponsible deregulation of financial institutions that encouraged bankers to create and market high-risk instruments, both at home and abroad, that bore little relationship to underlying values. Thus, none of the goals questions deal with that aspect of international economic policy.

At the other end of the importance spectrum, the public has generally expressed lukewarm enthusiasm for promoting and defending American values and institutions abroad, including human rights and a democratic form of government. These responses probably reflect in part the difficulties that the United States encountered in trying to achieve these goals. The post–World War II occupations of Germany and Japan transformed these two countries into stable democracies with strong institutions and effective protection of human rights, and American support for India and Israel played a role in their

TABLE 4.6. The Importance of American Foreign Policy Goals: Assessments by the General Public in 1998, 2002, 2004, 2006, and 2008, Chicago Council on Foreign Relations Surveys (percentage of "very important" ratings)

For each [foreign policy goal], please say whether you think that it should be a very important foreign policy goal of the United States, a somewhat important foreign policy goal, or not an important goal at all.

	1998	2002[a]	2004	2006	2008	Change, 1998–2008
World order security issues						
Preventing the spread of nuclear weapons	82	86	73	74	73	−9
Combating international terrorism	79	83	71	72	67	−12
Strengthening the United Nations	45	55	38	40	39	−6
Protecting weaker nations against aggression	32	35	18	22	24	−8
World order economic and environmental issues						
Combating world hunger	62	54	43	48	46	−16
Improving the global environment	53	55	47	54	—	1[b]
Helping improve the standard of living in less developed countries	29	28	18	22	—	−7[b]
Limiting climate change	—	—	—	—	42	—
Promoting international trade	—	—	—	—	34	—
U.S. economic interest issues						
Stopping the flow of illegal drugs into the U.S.	81	72	63	—	—	—
Protecting the jobs of American workers	80	81	78	76	80	0
Securing adequate supplies of energy	64	69	69	72	80	16
Controlling and reducing illegal immigration	55	70	59	58	61	—
Protecting the interests of American business abroad	—	51	32	—	—	—
Promoting economic growth	—	—	—	62	—	—
U.S. values and institutional issues						
Promoting and defending human rights in other countries	39	41	—	28	31	−8
Helping to bring a democratic form of government to other nations	29	24	14	17	17	−12
Improving America's standing in the world	—	—	—	—	83	—
Cold War/Security issues						
Maintaining superior military power worldwide	59	67	50	55	57	−2

Source: John E. Reilly, ed., *American Public Opinion and U.S. Foreign Policy, 1999* (Chicago: CCFR, 1999); Marshall Bouton and Benjamin Page, *Worldviews 2002: American Public Opinion and Foreign Policy* (Chicago: CCFR, 2002); and Chicago Council on Foreign Relations (CCFR), *Global Views 2004: American Public Opinion and Foreign Policy* (Chicago: CCFR, 2004); CCFR, *Global Views, 2006* (Chicago: CCFR, 2006); Chicago Council on Global Affairs, *Global Views 2008* (Chicago: CCGA, 2008).

[a]Figures are from the Internet rather than telephone survey.
[b]Change 1998–2006 rather than 1998–2008.
— = No data.

emergence as democracies after they had achieved independence. Elsewhere the record is rather bleak, however, as few other efforts in the Third World, notably in Vietnam and Central America, have matched those impressive successes. Moreover, a number of postwar U.S. interventions abroad sought to *overthrow* rather than promote or sustain democratically elected governments.

The Bush administration and its supporters defended the Iraq War as a necessary step toward bringing democracy to the entire Middle East region. That transformation would, it was asserted, bring peace and stability to a region that has known little of either. Although Iraq has achieved a new constitution and an elected parliament, expectations of stability, security, or levels of effectiveness of police and military units have proved to be too optimistic, a point that even President Bush has conceded.[9] That experience may help to explain why only about one in six participants in the 2006 and 2008 Chicago Council surveys expressed the view that "helping to bring a democratic form of government to other nations" is a vital foreign policy goal. In the absence of some clearer evidence that the long and costly U.S. intervention has given root to a government in Baghdad that is able to gain effective levels of public support from all sectarian groups with minimal levels of violence and corruption, there is little reason to believe that the Iraq experience will cause many Americans to attribute greater importance to democracy promotion abroad on the country's foreign policy agenda. Although the turnout in the 2010 elections was quite impressive and it included participation by the Sunni minority, the postelection stalemate among party leaders, resulting in an inability to form a government in a timely manner, is a major cause for concern about the future of democracy in Iraq. Nor is the modest support the American public accorded to promoting human rights likely to improve dramatically.

The most recent Chicago Council studies also revealed slightly declining support for some world-order economic issues—sometimes described as "compassion fatigue"—including combating world hunger and dealing with the standard of living in less-developed countries. That said, on balance the general public has shown few inclinations to retreat indiscriminately into a new phase of withdrawal from world affairs during the period encompassing the invasion of Iraq and the turbulent occupation of that country. An item on "improving America's standing in the world" only appeared in the 2008 Chicago Council study, in which it received an exceptionally high rating as 83 percent judged it to be "very important." This is consistent with the finding cited earlier (table 4.3) that many Americans are aware of the sharp decline in America's reputation abroad during the period since the invasion of Iraq. It also reveals a significant public concern for relations with other countries, and a rejection of the view held by a number of Bush administration officials and conservative pundits that the United States is better off pursuing a unilateralist course in foreign affairs rather than trying to cooperate or coordinate policies with less red-blooded allies or, worst of all, with various international organizations.

The overall stability of public opinion on goals for American foreign policy can be summarized by some rank-order statistics. The rank-order correlation across the entire ten-year span of 1998–2008 is a very high 0.91. The 1998–2002 comparison, which provides some indication of the impact of the September 11 terrorist attack, yields a very similar rank-order correlation of 0.90, whereas the correlation between the goal rankings in 2002 and in 2008, surveys that bracket the Iraq War, is also a very high 0.88.

The Pew Research Center also included a "long range goals" item in eight of its surveys spanning more than a decade and a half. Although the dates of the surveys and the exact wording of some items differ from those of Chicago Council studies, the results are generally quite similar. Protection from terrorism, preventing the spread of weapons of mass destruction, protecting American jobs, and energy independence consistently ranked among the top priorities for American foreign policy, with 60 percent or more of respondents rating them as "top priority" goals. In contrast, the importance attached to two global order issues—strengthening the United Nations and dealing with global climate change—fell somewhat. At the other end of spectrum, the evidence once again indicates that promoting and defending democracy and human rights in other countries is not deemed to be a high foreign policy priority, even if doing so involves protecting groups that are threatened with genocide.

The evidence about foreign policy priorities summarized in table 4.7 on balance reveals more continuity than change although the 16-year period spanned the 9/11 attacks and the first 6 years of the Iraq War. There is, however, one *very important* exception to this generalization. When the 2001, 2005, and 2008 Pew surveys asked respondents to assess the goal of "reducing U.S. military commitments overseas," their responses reveal a striking and significant trend. Whereas in the first of the three studies only about one respondent in four judged that to be a "top priority," by 2008 that figure had increased to 45 percent. It takes no stretch of imagination to attribute the increasing disenchantment with military commitments abroad to the Iraq War and, perhaps, to a somewhat lesser extent, to the conflict in Afghanistan since 2001.

In response to demands by Iraqi prime minister Nuri al-Maliki, President Bush agreed in 2008 to a planned withdrawal of most American forces from

TABLE 4.7. Long-Range Goals for American Foreign Policy in Pew Research Center Surveys, 1993–2009 (percent "top priority")

	1993	1995	1997	2001	2004	2005	2008	2009	Change, 1993–2009
Reducing our dependence on imported energy sources	—	—	—	—	63	67	76	64	—
Preventing the spread of weapons of mass destruction	69	68	70	80[a]	71	75	62	74	5
Finding a solution to the conflict between Israel and Palestinians	34	—	—	—	28	—	25	—	—
Improving relations with our allies	—	—	—	—	54	—	54	—	—
Protecting groups that are threatened with genocide	—	—	—	49[a]	47	46	36	—	—
Reducing U.S. military commitments overseas	—	—	—	26	35	—	45	—	—
Protecting the jobs of American workers	85	80	77	74	84	84	82	85	0
Strengthening the United Nations	41	36	30	44[a]	48	40	32	37	−4
Reducing the spread of AIDS and other infectious diseases	—	—	—	66[a]	72	72	53	—	—
Promoting and defending human rights in other countries	22	21	27	28[a]	33	37	25	29	7
Dealing with global climate change	56	56	50	38[a]	36	43	43	40	−16
Taking measures to protect the U.S. from terrorist attacks	—	—	—	87[a]	88	86	82	85	—
Combating international drug trafficking	—	—	—	64	—	59	—	56	—
Helping to improve the standard of living in developing nations	—	—	—	25	—	31	—	26	—
Promoting democracy in other countries	—	—	—	29	—	24	—	21	—
Reducing illegal immigration	—	—	—	—	—	51	—	46	—

Source: Pew Research Center surveys; a report released September 24, 2008, includes results of the earlier surveys. Pew Research Center, *America's Place in the World*, Washington, DC, 2009.

[a] Average of surveys in September 2001 and October 2001.

— = No data.

Iraqi cities in mid-2009 and from Iraq by end of 2011, a timetable not dramatically different than that proposed by President Obama shortly after he took office. The Obama plan leaves some 50,000 troops in Iraq, mostly for continued training of the Iraqi military. Although they are no longer designated as "combat brigades," there is no assurance that they can avoid a combat role or avoid casualties. Indeed, some American troops were killed within days after the withdrawal of combat brigades. Whether the Iraqi army and police forces can maintain a decent level of security in their country will no doubt depend in part on whether the sectarian groups can resolve their still significant differences by political processes rather by a resumption of the violence that brought their country to the brink of civil war. Should that happy outcome take place, it might stanch the clearly increasing public desire to reduce military commitments abroad. In accordance with the Bush–al-Maliki agreement of 2008, all U.S. forces were withdrawn from Baghdad and other major urban centers on June 30, 2009. Even though the previous month had witnessed a rather sharp increase in sectarian violence, Prime Minister al-Maliki was adamant that the U.S. withdrawal must take place on schedule. In a somewhat less-than-gracious commentary on American policy in his country, he declared a national holiday to celebrate the withdrawal from cities, and he lauded the "repulsion of foreign occupiers" as comparable to the rebellion against British troops in the 1920s.[10] Policymakers in Washington and American officers in Iraq wisely did not get drawn into a debate about those statements, accepting them as not very subtle efforts by al-Maliki to strengthen his domestic political base in Iraq in preparation for the 2010 elections.

The conflict in Afghanistan presents the other big question mark in this respect. Can the deployments of additional U.S. troops—21,000 troops in the spring of 2009 and a further deployment of 30,000 Americans toward the end of the year—to that troubled country prevent Afghanistan from spiraling into a failed state, a narco state, a refuge for Taliban insurgents, or some combination of those undesirable outcomes? Even with the additional troops, by early 2011 that happy outcome seemed increasingly uncertain. Should the situation in Afghanistan improve substantially without incurring increasing American casualties, it might, but is certainly not guaranteed to, stem the tide of growing public disenchantment with U.S. military commitments overseas. Secretary of Defense Robert Gates probably expressed a popular opinion when he told West Point cadets in February 2011 that if any future holder of his office proposes to send the military to a big land war in Asia or the Middle East, he "should have his head examined."[11]

USES OF ARMED FORCES ABROAD

American armed forces have been deployed abroad since almost the time of the birth of Republic—for example, Thomas Jefferson sent the small U.S. navy to Africa to deal with the Barbary pirates—but rarely without controversy. The Japanese attack on Pearl Harbor catapulted a united country into World War II, but in this respect it was almost unique. The War of 1812, the Mexican War, and American entry into World War I engendered often-bitter debates in Congress about the wisdom and justice of going to war. Had public opinion surveys on declarations of war been available at those times, they almost surely would have revealed sharp divisions in the country at large. Since World War II, declarations of war by Congress have gone out of style, in part because the Constitution stipulates that the war-making prerogatives are shared between the executive and legislative branches, and the former has clearly come to dominate the latter. Despite efforts to redress the balance between the two branches—for example, through the War Powers Act of 1973—in practice expansive presidential interpretations of prerogatives arising from the constitutional role of commander in chief of the armed forces have generally trumped occasional calls for restoring a central congressional role, as stipulated in Article I, Section 8 of the Constitution, in decisions about war.

The Chicago Council surveys have posed a cluster of items about circumstances that would justify the use of American armed forces abroad, and some similar questions appeared in a 2009 Pew study. Some of them concern situations covered by such alliance commitments as the U.S.–South Korea pact, whereas others pose hypothetical scenarios that might give rise to demands that the United States intervene with its armed forces. Responses to these questions in the Chicago Council and Pew surveys are summarized in table 4.8.

The Iraq War represented the largest deployment of U.S. troops into a combat situation since the Vietnam War. There is growing evidence, however, that the postinvasion Iraq quagmire can be traced in large part to Washington's decision to deploy forces sufficient to defeat Saddam Hussein's second-rate military but without serious attention to the manpower requirements of maintaining security in post-Saddam Iraq. Defense secretary Donald Rumsfeld, Paul Wolfowitz, and other top decision makers in the Bush administration persuaded themselves that U.S. troops would be greeted as liberators rather than conquerors, thus trumping the arguments of army chief of staff Eric Shinseki and many experts on the region about the need for "several hundreds of thousands" of military personnel to maintain security in Iraq.

Despite the growing unpopularity of the Iraq War, the evidence does not indicate that the American public has become reflexively gun-shy about all deployments of U.S. forces into conflict situations. Even before the 9/11 terrorist attacks, most surveys revealed that the public had selective views on the question, and that it would usually support using American armed forces to deter or repel the invasion of friendly countries, as in the case of Iraq's invasion of

Kuwait in August 1990, or an attack on Israel. There has also been strong approval of deploying troops to prevent humanitarian disasters arising from natural catastrophes such as the 2010 earthquake in Haiti or genocidal actions of governments against their own people. Conversely there has been very limited enthusiasm for using the armed forces to export democracy. Indeed, as indicated earlier, Americans have rarely given top priority to such foreign policy goals as international promotion of American values and institutions such as democracy, human rights, or market economies.[12]

As shown in table 4.8, six surveys by the Chicago Council and one by the Pew Research Center provide evidence that, the unpopular Iraq War notwith-

TABLE 4.8. Public Support for Use of Troops Abroad: Chicago Council on Foreign Relations and Pew Surveys, 1990–2009 (percent favor)

	1990	1994	1998	2002	2004	2006	2009
To stop a government from committing genocide and killing a large number of its own people[a]	—	—	—	77	75	71	58
To deal with humanitarian crises	—	—	—	—	72	66	—
To be part of an international peacekeeping force in Afghanistan	—	—	—	76	60	—	—
To ensure the supply of oil	—	—	—	—	54	45	—
To be part of an international peacekeeping force to enforce a peace agreement between Israel and the Palestinians	—	—	—	65	52	51	—
If the government of Pakistan requested our help against a radical Islamic revolution[b]	—	—	—	61	51	—	51
To be part of a UN-sponsored force to help keep peace between India and Pakistan	—	—	—	—	51	40	—
To fight drug lords in Colombia	—	—	—	66	51	—	—
If North Korea invaded South Korea	26	39	30	36	43	45	—
If Arab forces invaded Israel	45	42	38	48	43	—	—
If China invaded Taiwan	—	—	27	32	33	32	—
To install democratic governments in states where dictators rule	—	—	—	—	30	29	—
To be part of an international peacekeeping force to stop the killing in Darfur	—	—	—	—	—	65	—
If Iran attacked Israel	—	—	—	—	—	53	—
To stop Iran from obtaining nuclear weapons[c]	—	—	—	—	—	62	63

Source: Chicago Council on Foreign Relations (CCFR), Global Views 2004: American Public Opinion and Foreign Policy (Chicago: CCFR, 2004); CCFR, Global Views 2006 (Chicago: CCFR, 2006); and Pew Research Center, America's Place in the World, Washington, DC, 2009.
[a]2009 wording: "If an ethnic group in Africa were threatened by genocide."
[b]2009 wording: "If extremists were poised to take over Pakistan."
[c]2009 wording: "If it were certain that Iran had produced a nuclear weapon."
— = No data.

standing, the pattern of support for the use of armed forces has remained relatively stable, with prevention of humanitarian disasters, including the killing in the Darfur region of Sudan, gaining approval from more than half of the respondents. Those responses are not quite consistent, however, with the finding reported in table 4.7 above, in which those taking part in Pew surveys gave a rather low priority to the goal of protecting groups that are threatened with genocide.

The steady lack of strong support for using the military to protect Taiwan from a Chinese invasion probably arises in part from the long-standing Shanghai communiqué signed by President Nixon in 1972 stipulating that there is only one China, the subsequent abrogation of the Taiwan security treaty, and by a general lack of enthusiasm for engaging in a conflict over the security of Taiwan with a nuclear-armed country of some 1.3 billion people. China has also become a major trade partner, and it gains at least some leverage from its vast holdings of U.S. securities—the official Treasury Department figure at the end of 2010 was $1.16 trillion, but a Reuters report calculated that the actual amount was closer to $2 trillion—which, if sold off, would create havoc on Wall Street and other financial markets. Although relations between China and Taiwan have generally stabilized in recent years, those between Washington and Beijing have hit a number of rough patches. American requests for Chinese cooperation on China's undervalued currency, at the Copenhagen conference on global warming, and on Iran's nuclear program have largely gone unheeded. When in early 2010 the United States announced a $6 billion arms package of defensive arms for Taiwan—including helicopters and Patriot missiles, but excluding F-16 fighters and diesel submarines—in accordance with a Bush administration plan and long-standing congressional mandate on Taiwan's security, China vehemently expressed its displeasure and threatened to punish American arms companies that sell to Taiwan and to cancel some high-level meetings between Washington and Beijing. However, unless this marks the beginning of a protracted new cold war between the United States and China, it seems unlikely that public support for military deployments in support of Taiwan will increase substantially.

Although the United States has a security treaty with South Korea, earlier surveys found very limited support for coming to Seoul's aid in case of another invasion by North Korea, but there is a clear trend toward higher approval of such assistance. As revealed in table 4.8, whereas only about a quarter of respondents to a 1990 Chicago Council survey supported the deployment of American troops "if North Korea invaded South Korea," that number climbed fairly steadily in five subsequent polls, reaching 45 percent in 2006. North Korea's belligerent behavior, including firing missiles into the Sea of Japan and achievement of nuclear weapons capabilities, has probably had an impact on public opinion. Its sinking of a South Korean naval ship, the *Cheonan,* in the spring of 2010, resulting in the death of 46 sailors, is also certain to have an impact on how Americans view North Korea. When the ship was raised to the surface, the torpedo that sank it was found to bear North Korean markings. However, when the issue came before the United Nations Security Council, owing to China's insistence a resolution on the sinking failed to mention North Korea as the guilty party.

Iran was identified by President Bush in his 2002 State of the Union message as part of the "axis of evil," and since the hostage crisis of 1979–81, most Americans have had strong negative opinions of the Tehran regime. In the wake of the U.S. invasion of Iraq, in May 2003 the Iranian government sent a secret proposal, via the Swiss ambassador, for settling issues between Tehran and Washington as part of a "grand bargain." The proposal included full Iranian cooperation with the United States and the International Atomic Energy Commission on nuclear safeguards; decisive action against terrorists on Iranian soil, "especially al Qaida"; ending material support for Palestinian militias and support for a two-state solution of the Israeli-Palestinian conflict; and active support for Iraqi stabilization, including establishment of democratic institutions and a nonreligious government. In return, the United States would have to lift economic sanctions on Iran; support Iranian reparations claims against Iraq; provide access to peaceful nuclear technology; assist in action against anti-Iranian terrorists, above all, MKO (People's Mujahedin of Iran); and issue a statement that "Iran does not belong to the axis of evil." President Bush's inclusion of Iran in the "axis of evil" had made cooperation much more difficult and ultimately ended it.

Some U.S. officials, including Richard Haass in the State Department, felt that there was nothing to lose in pursuing the Iranian initiative even if, on further exploration, it resulted in a "dry hole." Vice president Cheney and defense secretary Rumsfeld strongly opposed such a course of action even though the United States would enter into any discussions with a decided advantage, including a large army of occupation in neighboring Iraq, and they reprimanded the Swiss ambassador for even forwarding it.[13] Ryan Crocker, the American ambassador in Afghanistan, recently confirmed that during 2001 through 2003, Iranian diplomats were eager to work with the United States and the new Karzai government in Kabul on issues of common interest, including arrest and detention of al Qaeda leaders. It is far from clear whether the 2003 Iranian initiative might have led to some easing of the fraught relations between the two countries, but the subsequent insurgency in Iraq—to which Iran contributed—and skyrocketing oil prices certainly did not reduce Tehran's relative bargaining position.

Although Iran denies that its nuclear program is aimed at developing weapons, a substantial majority of those taking part in the 2006 CCFR and 2009 Pew surveys would approve using troops to prevent Tehran from obtaining nuclear weapons. Concern with Iran also shows up in another context. When respondents were asked about protecting Israel from an invasion by its Arab neighbors, support for using American troops in such a conflict remained steady, averaging in the low 40 percent range through 2004. When the 2006 survey rephrased the question, positing a hypothetical invasion of Israel by Iran, support increased to 53 percent.

More recent surveys revealed that most Americans (88 percent) believe that Iran, despite its repeated denials, is in fact trying to develop nuclear weapons, but opinions about taking military action against Iran indicated the lack of a similar consensus. Several surveys during October 2009 found those favoring military action ranged from 29 percent to 54 percent. When asked whether U.S. forces should be used to remove the Iranian government from power, there was limited enthusiasm for doing so; an ABC/*Washington Post* survey found that 62 percent opposed such action, and 82 percent responding to a CNN/Opinion Research poll expressed opposition to military intervention.[14]

The highly controversial Iranian presidential election of 2009, in which incumbent president Mahmoud Ahmadinejad was declared the winner only two hours after the polls closed with an improbable 62 percent of the vote, did little to improve relations between the United States and Iran. In another example of the dictum that "politics makes strange bedfellows," some conservative American pundits were openly supporting the election of the hard-line Iranian incumbent over the modestly more reformist Mir Hussein Mousavi for any of several reasons. In a speech to the Heritage Foundation, Daniel Pipes expressed a preference for an Ahmadinejad victory because that outcome would make it easier for Israel to launch an air strike against Iranian nuclear research facilities. Michael Rubin told a *National Review* reporter that an Ahmadinejad victory would discredit the Obama administration policy of seeking diplomatic solutions in foreign affairs. Martin Peretz in the *New Republic* and Ilan Berman in the *American Spectator* asserted that there was no difference between the two Iran presidential candidates.[15]

President Obama condemned the violence against postelection protesters in Tehran but wisely refused to take sides on the election, thereby accentuating the rifts between the "death to America" faction in Iran and those who oppose that view. No doubt public assessments of the Iranian regime will decline as a consequence of the controversial election and its immediate aftermath, including numerous arrests and some executions of protesters who openly defied the regime, but it is also possible that widespread reports of the protests in Tehran may result in more favorable views of Iranian society. It remains to be seen if that would be accompanied by an increased or decreased willingness to engage in possible military action against Tehran.

In summary, the data in table 4.8 fail to provide substantial evidence that the September 11 terrorist attacks and the subsequent wars in Afghanistan and Iraq have fundamentally transformed public views on the uses of armed forces abroad. Americans continue to be selective in that respect, rejecting both a retreat into isolationism and an expansive definition of national security that employs the country's unquestioned standing as the world's only superpower as a springboard for an ambitious agenda of global transformation, especially if such efforts were undertaken unilaterally. The data once more serve to rebut the charge that American public opinion is volatile and that the changes bear little relationship to important international developments.

That said, there are also some indications in the latest Pew Research Center survey of public disenchantment with international affairs. When asked whether "The U.S. should mind its own business internationally and let other countries get along as best they can on their own," a plurality of 49 percent agreed. That is a sharp increase from the 30 percent who gave that answer, shortly prior to the invasion of Iraq, in December 2002. Another item in the same survey—"We should not think so much in international terms but concentrate more on our own national problems and building up our strength and prosperity here at home"—yielded agreement from 76 percent of the respondents.[16] However, since that question was first posed by Gallup in 1964, it has never failed to gain support from very substantial majorities. The 2009 responses did not differ strikingly from those of three Pew surveys in 2004–6, which averaged 70 percent, and they are exactly the same as in an April 1993 study. The financial meltdown of 2008 and the resulting increase in unemployment no doubt reinforced the public preference that domestic issues should take a priority. Finally, another item in the 2009 Pew survey asked whether it was more important for the president to focus on domestic or foreign policy. Those favoring the former option prevailed by a very large 73 percent to 12 percent margin. It is also important to note, however, that only once since Pew began posing the questions in 1993 has foreign policy been cited as more important, and then by only a slim margin of 40 percent to 39 percent in January 2007, when the situation in Iraq threatened to turn into a full-scale civil war. In summary, although the evidence does not indicate a public preference for withdrawal from an active international role, it does suggest something akin to "internationalism fatigue." In the light of two long and costly wars, the outcomes of which do not yet warrant triumphant assertions of "mission accomplished," that is hardly surprising, nor should it be construed as evidence of public irresponsibility.

CONCLUSION

This chapter has explored the question of whether the public's growing dissatisfaction with the situation in Iraq has spilled over to reshape a broader set of opinions about American foreign relations. Most of the evidence suggests a limited spillover rather than a dramatic transformation of public opinion, at least through the end of 2010. In the 1995 essay cited earlier, Arthur Schlesinger perceived declining support for internationalism across the entire spectrum of American society, from "the housewife in Xenia, Ohio," to members of the Council on Foreign Relations and many officials in Washington.[17] The evidence reviewed here suggests that if the Ohio housewife represents the public at large, she is pretty sensible in her appraisal of the global situation and America's role in it. She is almost certainly disenchanted with the Iraq War, and she may well have some serious reservations about future deployments of American troops abroad, including those used to support weaker allies, but she does not seem prepared to advocate a wholesale retreat from engagement in the global system, not even from major military actions if such undertakings have the support of allies. Contrary to Schlesinger's fears, she strongly seems to prefer burden sharing to unilateralism in foreign policy. As this is being written, Libya appears to be on the verge of a bloody civil war as Colonel Muammar el-Qaddafi seems willing to unleash his military forces, including the use of airstrikes against rebels demanding that he step down. She is not likely to support any military intervention unless it is part of a multinational effort.

In light of the evidence that most Americans are not prepared to withdraw from an active role in world affairs, why have many post–World War II public officials been concerned that there may be a resurgence of isolationist sentiments? There are probably many explanations. A long tradition in American thought, going back at least to James Madison, identifies international activism, especially if it takes a military form, as a threat to democratic institutions at home. According to Madison, "Perhaps it is a universal truth that the loss of liberty at home is to be charged against provisions of danger, real or pretended from abroad. The management of foreign relations appears to be the most susceptible of abuse of all the trusts committed to a Government, because they can be concealed or disclosed, or disclosed in such parts and at such times as will best suit particular views; and because the body of the people are less capable of judging, and are more under the influences of prejudices, on that branch of affairs, than of any other."[18] Senators Robert A. Taft, who narrowly missed gaining the Republican presidential nomination in 1952, and George McGovern, the Democratic nominee in 1972, strongly espoused these views. Moreover, the "conventional wisdom" that public opinion is volatile and often out of synch with international realities has never fully died out, despite strong evidence to the contrary. Walter Lippmann was not only a founding father of public opinion research, but he was also a widely read syndicated columnist who frequently expressed his skeptical views of the public. Lippmann has long since passed from the scene and his theories have not held up well in light of extensive empirical research on post–World War II public opinion, but his views nevertheless live on in the writings of some pundits and other opinion leaders. All of this is not to rule out the possibility that at some future point there may be a significant reversal of public opinion, especially if the economic difficulties arising from the 2008 financial meltdown, including high unemployment, persist over an extended period. Such a scenario might make it easier for opinion leaders to argue that the best solution to domestic difficulties is to reduce international involvement, not only on security concerns but even more significantly on trade, finance, immigration, and many other economic issues.

In conclusion, however, it is also worth pondering an important question that can only be answered in the future. Will the fact that the Bush administration took the country into a long and costly war on the basis of faulty arguments and highly flawed use of intelligence color how the United States is able to respond to future situations in which the alleged threat to vital national interests lacks the clarity of a Pearl Harbor or September 11 type of attack? Leaving aside constraints arising from evidence that American armed forces are stretched very thin; West Point graduates are leaving the military in record numbers as soon as their five-year service obligations are fulfilled; the increasing physical and psychological toll arising from repeated deployment to Iraq and Afghanistan; military suicides that are at a record level; rising postdeployment alcoholism, domestic violence, and murders; difficulties in meeting military recruitment quotas that have given rise to significant reductions in education, fitness, and criminal background standards; and the gigantic budget deficits of recent years, are there limits on the willingness of the American public to "rally 'round the president" in support of military interventions?[19] At some point significant numbers among the public and opinion leaders may well recall the story of the boy who cried wolf too often. While that may prevent unwise interventions, one of the long-term costs of the Iraq invasion may be that its example serves as a constraint when the threats are in fact real.

CHAPTER 5

The Impact of Public Opinion on Iraq Policy

Not long after assuming the presidency, George W. Bush asked a top aide, "What's all this NBC/*Wall Street Journal* poll b.s.?" Later Bush told Dee Dee Myers, press secretary for President Clinton, "In this White House, Dee Dee, we don't poll on something as important as national security." These statements echo claims he had made while campaigning for the presidency—that he leads "based upon principle and not on polls and focus groups."[1] These assertions also have something of a "dog bites man" flavor to them. Whatever their private views about the relevance or utility of public opinion, if there have been presidents who proclaimed publicly, "We chose policy X because the public demanded it," or "I decided not to undertake action Y because it would have run into strong public opposition," it has escaped my notice.

That said, most presidents recognize the truth of Theodore Roosevelt's observation that the White House gave him a "bully pulpit" with which to persuade Congress, the media, other opinion leaders, and the general public about the virtues of his policies and the deficiencies of those espoused by his opponents. Walter Lippmann, one of the founding fathers of public opinion research, served as an adviser to Woodrow Wilson and helped to write the president's famous "Fourteen Points" speech during World War I. Shortly thereafter Lippmann wrote that, owing to widespread public ignorance of and indifference to public affairs, modern governments must necessarily engage in the process of "manufacturing consent" from the public.[2] Three decades later Lippmann came to fear what he perceived as the growing ability and willingness of legislatures to hamstring executives, especially in the conduct of foreign affairs.

According to Lippmann, this dangerous derangement of powers was sustained by publics, whose opinions are fickle, volatile, and usually out of synch with realities.

> The unhappy truth is that the prevailing public opinion has been destructively wrong at the critical junctures. The people have impressed a critical veto upon the judgments of informed and responsible officials. They have compelled the government, which usually knew what would have been wiser, or was necessary or what was more expedient, to be too late with too little, or too long with too much, too pacifist in peace and too bellicose in war, too neutralist or appeasing in negotiations, or too intransigent. Mass opinion has acquired mounting power in this country. It has shown itself to be a dangerous master of decision when the stakes are life or death.[3]

Lippmann was not alone in his cry of despair about the impact of public opinion on American foreign policy. Diplomat-historian George F. Kennan, political scientist Gabriel Almond, and diplomatic historian Thomas A. Bailey were among the prominent students of American foreign policy who expressed very similar concerns. Indeed, the growing availability of survey data reinforced rather than assuaged their fears.[4]

A good deal of research during the past three decades has seriously challenged Lippmann's dismal conclusions about the nature and impact of public opinion.[5] It has also shown that presidents have varied widely in their beliefs about the nature and legitimacy of public opinion, as well as in their sensitivity to information about public preferences and survey data.[6] As noted earlier, two Democratic presidents of approximately the same generation, Franklin Roosevelt and Harry Truman, differed widely on these questions. Nevertheless, during recent decades, all presidents with the possible exception of George H. W. Bush have made extensive use of private pollsters to provide information about public sentiments.

What about the impact of public opinion in the George W. Bush administration and, more specifically, on its Iraq policy? Although it is far too soon to offer a definitive answer, the evidence to date suggests that President Bush resembled Truman in his public derision of pollsters and those who believe that policy decisions should be affected by surveys. At the same time he resembled Roosevelt in using polls—generated by Jan van Lohuizen (Voter/Consumer Research) and Fred Steeper (Market Strategies)—while going to great efforts to keep that fact private. But the survey data were not used as guides to policy;

rather, "Policies are chosen beforehand, polls used to spin them." This was especially true of unpopular policies.[7] In short, the administration could not be accused of pandering to the public.

Interviews with a member of the administration brought forth several observations that seem to lend some credence to President Bush's denial that he made policy decisions with an eye to polling data.[8] The president had a very low regard for pollsters and was skeptical of evidence from their surveys, believing that his own instincts provided a better guide to the public mood. In a 2002 interview with Bob Woodward, Bush "referred a dozen times to his 'instincts' or his 'instinctive' reactions as a guide for his decision. . . . 'I'm not a textbook player, I'm a gut player.'" This is apparently a trait in which he took considerable pride because he repeated it to others who described his decision-making style.[9]

Among staff members who kept track of polls other than those commissioned by the White House or National Republic Committee, the prevailing view was that owing to samples and questions that are often alleged to reveal an antiadministration bias, most polling organizations provided little useful feedback or guidance on foreign policy issues. For example, although Pew Research Center polls abroad were highly regarded, its domestic surveys were seen as partisan and antiadministration. Even the Gallup Organization, sometimes thought to have a pro-Republican slant, was suspect. The Program on International Policy Attitudes (PIPA) was charged with having a consistent "liberal internationalist bias" in its choice of issues and questions. Zogby International, although seen as antiadministration and anti-Israel, was cited as a good source on a narrow range of Middle East issues, and the Defense Department did some useful polling of publics abroad. On balance, however, survey data apparently played little role in *policy decisions* but they helped shape *how issues were framed* in what was a relentless effort to gain public support for the administration's policies on Iraq.[10]

PHASE I (2001–3)

The thesis to be developed here is that the Bush administration pursued a very active public relations campaign to promote and sustain support for its Iraq policy, but the flow of influence in the other direction—from public opinion to policy—was at best quite limited. This discussion divides the relationship between public opinion and Iraq policy into two phases. During the period beginning with the September 11 terrorist attacks and ending slightly less than two years later there was a moderately high correspondence between administration policies and public opinion on Iraq for at least three reasons: (1) The American public had long been predisposed to believe the worst about the Saddam Hussein regime; (2) top administration officials engaged in a relentless overt and covert public relations campaign to link its Iraq policy to the "global war on terrorism"; and (3) the media and Congress, which might have been expected to raise probing questions about an issue as important as the invasion of Iraq, generally played a quiescent role.

The decision to oust the Saddam Hussein regime in Iraq had its roots in the opening weeks of the Bush administration, but the September 11 terrorist attacks almost completely dominated the societal and institutional context within which the Iraq policy was formulated and executed.[11] Even before the terrorist attacks, the public had harbored overwhelmingly negative views of Saddam Hussein as a result of the invasion of Kuwait that led to the 1991 Gulf War and because of growing evidence about his brutal reign. As revealed in table 2.2, Pew, Gallup, and CBS/*New York Times* surveys between 1992 and 2003 found majorities ranging from 52 percent to 74 percent favoring the use of force to remove Saddam, although in no case did as many as two respondents in five favor doing so "even if allies won't join." Thus the administration's active campaign to link Iraq with weapons of mass destruction and al Qaeda found an audience ready to believe the worst about the Baghdad regime.

Perhaps even more important, the administration received a virtually blank check from the media following the September 11 attacks. One perspective on the role of the media emerged from one journalist's interview with an "unnamed administration official."

> The aide said that guys like me were "in what we call the reality-based community," which he defined as people who "believe that solutions emerge from your judicious study of discernible reality." I nodded and murmured something about enlightenment principles and empiricism. He cut me off. "That's not how the world really works anymore," he continued. "We're an empire now, and when we act, we create our own reality. And while you're studying that reality— judiciously as you will—we'll act again, creating other new realities, which you can study too, and that's how things will be sort out. We're history's actors . . . and you, all of you, will be left to just study what we do."[12]

Six days after the 9/11 attacks, CBS news anchor Dan Rather, often derided by conservatives as part of "the liberal media establishment," told David Letterman,

"George Bush is the President. . . . wherever he wants me to line up, just tell me where." Less than three weeks later Rather repeated his patriotic willingness to support the president on *Entertainment Tonight:* "If he needs me in uniform, tell me when and where—I'm there." Not be outdone, another of the country's most visible and credible newspersons, Cokie Roberts of ABC, told Letterman, "Look, I am, I will confess to you, a total sucker for the guys who stand up with all the ribbons and stuff and they say it's true and I'm ready to believe it."[13] The passive view of the media role was also reflected in the explanation by Jim Lehrer, host of Public Broadcasting System's *News Hour,* for the lack of prewar attention to the possible challenges presented by the post-Saddam era: "The word occupation . . . was never mentioned in the run-up to the war. It was about liberation. It was a war of liberation, not a war of occupation. So, as a consequence, those of us in journalism never even looked at the issue of occupation."[14]

Most of the media also fell into line. Repeated administration claims about Iraqi weapons of mass destruction (WMDs) and ties to al Qaeda—neither of which was conclusively proven valid—were largely allowed to go unchallenged during the run-up to the war. Although there were some honorable exceptions, including the McClatchy newspapers, Judith Miller of the *New York Times* was the poster child for a complacent media. A December 2001 story featured information from an Iraqi defector who claimed to have worked on renovations of Iraqi chemical, biological, and nuclear weapons facilities. All of those claims were later shown to be totally false. Her byline appeared in 64 articles about Iraq's alleged WMDs, the most important of which was a 2002 article asserting that Saddam Hussein was increasing his quest for atomic bomb parts.[15] The article appeared almost simultaneously with the start of the administration public relations campaign on Iraq's weapons of mass destruction and ties to al Qaeda. She did not inform the *Times* or her readers that she relied heavily on a highly questionable source, Ahmed Chalabi, an ambitious Iraqi exile who was the favored Pentagon candidate for a major post-Saddam leadership role in Iraq. The U.S. government paid Chalabi's organization, the Iraqi National Congress, $36 million from 2000 to 2003. Chalabi had asserted that his plan for an insurgency would easily prevail, and the outcome "would turn Iraq into a good, stable, modern, pro-Western free market country."[16] Aside from his doubtful reliability as a source on Iraq's WMD programs, Chalabi had been indicted for embezzlement in Jordan. He fled Jordan in the trunk of a car and was later sentenced, in absentia, to a 22-year prison term.

To its credit, the *Times* later conducted a self-critique of its reporting on the issue of Iraq's WMDs, but it buried the story on page 18.[17] In response to criticism of her reporting, Miller asserted, "My job [as an investigative reporter in the intelligence area] isn't to assess the government's information and be an independent intelligence analyst myself. My job is to tell readers of the *New York Times* what the government thought about Iraq's arsenal." She went on to insist that the problem was with the intelligence, not the reporting. "To beat up the messenger is to miss the point."[18] Charles Gibson of *World News* on the ABC network expressed a similar viewpoint about prewar coverage. "I think the questions [about the war] were asked. . . . It was just a drumbeat of support from the administration. It is not our job to debate them. Our job is to ask questions."[19]

There is also some evidence that newspersons were under corporate pressure in the post-9/11 environment to avoid being critical and, therefore, of seeming to lack sufficient patriotism. Katie Couric, a CBS news anchor, asserted that "she felt pressure from government officials and corporate executives to cast the war in a positive light." Jessica Yellin of MSNBC recalled that her producers "wanted their coverage to reflect the patriotic mood of the country."[20]

The *Washington Post* provides a good example of how even one of the country's best newspapers skewed its coverage of the Iraq issue. A newspaper that set the gold standard for investigative reporting of the Watergate break-in that led to President Nixon's resignation in 1974 provided a platform for administration claims while muting if not completely ignoring those who raised serious questions about those assertions. The *Post* editorial pages strongly supported the war, but there was a firewall between the editorial and news staffs. Nevertheless, between August 2002 and March 19, 2003—the day of the American invasion— the *Post* ran more than 140 front-page stories that focused strongly on claims by the president, vice president, and other top officials about Iraq. In contrast, a story on September 19, 2002, about independent experts questioning administration claims that the aluminum tubes were suitable for Iraq's alleged nuclear program ran on page 18. A month later, a Thomas Ricks story titled "Doubts" cited Pentagon officials, retired officers, and outside experts who were reluctant to support the planned invasion and were worried that its risks were being underestimated. The story was killed by Matthew Vita, the national security editor. According to Ricks, "There was an attitude among editors: Look, we're going to war, why do we even worry about all this contrary stuff?" Walter Pincus, a 32-year veteran staff member at the *Post,* had served in the counterintelligence corps during his two-year stint in the army and had won a Polk Award, a Pulitzer Prize, and a TV Emmy Award. He had established excellent contacts with the likes of Hans Blix, the chief UN weapons inspector for Iraq, but he also ran into similar difficulties with stories questioning administration claims on Iraqi weapons of mass destruction.[21]

The McClatchy newspapers provided an exception to the generally complacent media treatment of administration justifications for the use of force against Iraq. For example, two days before the September 8, 2002, front-page *New York Times* story about Iraq's alleged efforts to develop weapons of mass destruction, a McClatchy article cited some Washington officials about the lack of hard evidence to back up assertions by Dick Cheney and other administration leaders on this very important issue.[22] McClatchy spokespersons later charged that, owing to their skeptical reporting on prewar intelligence, their reporters were systematically excluded from secretary of defense airplanes. The Pentagon denied the charge.[23]

That most of the media took a pass on the administration's primary arguments for going to war—Iraq's alleged weapons of mass destruction and ties to al Qaeda—can perhaps be explained in part by the difficulties for those outside government in ascertaining the veracity of those claims. Given what was known of Saddam Hussein's behavior, including his use of chemical weapons against Iran during their long war as well as against his own Kurdish population, neither of the charges could be dismissed as beyond the realm of possibility. The task of ferreting out the truth was not made easier by CIA officials who said, "Look, we know what we're talking about, but we can't tell you."[24]

The same argument cannot be said to justify the widespread failure of the media to probe beyond the surface of claims by the president, Dick Cheney, Donald Rumsfeld, Paul Wolfowitz, and other administration officials that American forces would be greeted as liberators rather than conquerors, that sectarian differences in post-Saddam Iraq would disappear, and that most if not all of the costs of the occupation and reconstruction could be paid for by Iraqi oil revenues. Scrutinizing these premises would not have required access to top secret intelligence files, or even an advanced degree in history. How often have foreign occupying forces been greeted as liberators, even after overturning the regime of a brutal tyrant? Have Islamic countries historically been especially prone to welcoming foreign invaders? As Sunnis and Shiites have been at odds for more than a millennium, was it probable that occupation by armies from a country with a very different culture would make Iraqis of these religious persuasions forget those long-standing differences for the sake of Iraqi unity? Was it possible that if Sunnis and Shiites found it convenient to cooperate, at least temporarily, it might be to *oppose* the American occupation forces? And while Iraq does indeed have major oil resources, assertions that these would suffice to pay for the occupation and reconstruction of the country assumed a best-case postwar scenario: oil wells remaining intact during the conflict, no damage to infrastructure during air attacks on Iraq, and peaceful acquiescence to the invasion. It is hardly sufficient to assert that the prewar deliberations in Washington did not really engage issues of what happens after the fall of Saddam. Thomas Ricks, the author of an award-winning book on the Iraq War, was right on the mark when he wrote, "the media didn't delve deeply enough into the issues surrounding the war, most notably whether the administration was correctly assessing the threat presented by Iraq and the costs of occupying and remaking the country."[25]

Scott McClellan, who served as White House press secretary under President Bush (2003–6), reinforced the criticism of the media.

> If anything, the national press corps was probably *too* deferential to the White House and to the administration in regard to the most important decision facing the nation during my years in Washington, the choice of whether to go to war in Iraq. The collapse of the administration's rationale for war, which became apparent months after our invasion, should never have come as such a surprise. The public should have been made much more aware, before the fact, of the uncertainties, doubts, and caveats that underlay the intelligence about the regime of Saddam Hussein. The administration did little to convey those nuances to the people, the press should have picked up the slack but largely failed to do so because their focus was elsewhere—on covering the march to war, instead of the necessity of war.[26]

Finally, by framing the Iraq issue as a central part of the post-9/11 "global war on terrorism," the administration was largely able to free itself from congressional constraints. The October 2002 votes in the House and Senate authorizing the use of force against Iraq and the hated Saddam Hussein just prior to the midterm congressional elections was deliberately timed to force members to take a stand on Iraq. It placed skeptics who may have doubted claims about Iraqi WMD or ties to al Qaeda in an almost impossible position, especially when the president frequently framed issues as "you are with us or you are with the terrorists."[27]

The strategy of focusing on Iraq as an integral part of the war on terrorism seems to have borne fruit in the elections. Typically the party that controls the White House loses seats in the midterm elections—1902, 1934, and 1998 were the most recent previous exceptions—but in 2002 the Republicans regained control of the Senate by picking up two seats. The GOP also added eight House seats, increasing their majority from seven to twenty-three. Among the losers was Senator Max Cleland (D-GA), a Vietnam veteran who lost three limbs in that conflict. He was accused of insufficient commitment to protecting the country from the threat of terrorism because he supported collective bargaining rights for employees of the new Department of Homeland Security. His opponent, Saxby Chambliss, who unleashed a series of ads attacking Cleland's patriotism that even some Republicans found disreputable, had gained six deferments from military service that kept him out of the Vietnam War. Karl Rove, also the recipient of several draft deferments during the Vietnam era, supported Chambliss's campaign. One political observer who served for several years in the administration and who had been in the Naval Reserves, but never on active duty, justified the attacks on the grounds that Cleland was "pathetic."

Bush administration officials often portrayed questions from Congress about its policies as tantamount to aiding the enemy. A request from Senator Hillary Rodham Clinton (D-NY) about planning on Iraq, including the possibility of eventual troop withdrawal, would have seemed reasonable in light of the Defense Department's abysmal record of preinvasion planning, but it brought forth a spirited reply from Undersecretary of Defense Eric Edelman: "Premature and public discussion of the withdrawal of U.S. forces from Iraq reinforces enemy propaganda that the U.S. will abandon its allies, much as we are perceived to have done in Vietnam, Lebanon, and Somalia."[28] After the October 2002 votes to authorize the use of force against Iraq, Congress as an institution played almost no role on Iraq other than to approve a series of huge supplemental appropriations for the war. The use of supplemental appropriations also served to reduce the perceived size of deficits in the budget.

An important part of the administration's strategy to marginalize the Congress was the extensive use of "signing statements" on legislation indicating that, irrespective of clear congressional intentions, the president would interpret and execute the laws in accordance *with his own preferences.* Until recent decades, all previous presidents combined had issued only 75 signing statements, but their use has increased sharply since the Reagan years. Although the Supreme Court has ruled against the line-item veto in *Clinton vs. City of New York* (1998), President Bush achieved an effect somewhat similar to the line-item veto by challenging more than 1,100 provisions of federal laws.[29] For example, the Detainee Treatment Act of 2005 prohibited cruel, inhuman, and degrading treatment of detainees in American custody. The signing statement attached to this legislation stated, "The executive branch shall construe . . . the Act, relating to detainees, in a manner consistent with the constitutional authority of the President to supervise the military executive branch and as Commander in Chief and consistent with the constitutional limitations on the judicial power."[30] In short, presidential preferences were deemed to trump congressional intent, and the judicial branch was asserted to be powerless on the issue. In 2006, the American Bar Association issued a report unanimously condemning the use of signing statements as contrary to the constitutional system of separation of powers.[31] This is not the place to engage in the legal debate on the constitutionality of signing statements. Suffice it to say that their very liberal use represents another significant step in a long-term process of expanding executive powers, well beyond what the Founding Fathers had in mind when they crafted Article I of the Constitution, at the expense of Congress.

According to Jack Goldsmith, a Bush appointee who served as head of the Justice Department's Office of Legal Counsel, the administration made expansion of executive powers its top priority and made little effort to work with other institutions. The president ignored "the soft factor on [policy] legitimation—consultation, deliberation, the appearance of deference, and credible expressions of public concern for constitutional and international values—in his dealing with Congress, the courts, and allies." Republican Senator Lindsey Graham agreed: "The Bush administration came up with a pretty aggressive, bordering on bizarre, theory of inherent authority that had no boundaries. As they saw it, the other two branches of government were basically neutered in time of war." Perhaps the most succinct summary of President Bush's beliefs about executive-legislative relations on Iraq was his assertion, "I don't think Congress ought to be running the war. I think they ought to be funding the troops."[32]

There was a fairly close concordance between public opinion and Bush administration policies during the two years leading up to the fall of Baghdad, but it would be a mistake to conclude that, therefore, public opinion was an important driving force in Washington. After the overthrow of the Taliban regime in Afghanistan the president mounted a full-scale public relations campaign against Iraq, highlighted by his 2002 State of the Union address and a graduation speech at the United States Military Academy at West Point five months later.[33] Unbeknownst to the public, however, the decision to invade Iraq had been made by midsummer 2002, if not earlier. The secret "Downing Street Memo," dated July 23, 2002, based on meetings of British officials with members of the Bush administration, left no doubt on that score.

C reported on his recent talks in Washington. There was a perceptible shift in attitude. Military action was now seen as inevitable. Bush wanted to remove Saddam, through military action, justified by the conjunction of terrorism and WMD. But the intelligence and facts were being fixed around the policy. The NSC had no patience with the UN route, and no enthusiasm for publishing material on the Iraqi regime's record. There was little discussion in Washington of the aftermath after military action.[34]

A careful study of the months leading up to the invasion in Iraq in March 2003 has shown that, President Bush's protestations to the contrary notwithstanding, some leaders in the administration may in fact have taken public opinion into account with respect to tactics and timing.[35] For example, the Bush administration took some steps to build on and buttress public anti-Iraqi sentiments by going to Congress to garner support for the use of force against Iraq. British prime minister Tony Blair made it clear that his constituents wanted United Nations involvement on the issue. Despite opposition to involving the United Nations from Donald Rumsfeld, Dick Cheney, and Paul Wolfowitz, the United States did so, and in November 2002, it gained unanimous Security Council approval of Resolution 1441 demanding that Iraq readmit UN inspectors to determine whether it was still in compliance with post–Gulf War agreements not to acquire weapons of mass destruction. Leading administration officials also undertook a strenuous multifaceted overt and covert public relations campaign to rally American public support for the upcoming invasion of Iraq.[36] American leaders also hoped to gain international approval in early 2003 for another Security Council resolution authorizing the use of force against the Saddam Hussein regime.

Although Washington was pressing for a favorable Security Council resolution for using force against Iraq, President Bush made it clear at a White House meeting with British prime minister Tony Blair on January 31, 2003, that the decision to go to war—slated at that time to begin on March 10—had essentially been made. In his words, "The diplomatic strategy had to be arranged around the military planning." He was determined to invade Iraq even if weapons inspectors failed to find any evidence of weapons of mass destruction, but that failure would not divert his determination to go to war. Indeed, the president told Blair that he was so worried about a failure to find hard evidence about WMDs that he thought of "flying U-2 reconnaissance aircraft with fighter cover over Iraq, painted in United Nations colors," hoping to provoke Saddam into firing on them, thus justifying the planned attack. Bush and Blair, neither of whom was an expert on Iraqi society, also agreed that it was "unlikely that there would be internecine warfare between the different religious and ethnic groups."[37]

The search for support for a second Security Council resolution on Iraq in fact proved futile. Washington assumed that Russia, France, and Germany would oppose such a resolution because they had made it clear that no action should take place before the arms inspectors in Iraq had completed their work, but it hoped to get enough votes to isolate those three countries, while providing at least an added element of legitimacy for the imminent invasion. However, even Mexico and Chile, hemispheric neighbors with which the United States has special trade relationships, let it be known that they would oppose the resolution, as would the three African members of the Security Council. Facing the prospect of an embarrassing defeat, the United States withdrew it. The United States and Great Britain thus invaded Iraq without the UN authorization they had sought.

The capture of Baghdad less than three weeks after the onset of hostilities brought American public support for the invasion to new highs. As shown in chapter 2 (fig. 2.1), three Pew Research Center surveys found that more than 70 percent of respondents agreed that the United States "made the right decision in using military force against Iraq." Other surveys in mid-2003 revealed strong majorities for the propositions that the war was going well (fig. 2.2), that it had improved American security (fig. 2.3), and that its cost had been worth it (fig. 2.4).

PHASE II (2003–9)

If there had been any ambiguity about the impact of public opinion on Iraq policy up through the summer of 2003—the thesis here is that it had almost no impact because the administration would likely have invaded Iraq even in the absence of public support—evidence for the period since the president announced the successful conclusion of hostilities points rather clearly to the conclusion that the public was seen largely as an entity to be "educated" rather than as a source of useful policy guidance or even as a significant political barrier. The most telling point was the steadily widening divergence between public support for the Iraq War and the administration's repeated insistence that its actions were vital to American national security, that events such as the several successful Iraqi elections in 2005 proved the wisdom and effectiveness of those policies, and that the goal of "victory in Iraq" was realistically within reach if the United States stayed the course rather than caving in to defeatists at home.

Henry Kissinger, who was identified as a frequent visitor to the White House during the Bush administration, drew the parallel between Iraq and the Vietnam War that, in his self-serving interpretation of that conflict, was sabotaged by "liberals" on the home front. It remains to be seen whether this is the opening shot in a campaign to demonize administration critics if the ultimate outcome in Iraq falls short of complete success.[38]

Beginning in the latter part of 2003, lack of conclusive evidence on the administration's central rationale for invading Iraq—its alleged weapons of mass destruction and ties to al Qaeda—combined with bloody sectarian violence and mounting American casualties, began to erode the effectiveness of public relations efforts by the administration to sustain support for the war (figs. 2.1–2.4). The growing public disenchantment with the war had very limited impact on policy, but it did impel the administration to alter its ways of framing the Iraq issue in the course of its vigorous campaign to persuade the public that, despite difficulties in bringing peace and security to Iraq, its policies were essential to protecting American national security.

But even if the evidence indicates that public views on the Iraq War had a very limited role in the policy-making process, this is not to say that the administration was indifferent to public opinion. Most important, the long run-up to the 2004 election made it imperative for the president to rally public support for the war effort. Two careful studies agreed that Iraq was an important election issue. According to one, "The presidential election of 2004 was profoundly influenced by judgments about the war in Iraq." Opinions about the use of force and the likelihood of success were important determinants of votes.[39] The second study concluded that "the president's advantage on terrorism narrowly trumped his disadvantage on the economy and Iraq."[40] As shown in figures 2.1 and 2.4, the election came at about the time that public support for the war was eroding.

The administration was also quite proactive in attempting to shield the public from the true costs of the war. The costs of the war were taken "off budget," and the administration continued to defend its tax cuts, to suggest even deeper cuts in the face of ballooning war expenditures and deepening budget deficits, and to encourage consumers to continue shopping and spending as their contribution to national security. It tightened limits on media access to the Dover, Delaware, and Ramstein, Germany, air bases to prevent coverage of flag-draped coffins returning from Afghanistan and Iraq. The Pentagon also took steps to obstruct coverage of burial services for those killed in Iraq, even if grieving family members gave the media permission to attend so that the nation would learn about the sacrifice of their loved ones.[41] Although there was substantial evidence that the armed forces were stretched very thin and that repeated deployments to Iraq and Afghanistan had inflicted a heavy toll on the military, there was never any consideration of reinstituting the draft as a way of spreading the human costs of the war more equitably; in justice, it must be acknowledged that any such proposal on the draft would have been dead on arrival in Congress. Republican senator George Voinovich summarized the point succinctly: "The truth of the matter is that we haven't sacrificed one darn bit in this war, not one. Never been asked to pay a dime, except for the people that we lost."[42]

Highlighting the heroic actions of specific soldiers can provide another means of gaining public support for a war effort. The military exploits of Sergeant Alvin York, Audie Murphy, and the five Sullivan brothers during the world wars are good examples. Notable combat achievements by York and Murphy were also the subjects of successful movies following those conflicts. Perhaps the most poignant such episode occurred in the early days of World War II. The five Sullivan brothers of Waterloo, Iowa, enlisted in the navy shortly after Pearl Harbor. Navy regulations would not permit them to serve on the same ship, but the rules were waived at the insistence of the brothers. They were aboard the light cruiser *Juneau* during the battle of Guadalcanal in late 1942. The ship sank after being hit by two Japanese torpedoes and ultimately all five Sullivans perished as a result. Their loss was widely publicized, it served to promote the sale of war bonds, and a destroyer was named for them. A 1944 movie, *The Sullivans* (later, *The Fighting Sullivans*), dramatized their sacrifice.

A combination of poor luck, bad judgment, and failed cover-ups at the field level subverted similar efforts during the Iraq War. Photogenic Army Pfc. Jessica Lynch was credited with a heroic rescue from her Iraqi captors, but it was later revealed that the episode was staged. Pat Tillman had given up a successful career and a $ 3.6 million contract as a star National Football League player for the Arizona Cardinals to join the U.S. Army Rangers in the aftermath of the 9/11 attacks. His death in Afghanistan on April 24, 2004, in a firefight made him a very visible symbol of selfless sacrifice, and his death and funeral were widely publicized by the military. It was later revealed that Tillman was, in fact, the victim of friendly fire rather than enemy action. His senior commanders, apparently including General Stanley McChrystal, knew the facts of his death within days, but their elaborate cover-up efforts ultimately failed, and, indeed, they backfired when members of the Tillman family outspokenly expressed their outrage about the military handling of the entire episode. There is strong evidence that Tillman, who had taken part in the March 2003 invasion of Iraq, had come to feel that the war was illegal. His diary has apparently been lost. A well-received documentary film, *The Tillman Story,* dramatically reveals the anger felt by his parents.[43]

The vigorous public relations efforts begun in early 2002 to create a climate of domestic support for the war continued throughout the years of the Bush administration. The "Victory in Iraq" campaign launched on November 30, 2005, is a good case in point. As some of the repeatedly articulated goals—a stable, prosperous democratic Iraq that would prove a beacon of hope to all peoples of an embattled region that has, tragically, rarely experienced peace, prosperity, or democracy—seemed to recede further into an uncertain future in the light of a bloody insurgency bordering on an all-out civil war, the president apparently believed that the American public would continue to support the war effort if it could be persuaded that the administration in fact had an effective strategy to gain a victory. A 35-page National Security Council pamphlet spelled out a blueprint for victory, and President Bush kicked off the campaign with an address at the U.S. Naval Academy in which he emphasized that the American goal in Iraq was nothing less than victory.[44]

As noted earlier, evidence from several polling organizations suggest that the public relations campaign on the "victory" theme failed to gain a great deal of traction among the public, although in the absence of the president's effort approval of the war might have declined even more sharply. In any case, optimism about America's ability to achieve its goals—a stable and democratic Iraq—declined markedly during the following months. A June 2007 *U.S. Today*/Gallup poll revealed that only 30 percent of respondents believed that the United States would "definitely" (10 percent) or "probably" (20 percent) "win the war in Iraq," whereas 41 percent stated that the United States could not win. More worrisome for the administration was the fact that several thoughtful senior Republican senators—including Gordon Smith (OR), Chuck Hagel (NE), George Voinovich (OH), John Warner (VA), Richard Lugar (IN), and Olympia Snowe (ME)—had by mid-2007 become increasingly vocal and public in questioning the administration's entire Iraq policy. Senator Hagel was especially outspoken in charging that the administration's salesmanship for invading Iraq included doctoring the intelligence. "Oh yeah. All this stuff was doctored. Absolutely. But that's what we were presented with. And I'm not dismissing our [Congress's] responsibility to look into the thing because there were senators who said, 'I don't believe them.' But I was told by the president—we all were—that we would exhaust every diplomatic effort." A wounded Vietnam veteran, Hagel asserted that administration advocates for the invasion had little understanding of war. "Look, it has not gone unnoticed that President Bush served a little time in the National Guard. Secretary Rice never served. Wolfowitz never served. Feith never served. Cheney had five deferments. Rumsfeld might have done something at one time. But the only guy with real experience was Colin Powell. And they cut him off. That's just a fact. That's not subjective. That's the way it was."[45]

THE IRAQ WAR AND ELECTIONS

Presidential and congressional elections are rarely referenda on a single issue but, as noted earlier, the Iraq War appears to have played a role in the 2002 midterm elections in which Republicans gained seats in both houses of Congress, and the 2004 elections in which president Bush narrowly defeated Democratic challenger John Kerry, and the Republicans maintained control of both the House of Representatives and Senate.

There is also some evidence that the war was a factor in the 2006 elections that gave Democrats control of both the House of Representatives and the Senate. Largely owing to the increasingly unpopular war, President Bush's job ratings were well below 50 percent on election day. In the House, which had been controlled by Republicans since 1994, Democrats retained all the seats they had won two years earlier and added 31 new members for a total of 233; Republicans in the House were reduced to 202. In the Senate, the Democrats defeated 6 Republican incumbents; when independents Bernie Sanders and Joseph Lieberman caucused with the Democrats, they gained a 51–49 margin. For the first time, the GOP failed to win any seats held by Democrats in either the House or the Senate. Iraq was not the only concern of voters in 2006, however, as CNN exits polls revealed that the four most important issues were corruption (42 percent), terrorism (40 percent), the economy (39 percent), and Iraq (37 percent). Moreover, as is often the case, individual races at times reflected issues far removed from foreign affairs. For example, Rick Santorum (R-PA) lost by a landslide after attacking schools and mothers who work outside the home, and George Allen (R-VA) was defeated by a narrow margin on questions regarding his ownership of stock in Barr Labs, maker of a "plan B" abortion pill, and his repeated use of racial slurs, for example, describing a critic as "macaca." Nevertheless, President Bush reinforced the view that the war had contributed to what he called "a thumping" for the GOP by dismissing Donald Rumsfeld, the highly unpopular defense secretary who had been a primary architect of the war plans for Afghanistan and Iraq, the day after the election.

On the face of it, it might appear that the 2008 presidential election that brought Barack Obama to the White House was first and foremost the result of a powerful public backlash against the Iraq War. Certainly the war played a large role in sinking the popularity and favorable job ratings of President Bush to near record lows—to the 20 to 30 percent range. Obama had been a vocal critic of the decision to invade Iraq even prior to his election to the U.S. Senate while he was still a member of the Illinois legislature. During the long marathon of primary elections that resulted in his winning the Democratic presidential nomination over Senator Hillary Clinton—she had voted in October 2002 to support the use of force against Iraq—as well as in the general election, Obama made clear if elected his administration would pursue a different policy on Iraq. In contrast, Senator John McCain, the Republican nominee, had remained a staunch supporter of the war and of the "surge" of American forces in 2007, even when a number of leading moderate Republican senators were becoming increasingly vocal in their criticism of the administration's policies. In short, two senators with sharply different views on the war faced each other in the presidential election.

There are, however, also important reasons to question whether the 2008 election was in fact *primarily* a referendum on the war. One basis for doubts on this score was the massive 2008 financial crisis that wrought havoc on both Wall Street and Main Street. It required unprecedented massive government bailouts by the Bush administration to save some of the bluest of blue chip firms in the financial industry, including Bear Stearns, American International Group, Merrill Lynch, Citigroup, Wachovia Bank, and Bank of America; the venerable Lehman Brothers investment bank was allowed to go bankrupt in September; and there were very real doubts about whether such icons of American manufacturing as General Motors and Chrysler could avoid a similar fate. A collapse of the housing price bubble brought down such major mortgage lenders as Countrywide and Washington Mutual, while resulting in mortgage defaults at levels not seen since the 1930s.

Some economic data for the twelve months prior to the 2008 election provide a few salient indicators of the background against which Senators McCain and Obama competed for the White House.[46]

Dow Jones Industrial Average:
      November 2, 2007: 13,595
      November 3, 2008: 9,320
Nonfarm unemployment rate:
      November 2007: 4.7 percent
      November 2008: 6.5 percent

Housing starts—adjusted annual rate:
November 2007: 1,187,000
November 2008: 616,000

There were, moreover, no credible signs on election day that these dismal figures represented a bottom from which the economy was on the verge of an imminent upturn. The Dow Jones Industrial Average fell below 7,000 during the next four months, and unemployment continued to creep up toward double digits.

In the light of these numbers, it is scarcely surprising that, according to exit polls, voters cited the economy (63 percent) as the most important issue in choosing between McCain and Obama, easily outdistancing the Iraq War (10 percent) and terrorism (9 percent). Among voters who rated Iraq as their top issue, Obama won in all but two states, whereas McCain was favored by those for whom terrorism was most important. Obama outpolled McCain 53 percent to 44 percent among those who cited the economy as the most important issue, as well as on Iraq (69 to 30 percent), health care (73 to 26 percent), and energy (50 to 46 percent), but those who cited terrorism as the most important issue favored McCain by a huge 83 to 13 percent margin.[47]

That said, in the absence of the Iraq War it seems unlikely that the election would have pitted Obama versus McCain as the nominees of the two major parties. Obama would most likely have remained a very junior senator from Illinois facing a very long uphill battle to wrest the Democratic nomination from Senator Clinton. McCain would have been hard put to best such Republican rivals as Mitt Romney, whose credentials on economic issues far outdistanced his. Indeed, while McCain admitted that economics is not his strong suit, his experience and status as a Vietnam War hero were important assets in gaining the GOP nomination, helping him to overcome the view among some Republicans that he was something of a maverick, as well as attacks on his positions on immigration reform and some of the hot-button social issues by such outspoken conservative leaders as talk show host Rush Limbaugh, political commentator Ann Coulter, and James Dobson of Focus on the Family.

CONCLUSION

What can account for the growing public disenchantment with American policy in Iraq? One answer is that the costs in both blood and treasure, in the eyes of an increasing number of Americans, outstripped the promised benefits of "staying the course."[48] According to this explanation, events are ultimately the driving force behind public opinion, trumping vigorous public relations efforts to paint the war as an indispensable and winnable effort to protect the most vital national interests. That is especially the case when the administration faces a growing credibility gap. As was the case in the later years of the Vietnam War when presidential pronouncements about "the light at the end of the tunnel" fell on increasingly skeptical ears, administration rhetoric about "victory" in Iraq apparently became less and less persuasive, even to distinguished Republican stalwarts such as Senator Richard Lugar. Moreover, by February 2008, 53 percent of respondents in a CNN/USA Today/Gallup poll stated that the administration "deliberately misled the American public about whether Iraq has weapons of mass destruction, or not."

A second possible explanation, one that had strong support among administration officials, traced declining public support for the war largely to what they asserted was an overwhelmingly biased and adversarial media that rarely missed an opportunity to highlight bad news from Iraq and Afghanistan, infrequently issued follow-up corrections to their highly misleading stories, and often deliberately slanted their reporting in ways that cast doubts on the administration and its policies. The president expressed the view that journalists were simply not seeing the progress in Iraq. In a similar vein, Wolfowitz unleashed the harshest critique of the media when he asserted that American reporters in Iraq were too cowardly to venture out where they might encounter good news: "Frankly part of our problem is [that] a lot of the press are afraid to travel very much, so they sit in Baghdad and they publish rumors, and rumors are plentiful. Our own media have some responsibility to try to present a balanced picture, instead of gravitating toward the sensational." Dick Cheney asserted, "The press is, with all due respect—there are exceptions—oftentimes lazy, often simply reporting what someone else in the press says without doing their homework." The charge of personal press cowardice was so outlandish—84 journalists had been killed in three years in Iraq, more than the 66 who died in twenty years in Vietnam—that Wolfowitz had to issue a letter of apology two days later.[49]

An even more serious charge is that of media bias. The sense of victimization was dramatically clear in the words of one former administration official who asserted that from 2003 on, there existed "a vigorous and well-funded public relations campaign against the Administration and against the Iraq war." The antiwar Move On organization was cited as the key piece of evidence, although that organization was very modestly funded compared to such administration cheerleaders as Fox News, Rush Limbaugh, the Wall Street Journal, or the Pentagon's public relations programs.[50] When queried about specific major newspapers, the *New York Times* and Carlotta Gall were cited as especially egregious offenders. Even the staunchly conservative *Wall Street Journal* received a mixed report card; its editorial pages were cited as "fair" while its reporting—specifically by Carla Anne Robbins—was also described as sharing a strong anti-administration bias.[51] At one of his press conferences Secretary of Defense Rumsfeld blasted the reporting from Iraq as inaccurate, harmful, and aiding the cause of terrorists: "Interestingly, all of the exaggerations seem to be on one side. It isn't as though there simply have been a series of random errors on both sides of the issues. On the contrary, the steady stream of errors all seems to be of a nature to inflame the situation and to give heart to the terrorists and to discourage those who hope for success in Iraq."[52] In his memoir he repeatedly attacks the media for their highly biased reporting of events bearing upon his time as head of the Pentagon.

General Tommy Franks, who led the invasion of Iraq, offered a diametrically opposed criticism of the media in his memoirs—that they had created false favorable expectations after the fall of Baghdad: "And pretty soon there was created—and I would not take credit as the guy who created an expectation, I will just say that all the reporting, and none of it was evil—but the reporting we all saw created a kind of expectation, 'Well peace is probably going to break out very, very quickly.'"[53]

One of the president's strategies for dealing with what he perceived as a largely hostile press—"I see the headlines. I sometimes read the stores. I've gotten to the point I can tell you what's going to be in the news prior to the news being printed"—was to meet with small groups of influential conservative and reliably proadministration columnists, knowing that they would faithfully convey his case to a wide audience. The strategy could be quite effective. For example, the president's 110-minute meeting with nine columnists, including David Brooks, William Kristol, Michael Barone, Fred Barnes, and Rich Lowry on July 13, 2007, led to highly favorable columns from all of them. David Brooks of the *New York Times* described a self-confident President Bush as "assertive and good-humored," and "a smart and compelling presence in person." Brooks admitted to being slightly held back by Leo Tolstoy's doubts about the "great leader theory of history," but the overall thrust of his widely read column was that the country and its policies in Iraq are in excellent hands.[54]

The Pentagon was also very proactive in cultivating "military analysts"—some six dozen high-ranking retired officers described as "message force multipliers"—who could be instructed to paint a glowing picture of the administration's prewar and wartime policies, whether about conditions at the Guantánamo prison facility or the conduct of operations in Iraq. According to a Pentagon spokesperson, "The intent and purpose of this is nothing other than an earnest effort to inform the American people." During the months prior to the invasion of Iraq, the Pentagon provided analysts "with a familiar mantra: Iraq possessed chemical and biological weapons, was developing nuclear weapons, and might one day slip some to al Qaeda; an invasion would be a relatively quick and inexpensive 'war of liberation.'"

The program continued during the difficult post-Saddam occupation. In addition to their generous stipends from the media, those taking part in the program received private briefings—which they were not to disclose, not even to the networks airing their commentaries—and trips to Guantánamo, Iraq, and other important sites. Most important, those taking part in these media efforts were also provided excellent business opportunities because members of this group represented more than 150 military contractors as lobbyists, senior executives, board members, or consultants. Many of them thus had important vested interests in the policies they were asked to assess. Retired four-star general Barry McCaffrey, who made almost one thousand appearances on NBC and its affiliates, made very good use of the program for personal gain. As a paid consultant for a small firm, Defense Solutions, he contacted General Petraeus urging that Iraq purchase five thousand armored vehicles from Defense Solutions. McCaffrey also had many other business connections with firms hoping to deal with the Pentagon.

Defense secretary Rumsfeld met with these military analysts to orchestrate a campaign against those taking part in the 2006 "revolt of the generals" against his policies. The message was aimed at trivializing Rumsfeld's critics by emphasizing that they represented only a statistically insignificant fraction among retired flag-rank officers. It was also clear to the officers taking part in the program that any expressions of dissent or even of mild doubts about Pentagon policies were unacceptable. The analyst who stated that the United States is "not on a good glide path right now" in Iraq was summarily fired. If Walter Lippmann's term about government efforts to "manufacture consent" seems a bit strong to describe the normal public relations efforts that are a part of every administration, it would seem to be a quite accurate, or perhaps even an understated, description of this covert Pentagon program.

In the face of congressional criticism, the Pentagon suspended the program in 2008 pending an internal review. An initial assessment by the inspector general cleared the Pentagon's use of the television analysts, but a second review concluded that the earlier report was "so riddled with flaws and inaccuracies that none of its conclusions can be relied upon." The inspector general's report was removed from the Pentagon website, and the television analyst program was terminated.[55] It is interesting to speculate how President Eisenhower, who famously warned of the acquisition of undue influence by a "military-industrial complex" in his January 17, 1961, Farewell Address, might have reacted to a program that might appropriately be called the "military-industrial-media complex."

These extraordinary efforts to generate public support for the Iraq War give rise to an important question: Why were they not more successful? Why did much of the American public continue to regard the invasion of Iraq as a mistake, even in the face of evidence that the introduction in 2007 of additional troops into Iraq and the change of strategy and tactics to cope with the insurgency had in fact reduced the violence in Iraq? What are the implications of these findings for our understanding of the relationship between public opinion and foreign policy? The final chapter will address these and some other broader issues arising from this study.

CHAPTER 6

Broader Issues Concerning Public Opinion

It is time to step back from the vast volume of public opinion data to consider three questions arising from the Iraq War, the implications of which may extend beyond the conflict itself.

Public opinion and foreign policy.   How, if at all, does this case address broader issues about public opinion and the conduct of American foreign policy? Do the data on public opinion in the long conflict in Iraq give rise to findings of a more general nature that may contribute to the long-standing debates about the role of public opinion in foreign-policy making? More specifically, do they tend to support or refute the theories that depict public opinion as volatile and subject to random changes that may have little or no relationship to real world developments, and thus are a serious hindrance to the effective pursuit of vital national interests?

The role of the media.   For the vast majority of Americans, the media serve as the sole source of information about foreign affairs, and the media, in turn, are highly dependent on government officials for the news that they report. One of the venerable issues in democratic governance is the proper balance between the media (the right of citizens to be informed about the major decisions and policies that are being conducted in their names) and the government (the need of public officials, especially on matters vital to national security, to be able to deliberate some important issues away from the constant glare of public scrutiny). How, if at all, does the Iraq War shed significant light on the age-old tensions between these competing claims of the media and government officials?

Possible stab-in-the-back explanations.   Are there any possible dangers of a stab-in-the-back myth emerging from the Iraq War—or from the concurrent conflicts in Afghanistan and against terrorist organizations such as al Qaeda—to explain any perceived shortfalls from the ambitious goals set forth by Bush administration officials during the run-up to the war? We know from earlier wars—including, most recently, the conflict in Vietnam—that for some there may be irresistible temptations to locate the cause of defeat, or even setbacks short of defeat, not in events on the ground, nor in the performance of military but in the actions of "enemies" on the home front. Whether or not such claims are strongly rooted in the facts of the situation, they may live on well beyond the conflict itself, continuing to poison domestic political processes and seriously hampering the effective conduct of foreign affairs.

PUBLIC OPINION: RANDOMLY VOLATILE
OR SENSIBLY STABLE?

The nature of public opinion is among the key issues that divides "realist" foreign policy theories from those of "liberals." Realists typically view public opinion as volatile, ill-informed, uninterested except during crises or other dramatic events, and thus a very slender reed upon which to rely in efforts to pursue vital national interests. To buttress their skepticism, realists can point to substantial evidence that even in the "information age," most Americans have rather limited factual knowledge about world affairs, and also to studies revealing that they fare poorly in this respect compared to publics in other developed countries.[1] Among the most damning evidence, according to some realists, are surveys showing that when asked about what they regard as the "most important issues" facing the country, public views may change fairly rapidly. During World War II, polls repeatedly showed that issues relating to that conflict ranked at the top of most Americans' concerns, but soon after the guns had cooled in 1945 such domestic economic issues as postwar employment prospects took the top spot. In his pioneering study of public opinion and American foreign policy, Gabriel Almond cited such evidence as buttressing his fears about a postwar return to isolationism, as had occurred following World War I.[2]

The realist depiction of public opinion as volatile and subject to random changes that bear little relationship to careful assessments of vital national interests has come under serious empirical challenge. Although there remains little doubt that most Americans are poorly informed about world affairs, a multitude of studies during the past several decades have shown that changes in public opinion, in the aggregate, are not merely random fluctuations; rather, they usually reflect events on the ground quite faithfully and sensibly.[3] Moreover, reasonable doubts can be raised about inferences from responses to the "most important issues" survey question. Did the post–World War II public concerns with domestic economic issues reflect mindless volatility and a concomitant loss of interest in world affairs, thus paving the way for a possible reversion to isolationist sentiments and withdrawal from international responsibilities? Or were they reasonable responses arising from the possible economic consequences of the rapid demobilization of the thirteen million Americans who had been in uniform during the war, especially as some economists had forecast that the postwar era might witness a return to the high prewar levels of unemployment? As noted earlier, the term *low information rationality* has been used to describe the perspective that even poorly informed publics may, in the aggregate, express sensible judgment, and that changes in public opinion are not merely "off the top of the head" responses rooted in the moods of the moment.[4]

How, if at all, does the evidence from the Iraq War shed light on this venerable debate about the nature of American public opinion? There is, on balance, a rather strong correspondence between the key events surrounding the Iraq War described in table 2.1 and the various trends in public opinion on the conflict analyzed in chapter 2. Although there were some divisions among the public about the decision to undertake the March 2003 invasion—hardly surprising given that it was a "war of choice" and launched in the absence of support for Washington from either NATO or the UN Security Council—the successful military campaign that led to the capture of Baghdad and the ouster of the Saddam Hussein regime in less than three weeks was reflected in surveys revealing that substantial majorities of Americans approved of the invasion and assessed the situation in Iraq as going well. Given the almost universal distaste for Saddam Hussein and his regime, it is hardly surprising that even among those who may have had doubts about the wisdom or legality of the invasion, his defeat was widely welcomed.

The onset of an insurgency not long after the fall of Baghdad that began to take its toll in American casualties, as well as sectarian violence that threatened to morph into a civil war, were also mirrored in polls that revealed declining enthusiasm for the war and growing doubts about how well it was going. Moreover, despite repeated administration claims about Iraqi WMDs and ties to al Qaeda as justifications for the invasion, it became increasingly clear that these assertions had no basis in fact. To be sure, such a dramatic event as the capture of the almost universally hated Saddam Hussein in December 2003 rekindled support for the war, but only over the short run. Despite some encouraging events such as Iraqi elections in 2005 and heightened overt and covert public relations activities by the administration, survey evidence from a multiplicity of polls revealed declining approval of the war during the period 2004 through 2007.

When the 2007 "surge" of American troops and the accompanying changes in strategies for their use resulted in declining violence and U.S. casualties, the public was paying attention. Various polls asking some variant of questions about how well the war was going found that the "going well" responses were increasing accordingly. Yet, even in the face of these more favorable appraisals, doubts about whether the United States had done "the right thing" in launching the invasion persisted. Is this an example of public irrationality, or was it a reasonable response, especially as the stated reasons for going to war had by then been wholly discredited? Perhaps a simple analogy will illustrate the point. A smoker who has undergone successful surgery and chemotherapy for lung cancer is likely to respond that his medical situation is "going well," and yet he may also regret his original decision to start smoking as a "mistake" and the "wrong thing" to do.

Given the nonquantitative nature of the evidence in table 2.1, it would be overstating the evidence presented here to say that there was a high correlation between events and opinions, but it is hard to fault the public, in the aggregate, as unreasonable and mindlessly volatile in its responses to the developments in the Iraq War. Indeed, it appears that changes in opinions on the war reflected events on the ground rather faithfully, despite almost unprecedented public relations efforts by the administration to generate support for its policies and to attack the patriotism of those who might question any aspect of its strategy or tactics.

Partisanship and Perceived Threats

The years since the Vietnam War have generally witnessed growing partisan discord on foreign policy, as shown in chapter 3. A previously cited study developed the hypothesis that the degree of bipartisan cooperation on foreign policy is correlated to the level of threat from abroad.[5] The Iraq War supports this hypothesis.

On the eve of the Pearl Harbor attack the American public was deeply divided on the country's proper stance toward the wars that were engulfing Europe and Asia. Some isolationists derided America's entry into World War I, a war that was supposed to end all wars, and urged that the country not be lured into another such fool's errand. A Congressional Special Committee on Investigation of the Munitions Industry headed by Senator Gerald Nye (R-ND) concluded that activities by such munitions makers as DuPont had dragged the United States into the war. Others, including Senator Robert Taft (R-OH), espoused the more fundamental proposition that participation in wars abroad, in distinction to the use of the military to protect the home territory, is fundamentally incompatible with the preservation of democratic institutions at home. The noted aviator Charles Lindbergh, a member of the isolationist America First organization that Senator Nye had helped to establish, had been highly impressed by the might of the German military after being invited by Hermann Goering, head of the Luftwaffe, to witness various air maneuvers while he was Goering's guest at the 1936 Berlin Olympic Games. In a speech in Des Moines less than two months before the Pearl Harbor attack, Lindbergh stated, "If any of these groups—the British, the Jewish, or the administration—stops agitating for war, I believe there will be little danger of our involvement."[6] Those opposing any American involvement in conflicts abroad thus defined the primary threat to this country as arising from entanglement in conflicts that had little if anything to do with this country's vital interest, rather than from German ambitions and aggressions.

Internationalists, including both President Franklin Roosevelt and his Republican opponent in the 1940 presidential election, Wendell Willkie, were convinced that German domination over Europe was such a threat that ultimately the United States could not avoid becoming involved in the war. They both supported such decidedly nonneutral actions as the Lend-Lease Act and sending 50 aged surplus American destroyers to Great Britain in exchange for long-term leases of British naval bases in the Atlantic and Caribbean. Important groups supporting active aid to Germany's opponents included the Committee for Peace through Revisions of the Neutrality Laws and the Committee to Defend America by Aiding the Allies. Both were nonpartisan, and the latter was headed by William Allen White, a noted newspaper editor with impeccable Republican credentials.

The domestic foreign policy divisions in 1940–41 thus were largely ideological—pitting isolationists against internationalists, groups who perceived threats to vital national interests quite differently—rather than partisan, in part because Roosevelt had effectively reached out to internationalist Republicans in seeking support for his policies. But whatever divisions existed on December 6 were wholly bridged by the Japanese attack on Pearl Harbor the next morning. Roosevelt's request for a declaration of war against Japan on December 8 passed unanimously in the Senate and with a single dissenting vote in the House. The potentially divisive issue of what to do about Germany was resolved when, three days later, Hitler inexplicably resolved any possible dilemmas in Washington by declaring war on the United States. As summarized in table 3.1, Pearl Harbor ushered in a period during which partisan cleavages among the American public on foreign policy issues were often muted.

The September 11 terrorist attacks resembled the events at Pearl Harbor in 1941 by dramatically bridging post-Vietnam partisan cleavages. Only ten months earlier President Bush had been declared the winner of Florida's electoral votes by the Supreme Court in a highly controversial election in which he lost the popular vote by more than 543,000 votes, but he enjoyed exceptionally high public support in all surveys during the months following the September 11 attacks, as did the invasion of Afghanistan to hunt down al Qaeda leaders and to topple their Taliban hosts in Kabul. To most Americans the invasion of Afghanistan in October 2001 was, like the response to Pearl Harbor, a "war of necessity." A *USA Today* poll two months later revealed that 93 percent of Americans supported the invasion. To seek evidence of partisanship in such overwhelmingly one-sided results would be a bit like debating the number of angels on the head of a pin.

Although Saddam Hussein had been viewed by the Reagan and Bush administrations as a valued regional quasi ally, and his regime had been the recipient of exceptionally generous American military aid and invaluable intelligence assistance during the long Iran-Iraq War, he had few supporters in this country following the 1990–91 Gulf War. The 1998 congressional resolution supporting his ouster by means short of U.S. military involvement had strong bipartisan support. Many Democrats in Congress supported the October 2002 resolution authorizing the use of force against Iraq, but not all of them did so, in part because they were not persuaded by the "evidence" of Iraq WMDs and ties to 9/11 terrorists. The skeptics included such establishment Democrats as Senators Robert Byrd, Ted Kennedy, and Bob Graham; Lincoln Chafee, the lone Republican; and also a young and obscure member of the Illinois legislature, Barack Obama.

Strong support for the successful invasion of Iraq overshadowed partisan differences. At that point the thesis that Saddam Hussein's regime represented a major security threat could not be disproved beyond any reasonable doubt. However, the year following the fall of Baghdad witnessed two major developments that contributed to a widening partisan gap on assessments of the war.

First, it became increasingly clear that conclusive evidence supporting prewar claims about Saddam Hussein's weapons of mass destruction and ties to al Qaeda and the 9/11 terrorist attackers—the rationales for the invasion—was not forthcoming and that Saddam was, in the apt description by Thomas Ricks, "an aging, almost toothless tiger"; he also described the Iraqi dictator as "dumb as a box of rocks." Marine general Anthony Zinni, who headed Central Command prior to his retirement in 2000 and thus had a good deal of experience in dealing with Iraq, made the same assessment when asked by Senator Richard Lugar (R-IN) in an appearance before the Senate Foreign Relations Committee prior to the invasion whether the threat from Saddam was imminent: "No, not at all. It was not an imminent threat. Nor even close. Not grave, gathering, imminent, serious, severe, mildly upsetting, none of these."[7] The alleged level of threat posed by his regime had thus been transformed into a source of debate. Second, a growing insurgency and rising American casualties indicated that administration scenarios of post-Saddam Iraq were in fact too sanguine and that the costs of the war to the United States would in fact far exceed those incurred in the defeat of Iraq's armed forces during the successful invasion. Thus, in the eyes of some, the major threat to American security—and to vital American values and institutions—in the entire Iraq undertaking was the invasion itself.

At that point, public assessments of the war began to diverge, and they did so largely along partisan lines. The strongest supporters of the war were strong Republican respondents who also asserted that they would support President Bush in his bid for reelection in 2004. They were also most inclined to continue believing, contrary to strong evidence, that Iraq had possessed WMDs, that it had ties to the 9/11 terrorists, and that the American invasion of Iraq was strongly supported by most publics abroad.

In contrast, increasing number of Democrats, although they may have been delighted by the overthrow of Saddam Hussein in 2003, began to express doubts about the wisdom of the invasion (was it "the right thing to do"?) and its consequences (is it "going well"?), in response to the Iraqi insurgency, and those doubts grew as the situation on the ground in Iraq deteriorated. In short, prior preferences, buttressed by partisanship, tended to affect what kind of information was deemed relevant to making judgments about the war. As one analyst noted, increasingly Democrats "forgot" that they had supported the invasion following the fall of Baghdad, whereas Republicans "forgot" that their support had been conditioned on accepting administration claims about Saddam Hussein's weapons of mass destruction.[8]

"Going Public"

The Iraq War also provides support for the hypothesis that administrations are most likely to: (1) "go public" in foreign policy episodes if (2) the stakes in the situation are perceived as high and (3) the prospects of victory are also highly favorable.[9] The Iraq situation was an almost perfect match on all three counts.

Long before taking office in 2001, key policymakers in the Bush administration, including Dick Cheney, Donald Rumsfeld, and Paul Wolfowitz, had been on record as giving top priority to the removal of the Saddam Hussein regime in Iraq. Although none had publicly disagreed with the elder President Bush's decision in 1991 to end the Gulf War before coalition forces reached Baghdad, thus leaving the Baath regime in power, Iraq's alleged violation of the Security Council–imposed prohibition against WMDs had, in their view, created a major threat to American national security. The 9/11 attacks on New York and Washington and Baghdad's alleged ties to the al Qaeda terrorist organization served to heighten dramatically the conviction within the administration that Saddam must go. As Wolfowitz noted, at key meetings during the days following 9/11, the debates were not about *whether* to use force against Iraq but *when,* that is, before or after the campaign against Afghanistan.[10] In short, with a very few important exceptions, notably Secretary of State Colin Powell, the beliefs of top leaders in the Bush administration met one part of the hypothesis—that the stakes in the situation were perceived as high.

There was also little doubt in Washington or among knowledgeable military analysts that any use of force in Iraq would result in a rapid American victory. To be sure, Iraq could field a large land army, as it had during the 1990–91 Gulf War, but it was hopelessly overmatched in most if not all other important respects. The largely flat, desert terrain of Iraq accorded significant value to air superiority, but Iraq had lost most of its air force during the Gulf War, and it had been unable to make up for that critical loss during the intervening years. The Soviet Union had once been the major supplier of military aircraft to Iraq, but after it had disintegrated in 1991, Moscow had shown little inclination to aid Baghdad, not even during the Gulf War. The terrain in Iraq also played to American advantages in crucial advanced military technology, including the ability to identify military installations and to track troop movements with great precision via satellite photography, as well as night vision technology that enabled it to conduct operations in the dark. American photographic intelligence assistance to Baghdad during the long Iran-Iraq War had played a major role in enabling the Saddam Hussein regime to avoid defeat against its larger and more populous enemy, but now the advantage lay fully with the United States. Finally, there were strong reasons to doubt the quality of Iraqi military leadership. In initiating and conducting wars against Iran and the U.S.-led coalition that opposed his invasion of Kuwait, Saddam Hussein had proved to be a less-than-brilliant military leader, and frequent purges of those suspected of being less than 110 percent in favor of Saddam had left subordinates who were often little more than pliant yes-men. Thus, the third condition of the hypothesis—the favorable prospect of victory—was in little doubt in this case.

In accordance with the hypothesis, then, the Iraq situation provided leaders in Washington with ideal conditions for "going public." Long before the actual invasion of Iraq, members of the Bush administration undertook a strong public relations campaign to build support at home and abroad for using force against the Baghdad regime. The annual State of the Union message provides presidents with a highly visible platform for outlining the administration's top priority goals. The president's speech is covered on prime-time television, and on the following day the speech will invariably be front-page news as well as the lead story on television and radio news broadcasts. In his 2002 address, President Bush left little doubt that a regime change in Iraq, dubbed a charter member of the "axis of evil," was at the top of his administration's foreign policy agenda. Subsequent speeches by the president, including an important graduation address at the U.S. Military Academy at West Point, may have received less public attention than the State of the Union address, but they underscored in a very public way the president's strong determination to deal with what he described as the top threat to U.S. national security.

Vice president Cheney and top Defense Department officials Donald Rumsfeld and Paul Wolfowitz frequently reinforced the message in public statements, and they were only somewhat less often joined by national security adviser Condoleezza Rice. To be sure, Secretary of State Colin Powell had doubts about the wisdom and necessity of attacking Iraq, especially when efforts to deal with Osama bin Laden and his al Qaeda colleagues had yet to result in complete success, as did some top-ranking military officers, but their views were usually conveyed in private rather than public settings. For those who did express doubts in public—including army chief of staff Eric Shinseki, army secretary Thomas White, national economic council director Lawrence Lindsey, and treasury secretary Paul O'Neill—doing so was essentially a career-ending move.

THE MEDIA, THE PUBLIC, AND FOREIGN POLICY

For most members of the public, the media are the sole source of information about international affairs. One perspective on the media is that they serve a vital watchdog role in the democratic governance—the so-called fourth estate. Some years after the French Revolution, Edmund Burke is said to have looked at the press gallery in the British House of Commons and stated, "Yonder sits the Fourth Estate, and they are more important than all of them." Before he assumed the presidency Thomas Jefferson wrote, "The basis of our governments being the opinions of the people, the very first object should be to keep that right; and were it left to me to decide whether we should have a government without newspapers or newspapers without a government, I should not hesitate a moment to prefer the latter."[11] That conception of the press was reflected in the writings of the "muckrakers," including Lincoln Steffens, Ida Tarbell, Upton Sinclair, Frank Norris, and many others who, during the Progressive Era, publicized misdeeds by industry and government. Their reports dealt with a wide array of problems, ranging from working conditions for women and children and sanitary conditions in food-production facilities to corruption in the Senate. More recent examples may be found in the investigative reporting of the Watergate crimes that ultimately led to the resignation of President Nixon in August 1974, and in the prize-winning exposé of the Bush administration's secret program to recruit and train retired military officers to sell its Iraq policies on television.[12] It was in this spirit that H. L. Mencken defined the proper role of journalism as "to afflict the comfortable and comfort the afflicted."

There is, however, also a long tradition among democratic leaders of various political persuasions to attack the media as unfair. The same Thomas Jefferson who extolled the vital importance of newspapers in 1787 bitterly denounced the press for mistreating him and his administration after he had assumed the presidency: "It is a melancholy truth, that a suppression of the press could not more completely deprive the nation of its benefits than is done by its abandoned prostitution to falsehood. . . . the man who never looks into a newspaper is better informed than those who read them, inasmuch as he who knows nothing is nearer the truth than he whose mind is filled with falsehood and errors."[13] Jefferson was far from alone in this respect. After losing the California gubernatorial election in 1962, Richard Nixon sneered that the press would miss no longer having "Nixon to kick around." In 1971, at the time of the Laos incursion during the Vietnam War, Nixon said, "Our worst enemy seems to be the press." Nixon's speech writer, William Safire, famously coined the phrase "nattering nabobs of negativism" for vice president Spiro Agnew to use in attacks on the media for their reporting on the Vietnam War. In the final days of his decade-long tenure as British prime minister, Tony Blair—whose manifest political skills included effectively "spinning the news"—described the media as a "feral beast" that undermines the ability of leaders to act.[14] And less than a year into his presidency, Barack Obama unwisely attacked Fox News for its nonstop critiques of his administration and for even questioning—falsely— the legitimacy of the birth certificate proving that he was born in the United States, thereby raising doubts about his eligibility to serve as president.

Many other examples of attacks by government leaders could be cited because there is often an inherent tension between the media and public officials. Few officials would accept H. L. Mencken's definition of the legitimate role of journalism as the last word on the proper role of the media, especially on foreign affairs and military issues. After a lecture at the National War College some years ago, I was told by a senior officer that he and many of his colleagues regarded their three most important enemies as the Soviets, Congress, and the media—and not necessarily in that order. Nor is it hard to find situations in which exclusion of the media was almost surely vital to the success of a major foreign policy undertaking.

When President Jimmy Carter invited Egyptian and Israeli leaders to the presidential retreat at Camp David in September 1978 for 12 days of secret meetings that led to a major breakthrough in relations between the two longtime enemies and, ultimately, the Israel-Egypt Peace Treaty of 1979, he excluded the media. It is almost certain that had the deliberations between Anwar el-Sadat and Menachem Begin been monitored daily by the press or, worse, shown in real time on television, the temptations to take a hard line for the home audiences in Egypt and Israel, rather than being seen as a compromiser—an "appeaser"—would have scuttled any possibilities of agreement. Nor would anyone reasonably argue for the right of reporters to reveal the Allied plan to invade the beaches in Normandy on D-day in June 1944, especially as one of the most successful counterintelligence undertakings of the war was an elaborate plan, Operation Bodyguard, to make Germany believe that the invasion forces would take the most direct route across the English Channel—from Dover for a landing at the Pas de Calais.

These rather dramatic one-sided examples do not, however, necessarily end the debate about the proper balance between demands of the media and government. During the opening months of the Kennedy administration, the *New*

York Times learned of a CIA plan, inherited from the Eisenhower administration, to train and transport Cuban exiles for an invasion of Cuba to overthrow the Castro regime. A combination of loose talk by the Cuban exiles and Soviet intelligence alerted Cuba and some of the media about the possibility of an invasion. Gilbert Harrison of the *New Republic* magazine sent the White House galley proofs of an article exposing the invasion. At the president's request, the article was derailed. Kennedy also urgently and successfully pleaded with the editors of the *New York Times* to suppress the story on the grounds that secrecy was vital to the entire undertaking.[15]

The invasion at the Bay of Pigs took place on schedule in April 1961, but it was an unmitigated disaster for the United States, partly because of almost amateurish CIA plans—for example, the failure to note the existence of major barriers such as swamps between the landing beaches and the mountains where the invaders were to gather to conduct their campaign against the Castro government—and also because the assumption that most Cubans would greet the invaders, many of whom had been associated with the corrupt pre-Castro Batista regime in Havana, as liberators turned out to be wishful thinking. In the end, most of the surviving 1,200 invaders were captured by Cuban forces. Many of their leaders were executed by Cuba, and the United States had to pay a significant ransom to gain the freedom of the others. Given the Cold War context, there was scant likelihood that either publication would have rejected Kennedy's demands to kill the story of the planned invasion, but is it possible that after the events unfolded, JFK might secretly have wished that they had? In any case, because the impending invasion was hardly a well-kept secret, he showed rather questionable judgment in allowing it to proceed.

"Indexing" the News

Without dismissing the importance of the watchdog role or investigative reporting by the media, any discussion of the links between public opinion, the media, and foreign affairs must also acknowledge three important points. It is a truism that the vast majority of the public must rely on the media for its information about foreign affairs. The mass media, in turn, rely on government officials for most of the daily news they report. Finally, there is compelling evidence that the mainstream media tend to "index" their reports according to the range of views in government debates on a given issue. For example, a careful analysis of U.S. policy toward Nicaragua in the mid-1980s found that news coverage was restricted within the bounds of institutional debate.[16] To the extent that these three points are valid, the theory that the media serve as the "fourth estate," playing a watchdog role in democracies and ensuring that the public is fully informed about the activities of its representatives, may at times be more fiction than fact.

The evidence about the role of the media during the run-up to the Iraq War cited in chapter 5 provides strong evidence for the "indexing" hypotheses. After the 9/11 attacks, it became increasingly clear that the Bush administration defined the ouster of the Saddam Hussein regime as a vital national security interest because of Iraq's alleged WMD program and ties to al Qaeda. Despite CIA chief George Tenet's assurance that the evidence against Iraq was a "slam dunk," there were at least a few legitimate reasons for doubt, if only because some sources for that evidence, including "Curveball" and Ahmed Chalabi, were, to put it charitably, hardly unbiased analysts or military experts. Nevertheless, during the months prior to the March 2003 invasion, top Bush administration officials spoke with one public voice on Iraq's alleged WMDs, and, consequently, even the *New York Times* and *Washington Post,* mainline national newspapers with well-deserved reputations for investigative reporting, largely followed suit. As noted in chapter 5, Judith Miller's many reports for the *New York Times* on Iraq's WMDs far outnumbered any stories expressing doubts. It should go without saying that staunchly conservative media outlets such as Fox News and the *Wall Street Journal, National Review,* and *Weekly Standard* were unswerving supporters of the administration on the Iraq issues.

After events in Iraq had conclusively failed to follow the optimistic post-Saddam scenario, and evidence supporting the war's rationale proved increasingly elusive, media reporting could not avoid giving voice to critics who pointed to rising American casualties and to increasing evidence of sectarian violence, thus raising questions about Pentagon planning for the post-Saddam era and, more generally, the conduct of military operations in Iraq. As significant numbers of the media took a more analytic stance toward events in Iraq, they also came under increasingly harsh criticism from members of the Bush administration. President Bush, Vice President Cheney, and Defense Department leaders Rumsfeld and Wolfowitz on more than one occasion charged the media with aiding and abetting the country's enemies, thus hampering the war effort in Iraq and playing into the hands of terrorists.

In contrast, the conservative military historian Max Boot, who supported the invasion of Iraq in 2003, gave the media rather high marks, noting, "Whatever the shortcomings of some reporting, there has been a lot of first-rate coverage by a heroic corps of correspondents that has persevered in the face of terrible danger." He went on to conclude, "If you wanted to figure out what was happening over the last four years [2003–7], you would have been infinitely better off paying attention to their writing than to what the president or his top generals were saying. If we fail to achieve our goals in Iraq . . . it won't be the fault of the ink-stained wretches or even their blow-dried TV counterparts. To argue otherwise deflects the blame from those who deserve it, in the upper echelons of the administration and armed forces. Perhaps that's the point."[17]

The Print and Electronic Media

There has been a vast proliferation of media sources during the past several decades, including cable television and the Internet, but news sources are not equal, especially with respect to providing their audiences with important and valid information about foreign affairs. Steven Kull and his colleagues undertook a careful study of public beliefs about three very significant points concerning the Iraq War that had demonstrably been disproved: that WMDs had been found in Iraq, that Saddam Hussein had proven ties to the 9/11 terrorist attackers, and that most publics abroad approved of the American invasion. They found that those who relied on the print media were much better informed than those for whom the electronic media was the primary source of information. It is not surprising that those relying on Fox News were most inclined to maintain their beliefs despite clear evidence to the contrary, but even those for whom the allegedly more liberal CBS television network was the primary sources of information did not fare much better. These results were supported by a Pew study that revealed that those whose primary news outlet was major newspaper websites were the best informed about current affairs, whereas those who relied on evening network news, local television news, Fox News, and network morning news were the least well informed.[18]

The importance of the print media for informing the public about international affairs also emerges from a list of the best reporters on the Iraq War, according to Max Boot: John Burns, Dexter Filkins, Michael Gordon, Greg Jaffe, Michael Philips, Tom Ricks, Tony Perry, John Daniszewski, Sean Naylor, Bing West, Robert Kaplan, and George Packer. The first nine reporters worked for newspapers as diverse as the *New York Times, Washington Post, Wall Street Journal,* and *Army Times,* whereas the last three wrote for the *Atlantic Monthly* and the *New Yorker.*[19] Michael Ware of *Time* also belongs on that list. Notably absent are reporters working for the electronic media, though he might well have included Anne Garrels, Peter Kenyon, Lourdes Garcia-Navarro, and Dina Temple-Raskin of National Public Radio. But even if Boot overlooked some excellent electronic reporters in compiling his list, there is no question that print reporters provided indispensable information and analyses of the war.

In light of the clear importance of the print media in providing the public with information about foreign affairs, it is more than somewhat troubling that newspapers in the United States are undergoing exceptionally difficult times. Their troubles arise in part from a serious decline in advertising revenues as a result of the economic meltdown of 2008, but the problems go deeper than that, as ad revenues had been eroding even before the crash. Revenues from retail and classified ads for the print media peaked in 2000 ($48.7 billion) and fell precipitously in 2008 to a total of $34.5 billion. Even when online revenues are included, the 2008 figure reached only $37.8 billion.[20]

Moreover, newspaper circulation, their other major source of revenues, has also been eroding steadily. It peaked in 1973, when a total of 1,774 newspapers enjoyed a circulation of over 63 million readers. Largely as a result of a sharp drop in the number of evening newspapers, by 2008 circulation totaled only 48.6 million readers.[21] According to the Audit Bureau of Circulation, midyear results for 2009 indicated that this declining trend continued. Of the top 25 newspapers, only the *Wall Street Journal* enjoyed increased circulation, whereas a number of them, including the *San Francisco Chronicle* and *Dallas Morning News* suffered declines of more than 20 percent. Several big city newspapers have gone into bankruptcy—for example, the Seattle *Post-Intelligencer,* Denver's *Rocky Mountain News,* the Minneapolis *Star Tribune,* and the *Philadelphia Inquirer*—leaving some major cities with only one newspaper. The *Christian Science Monitor* replaced its daily newspaper with a weekly edition, and the *Boston Globe* was put up for sale by its owner, the *New York Times,* but there were no reasonable offers, and it survives on life support. After *Globe* employees accepted large wage cuts, the *Times* withdrew the sale offer in October 2009. There have also been significant cutbacks in the newsrooms of the *New York Times, Los Angeles Times, Chicago Tribune,* and other major national newspapers. The ABC results for the six-month period ending March 31, 2010, were even worse, as newspaper circulation fell by 9 percent from year-earlier figures. To be sure, the number of online readers has increased sharply, but with some exceptions they can gain access to these sources without payment and thus they add nothing to newspaper revenues. The *New York Times* has announced plans to start charging for online access in 2011, but its success in increasing its revenues is uncertain.

From the perspective of informing the public about foreign affairs, the problems are not merely negative trends in advertising and circulation. Long before the Iraq War, the media had been cutting back on international coverage while increasing the amount of local and entertainment content.[22] Media leaders respond to critics by stating that as businesses they must offer what audiences want and that, except in times of crises or other attention-grabbing international events, there is only a limited market for international news. Although that is at least in part a rather self-serving response, it also contains more than a grain of truth. Until and unless the American public exhibits a strong demand for daily information about global challenges and opportunities, as well as options for dealing with them, the shrinkage of the international "news hole" is likely to persist.

STAB-IN-THE-BACK THEORIES

Germany and World War I

History is filled with explanations for tragic events in which the heroes are betrayed by those who proved unworthy of the trust placed in them. The classic and most familiar stab-in-the-back explanation for defeat in war was propagated to account for Germany's loss in World War I. According to one account, in a postwar discussion with British lieutenant general Neill Malcolm, field marshall Erich von Ludendorff was asked why Germany had lost the war. After Ludendorff listed what he believed to be the cause of his country's defeat, the British general summarized his account, "It seems that you were stabbed in the back." Ludendorff immediately agreed, and later field marshall Paul von Hindenburg told the German National Assembly, "As an English general has very truly said, the German army was stabbed in the back." He later wrote, "Like Siegfried, stricken down by the treacherous spear of savage Hagen, our weary front collapsed."[23]

Ludendorff and Hindenburg were not alone in espousing this theme as even some leaders of the democratic postwar Weimar regime did so. Most notoriously, Adolf Hitler made the stab-in-the-back theme a major part of his campaign for his Nazi Party, and he used it repeatedly after he came to power in 1933 to justify, first, the exclusion of Jews from important positions and, later, in launching the Holocaust. According to Hitler, Germany was not defeated on the battlefield but was betrayed on the home front by Socialists, Bolsheviks, and, above all, by Jews. Their treason had undermined the war effort at home and led the country to defeat.

Although the tide of battle had clearly turned against Germany on the Western front, and Ludendorff saw that defeat was imminent after the failure of the massive German offensive in September 1918, this explanation gained some plausibility among Germans for two reasons. Russia had pulled out of the war following the Bolshevik revolution in November 1917, and it had signed the draconian Treaty of Brest-Litovsk by which it ceded substantial territory, including one-quarter of its population and a similar proportion of its industry, to Germany. Moreover, German troops were still on French and Belgian soil when the armistice went into effect on November 11, 1918, and German military forces returned home in a fairly orderly fashion rather than as a disorganized and defeated rabble.

To prevent a recurrence of a stab-in-the-back myth to explain German defeat in World War II, at the 1943 Casablanca summit meeting Roosevelt and Churchill agreed on a policy of demanding that Axis countries be forced to accept an "unconditional surrender" rather than a negotiated settlement to end the war. Moreover, at the Yalta conference in 1945 the Allied leaders decided that Germany would be occupied by American, British, Russian, and French armies after the war.

The Vietnam War

Some proponents of the Vietnam War developed a similar line of reasoning to explain America's defeat in that long and bloody conflict. As in the case of Hitler's explanation for defeat in 1918, this version of history gained some plausibility from events on the ground. For example, the "Tet offensive" in 1968 was a military defeat for Viet Cong and North Vietnamese forces, but some observers also depicted it as a political defeat for the United States because the attackers were able to carry their assault into Saigon, the capital of South Vietnam, and into the grounds of the American Embassy in that city. Indeed, the United States never lost a major battle during the long war. According to this variant of the stab-in-the-back thesis, antiwar protestors—the hapless actress Jane Fonda, who made a trip to Hanoi during the war, was portrayed as the poster child for these dissidents—and the liberal media at home undermined the war effort. Moreover, the political leadership in Washington was accused of preventing the military from employing strategies that would have ensured victory—for example, unlimited bombing of North Vietnam, mining of Haiphong harbor from the outset of the war to prevent resupply of North Vietnam by its Soviet and Chinese allies, and, possibly, the use of nuclear weapons.

This is the myth that the military was forced to fight "with one hand tied behind its back."

According to this view, then, not only did dissidents sap the morale of the country and, more important, of the troops in the field, but the hands of the military were tied by civilian leaders, ultimately leading to the 1973 peace agreement that permitted North Vietnam to station 150,000 troops in the South and the American evacuation of Saigon in April 1975 in the face of an all-out North Vietnamese assault. According to a paper written by two army psychological operations officers in 1980, "We lost the war—not because we were outfought, but because we were out Psyoped [psychological operations]. Our national will to victory was attacked more effectively than we attacked the North Vietnamese and Viet Cong, and perceptions of this fact encouraged the enemy to hang on until the United States broke and ran for home."[24] Ronald Reagan, who had proposed bombing North Vietnam into "a parking lot" in 1965, made frequent references to the defeat in Vietnam during his successful presidential campaign in 1980. He described it as a war in which American soldiers "came home without a victory, not because they'd been defeated but because they'd been denied permission to win." In a similar vein, in a documentary film by the Accuracy in Media organization, the narrator, Charlton Heston, concluded, "We were wrong to think the outcome [in Vietnam] would be decided by military strength. In the end words, disinformation, [and] deception were the decisive factors."[25]

This explanation had and continues to have some vocal proponents. For example, Senator John McCain, who endured years of brutal captivity after his aircraft was downed over North Vietnam, cited a variant of this theme during his 2008 presidential campaign.[26] Although there were in fact increasing numbers of domestic critics of the war, even before the Tet offensive, they were not all "bums," as President Nixon described them. They included such important architects of America's Cold War policies to contain the Soviet Union as George F. Kennan and J. William Fulbright, as well as many others of the "realist" school of foreign affairs who doubted that the security of South Vietnam was a vital American interest. Noted television journalist Walter Cronkite, sometimes described as "the most trusted man in America," returned from a fact-finding trip to Vietnam in 1968 and expressed doubts about the course of the war and prospects of victory: "To say that we are close to victory today is to believe, in the face of the evidence, the optimists who have been wrong in the past."[27] Upon hearing Cronkite's assessment, President Johnson is reported to have said, "If I have lost Walter Cronkite, I have lost the war."

Among the general public, increasing casualties and skepticism arising from repeated less-than-prescient assertions by American policymakers that they could see "the light at the end of the tunnel" undermined support for the war.[28] As the United States had conscription until its abolition in 1973, few communities avoided sharing in the more than 58,000 Americans killed in the war. Moreover, the core rationale for the war, the thesis that sustaining the independence of South Vietnam was vital to containing a monolithic "communist bloc" and, most important, an aggressive and expansionist "Red China," lost much of its credibility when China and the USSR engaged in border clashes along the Ussuri River in March and August 1969. It was further eroded when, in February 1972, President Nixon and Henry Kissinger made their historic trip to meet Zhou En-lai and Mao Tse-tung in Beijing. Not only did that trip initiate a process that ultimately led to normalization of relations between the two countries, but the Shanghai Communiqué acknowledged that only one China existed and that Beijing, not Taipei, was its capital. In short, Nixon abandoned the long-standing shibboleth that the sole legitimate government of China resided in Taiwan.

The Vietnam War has long since passed from public consciousness, and, ironically, the Vietnamese people today have more favorable views of the United States than publics in some of America's allies have. The war nevertheless lives on in the firm convictions of some that the actions of domestic critics led to the country to defeat. Henry Kissinger has been among the most visible and consistent proponents of the thesis that "the Vietnam defeat was almost entirely a U.S. domestic affair." Twenty-eight years later he repeated that diagnosis in warning that the "lesson of Vietnam" is that because the "impasse [between the administration and protest movements] doomed the U.S effort in Vietnam," there must be strong bipartisan support for American policy in Iraq to avert another defeat.[29]

The Iraq War?

Most thoughtful observers of the situation in Iraq agreed that the ultimate outcome of the war was unlikely to be fully determined by the time the bulk of American forces were withdrawn at the end of August 2010, in accordance with the agreement between Washington and Baghdad negotiated during the closing weeks of the Bush administration.[30] A modest "best case" scenario for Iraq would be a country in which the three major sectarian groups tolerate each other, settle issues through political processes rather than by terrorist violence, avoid the kinds of gross injustices that might provoke neighboring countries—

for example, Iran, Syria, Turkey, or Saudi Arabia—to intervene on behalf of one or another group, and deal effectively with such important outstanding issues as the status of the city of Kirkuk and the division of oil royalties.

Even if Iraq falls considerably short of a model Jeffersonian democracy, as in the scenario above, it would be a vast improvement over Saddam Hussein's brutal regime, and it might possibly represent at least a small step toward peace and stability in a region that has historically known little of either. As Iraq moved toward important elections in 2010, there were both favorable and unfavorable signs. Even in the face of several bloody bombings some major Iraqi leaders, including prime minister Nuri al-Maliki, had taken steps to move past sectarian divisions, at least for the purpose of the elections. On the other hand, the original election date of January had to be postponed until March 7 owing to continuing disputes on election procedures. The disqualification of 499 politicians—many but not all of whom were Sunnis—by Iraq's Independent High Election Commission on January 14 also threatened the legitimacy of the election.

The parliamentary elections took place on March 7 with a respectable turnout and without a boycott from the Sunni minority, but the run-up to the election was not free from violence; for example, two car bombs on election day killed 33 and injured 55. The final results indicated that the al-Iraqiya coalition, a secular alliance of Shiites and Sunnis headed by former prime minister Ayad Allawi, garnered 91 seats, just 2 seats ahead of the State of the Law coalition, a Shiite group led by incumbent prime minister Nuri al-Maliki. The National Alliance, a Shiite group that included anti-American cleric Mokdata al-Sadr, garnered 70 seats, followed by the Kurdistan Alliance with 43 seats. The remaining 32 seats were divided among eight other parties.

After the results were announced, prime minister al-Maliki was quick to charge fraud, and there were demands that some members of the Allawi coalition be disqualified on charges that they had previous ties to Saddam Hussein's Baath Party. Later, al-Maliki asserted that fraud had cost his party 20 seats. As neither of the leading coalitions came close to a majority in the 325-seat parliament, both leaders were required to seek ties to other groups in order to form a government. Five months of negotiations had been required to form a government after the 2005 balloting, and after an even longer interval of political bargaining following the 2010 elections, Iraq was still without a government. Vice President Biden visited Baghdad in July, urging Iraqi leaders to negotiate the end of the political impasse, but he was not successful in doing so. Meanwhile, the violence that marked the election campaign persisted into the postelection period. Although it fell far short of the near–civil war that followed the balloting in 2005, bombings continue to destroy Iraq at very regular intervals. More than eight months after the election, amid a series of bombings in Baghdad, a new government was formed with Nuri al-Maliki as the prime minister for a second term. He expanded the number of ministers in his cabinet as a way of satisfying demands by members of his coalition. Although formation of the government was an important landmark, violence in Iraq has not completely abated. In February 2011, perhaps in response to the turmoil that ousted unpopular longtime leaders in Tunisia and Egypt, al-Maliki announced that he will not run for a third term, and he cut his own salary in half.

The best-case scenario from the U.S. perspective is the formation of a coalition government that is generally perceived as legitimate and is also capable of effectively reducing the violence in the country. That happy outcome would enhance the prospects of a U.S. withdrawal from Iraq along the lines of the Bush–al-Maliki agreement of November 2008, and the fairly similar Obama timetable. President Obama announced on August 31 that U.S. combat units had withdrawn in accordance with the Bush–al-Maliki agreement and his own presidential campaign pledge. He expressed the hope that "out of the ashes of war, a new beginning could be born in this cradle of civilization," but he wisely avoided any premature assertions of "mission accomplished."

Although a favorable outcome in Iraq would not settle the deep and lingering differences on whether the United States did "the right thing" in unleashing the 2003 invasion, it would be a significant step toward leaching some of the poison out of the bitter domestic debates of the past few years. It would also allow public attention to focus on other important issues, at least some of which might not arouse such sharp partisan divisions.

But what if the outcome in Iraq falls far short of even that very modest "best case" scenario? General David Petraeus, who is credited with successfully changing American strategy in Iraq after the 2007 "surge," has repeatedly described improvements of the 2007–10 period as "fragile and reversible."[31] What if there is a resumption of the violence that in 2006–7 brought the country to the brink of civil war? What if the approximately 50,000 U.S. troops who will remain in Iraq beyond the August 2010 drawdown in a largely training role are caught up in the violence and, as a result, suffer significant casualties? What if fragile political institutions prove ineffective, are seen by increasing numbers of Iraqis as lacking in legitimacy, and as a result, give way to a military government that might bear some resemblance to the Saddam Hussein regime? That would be an immense tragedy for the long-suffering Iraqi people, who by 2007 had endured upwards of 110,000 civilian casualties, some 930,000 internal displaced persons, and almost 3,000,000 refugees, mostly to Syria, Egypt, Jordan, Iran, and Lebanon.[32] The consequences of such unhappy developments might well go beyond Iraq.

Is there also the possibility that such an unfavorable outcome might further poison the already toxic tone of political debates in this country? There are several reasons for concern on this score. As shown in chapter 3, the Iraq War has given rise to partisan cleavages of unprecedented depth, and there is little indication, even as the situation in Iraq has given way to other issues as the highest priority to the public in the wake of the severe economic crisis of 2008—notably the state of the economy, the level of unemployment, and health-care reform—that the deep division across party lines has been bridged. Like all presidents, George W. Bush was at times the target of sharp partisan criticism, but the tenor and intensity of those attacks paled in comparison to those aimed at his successor. Most generally, quite aside from the Iraq issue, the post-2008 election atmosphere in this country reflects bitter divisions rather than significant signs of reconciliation. Finally, times of economic troubles such as the present may increase temptations to search for scapegoats.[33]

CONCLUSION

It is hardly surprising that the health insurance issue is controversial; that, after all, is precisely why the many previous efforts—going back to Theodore Roosevelt's unsuccessful presidential campaign in 1912—to expand coverage have foundered. But the tone of the 2009–10 debate, in which such terms as *liar, death panels, socialist, communist, fascist, National Socialist healthcare—Dachau 1945,* and the like were fairly common, has been marked by a level of vitriol far in excess of that seen by previous administrations who tried to deal with the problem. Before it was closed down, a Facebook site presented a survey that asked viewers whether President Obama should be killed. It offered four response options: *No. Maybe. Yes. Yes, if he cuts my health care.*

Unfortunately, other examples of similar sentiments can be cited. The *Warren Times Observer* accepted and published an ad that read: "May Obama follow in the steps of Lincoln, Garfield, McKinley, and Kennedy." One does not require a PhD in American history to decode the message, but publisher John Eichert excused its publication, saying that the newspaper's advertising staff did not make the historical connection. Former fundamentalist religious leader Frank Schaeffer told the Rachel Maddow news program that a new slogan has appeared on a popular bumper sticker and on the Internet: "Pray for Obama: Psalm 109:8." In that psalm, David tells of a wicked ruler, and verse 8 reads: "Let his days be few; and let another take his office." Lest that appear to be merely an early call for a change of leadership in the Oval Office as a result of the 2012 presidential election, verse 9 reads: "Let his children be fatherless, and his wife a widow." Perhaps these could be dismissed as the ravings of the lunatic fringe, but even if they do not energize a contemporary John Wilkes Booth or Lee Harvey Oswald, they are at least minor indicators of the deep discord in American society.

It is perhaps not surprising that such falsehoods as Barack Obama's alleged lack of American citizenship were a staple for some talk radio programs and Fox News commentators who have consistently sought to delegitimate that president, but the question was also raised in the mainline media by a CNN commentator—Lou Dobbs—and by Frank Gaffney, founder and head of the Center for Security Policy in Washington. The latter also suggested that Obama may be a Muslim with a covert agenda for promoting that religion. Jerome Corsi wrote, falsely, that the Muslim soldier who perpetrated the Fort Hood massacre in November 2009 served as a transition adviser to the president, and *Forbes* magazine published a cover story by Dinesh D'Souza asserting that Obama's socialist anticolonial worldview was derived from his Kenyan father.[34] Popular Fox News commentator Glenn Beck has repeatedly denied that Obama is a Christian. Aside from the falsity of that claim, there is some irony in that charge because Beck's own faith, Mormonism, has on occasion been criticized as non-Christian. Such repeated falsehoods have had an impact. According to a survey conducted in August 2010 for *Newsweek* magazine, 24 percent of respondents stated that Obama is a Muslim, and an equal number asserted that the president "sympathizes with the goals of fundamentalists who want to impose Islamic law around the world."

NewsMax.com is a financially successful website whose board has included such establishment figures as former secretary of state Alexander Haig and former chairman of the Joint Chiefs of Staff Admiral Thomas Moorer, and whose writers have included Arnaud de Borchgrave and Michael Reagan, son of the late president. It also publishes a magazine. On September 29, 2009, one of its authors, John L. Perry, wrote an article, "Obama Risks Domestic Military 'Intervention,'" which described an increasing possibility of military coup against President Obama because, among other things, he was quoted as saying, "I am not interested in victory" in Afghanistan.[35] Although the article was later pulled, its tenor was similar to the many other incessant attacks on Obama.

When the International Olympic Committee awarded the 2016 games to Rio de Janeiro rather than to President Obama's hometown—Chicago—that decision provoked great joy from some sectors of the right-wing media who chose to interpret the IOC site selection as a stinging personal defeat for the president. Many of the same critics who relished the Olympic decision as an international slap in the face for Obama expressed outrage when a few days later the president was awarded the Nobel Peace Prize. The reactions to the Olympic Games and Nobel Prize decision were hardly of world-shaking consequence, but they raise the question whether any setbacks on much more important issues such as Iraq or Afghanistan would give rise to a similar reaction as long as there was some way to blame anyone on the home front who may have expressed doubts about American policy.

Other examples could be cited. Given the horrendous human and financial costs of the Iraq War, should the situation there deteriorate into something approaching a worst-case scenario, temptations to develop a stab-in-the-back theory for that unhappy outcome may be irresistible to some. We have already witnessed some suggestions that such explanations may be lurking in the wings, just awaiting the right moment to enter center stage.

To assess the possibilities of a stab-in-the-back explanation for any shortcomings in Iraq, it is not necessary to identify and cite commentators from the lunatic fringes of American society because several warning signs have already emerged from some establishment figures. Consider, for example, a blistering critique of the media by the distinguished social scientist James Q. Wilson, who had served on the faculties of two top-tier American universities—Harvard and the University of California at Los Angeles. In Wilson's view, since the middle of the Vietnam War the media have systematically turned their writing and reporting *against* the United States, and in doing so, they have essentially become the witting allies of this country's enemies. Wilson praised such late nineteenth-century media leaders as William Randolph Hearst, Joseph Pulitzer, and Joseph Medill, who left no doubt about which side they supported in the Spanish-American War, and he also applauded the reporting during World War II and such patriotic media leaders of that era as Henry Luce of *Time* magazine.

But according to Wilson, since the Vietnam War and the reports about American policies by such media notables as Walter Cronkite, Morley Safer, and David Halberstam, it has been all downhill as reporters have abandoned any pretense of patriotism in favor of attacking the United States and its policies whenever possible. Part of the problem, according to his analysis, is that today 93 percent of reporters and editors have college degrees, whereas in previous times they had learned their trade not in universities, but by working up the journalistic ladder from the police beat.

> This change in the media is not a transitory one that will give way to a return to the support of our military when it fights. Journalism, like so much scholarship, now dwells in a postmodern age in which truth is hard to find and statements merely serve someone's interests.
>
> The mainstream media's adversarial stance, both here and abroad, means that whenever a foreign enemy challenges us, he will know that his objective will be to win a battle not on some faraway bit of land but among the people who determine what we read and watch. We won the Second World War in Europe and Japan, but we lost in Vietnam and are in danger of losing in Iraq and Lebanon in the newspapers, magazines, and television programs we enjoy.[36]

Wilson thus leaves little doubt that he is a member in good standing of the stab-in-the-back school with respect to the wars both in Vietnam and Iraq, and that in his view the knives have been and continue to be wielded by members of the American media.

John P. Hannah, national security adviser to Vice President Dick Cheney, published an opinion article stating that President Obama had inherited an excellent situation in Iraq based on President Bush's insightful understanding of the "imperatives of victory once U.S. forces were committed." Although Hannah acknowledged that Obama endorsed and acted upon the Bush timeline for reducing the U.S. military presence in Iraq, he asserted that "under Obama, Bush's commitment to winning in Iraq has all but vanished." In short, if the situation there falls short of rather ambitious goals: "a democratizing Iraq—aligned with the U.S. and endowed with vast oil reserves, water resources, and a large industrious population—could transform their region for the better, bolstering the forces of progressive reform at the expense of Sunni and Shiite extremists," the entire blame can be laid at Obama's doorstep owing to his alleged lack of sufficient attention to Iraq. As American combat forces were leaving Iraq in accordance with the Bush–al Maliki agreement of 2008, Rich Lowry, editor of the *National Review,* weighed in with a similar column, suggesting that Iraq may become "Obama's South Vietnam."[37]

Rush Limbaugh, whose talk radio program has a weekly nationwide audience of 13.5 million listeners, was interviewed on Fox News in November 2009. According to Limbaugh, "throughout the Iraq War, it was Barack Obama and the Democrat Party which actively sought the defeat of the U.S. military. . . . I do question their commitment to national security. I question their commitment to the U.S. military. They'll put their political survival and their political power being gained over anything else." When he had been asked just before inauguration day to join other prominent Americans in writing 400-word essays on their hopes for the Obama administration, Limbaugh replied: "Okay, I'll send you a response, but I don't need 400 words. I need four. I hope he fails."[38]

Most persistently, the former vice president has on numerous occasions attacked the Obama administration on such Iraq-related issues as the "enhanced interrogation methods" and the Guantánamo prison facility, asserting that any changes from policies of the Bush administration would open up the country to new terrorist attacks. According to Cheney, Obama's "half measures" have left the country "half safe." These themes were the core of one of the most widely publicized of his addresses, before a friendly audience at the American Enterprise Institute. A subsequent analysis of the speech revealed that it contained at least ten major errors of fact. General David Petraeus, head of Central Command, differed rather sharply from Cheney on the value of torture, asserting that methods approved by the Army Field Manual work well to gain significant information. "Whenever we have, perhaps, taken expedient measures, they have turned around and bitten us on the backside." Whenever Americans use methods that violate the Geneva Convention or the standards of the International Committee of the Red Cross, he said, "We end up paying a price for it ultimately. Abu Ghraib and other situations like that are nonbiodegradable. They don't go away. The enemy continues to beat you with them like a stick."[39] It remains to be seen whether the Petraeus assessment will cause the former vice president to back off on his vocal support for "enhanced interrogation methods."

Cheney also attacked the president for his "dithering" on the mid-2009 request by General McChrystal for a further deployment of American troops to Afghanistan beyond those he committed early in his presidency.[40] Yet Cheney was among Bush administration officials who supported the transfer of American forces from Afghanistan to Iraq during the months prior to the March 2003 invasion and who opposed nation-building efforts in Afghanistan by U.S. troops in the years following the overthrow of the Taliban regime in Kabul. It might also be noted that during the Vietnam War, Cheney "dithered" his way out of military service with five draft deferments. It would be highly inappropriate to suggest that Cheney relishes the prospect of major setbacks in Iraq, in Afghanistan, or in efforts to deal with terrorist threats, but one can be sure that, should such unfortunate developments occur, he would be well prepared to provide a powerful indictment, laying all the blame on the Obama administration. He and his daughter are establishing a consulting firm in Washington that will provide him with an institutional base for what are likely to be persistent attacks on the Obama administration and its policies.

Even in the face of setbacks abroad it is not writ in the stars that purveyors of stab-in-the-back myths will gain substantial traction among the American public, but history suggests that we cannot rule out that possibility. The Alien and Sedition Acts during the John Adams administration, the Palmer raids to round up and deport suspected radical leftist citizens and immigrants during the final years of the Wilson administration, and the McCarthy-era searches to identify the State Department traitors who allegedly "lost China" and gave the Soviets a free hand in Eastern Europe at the 1945 Yalta conference were not among the proudest moments in American history.

There will always be individuals and groups with explanations for complex problems that range from simplistic to absurd to totally false. Many of them will be little more than amusing curiosities, such as those who believe that the earth is shaped like a disk (Flat Earth Society) or that Noah's ark housed pairs of each kind of dinosaur (Answers in Genesis and its Creation Museum). But some, like Senator Joseph McCarthy, can become a serious menace and do considerable harm to the country's foreign policies. The imponderables are the extent to which they are able to gain a sufficient following among the public to become a menace; for example, McCarthy's witch hunt drove large numbers of China specialists out of the State Department for the "crime" of accurately reporting during World War II that Chiang Kai-shek's regime in China was incompetent and corrupt. To the extent that significant numbers among the American public may be imbued with the belief that, owing to its superior virtue—or perhaps even to God's design—this country is justly bound to prevail in all of its international undertakings, then the propensity to explain disappointments by pointing to domestic culprits is likely to increase.

In pondering such issues, we could do far worse than heed the words of Elihu Root, a conservative Republican who followed a highly successful legal career in New York with public service as secretary of war, secretary of state, and senator from New York. He also won the Nobel Peace Prize in 1912. Shortly after World War I, he contemplated with approval a world in which public opinion was likely to play an increasing role in foreign affairs.

> When foreign affairs were ruled by autocracies or oligarchies the danger of war was in sinister purpose. When foreign affairs are ruled by democracies the dan-

ger of war will be mistaken beliefs. The world will be the gainer by the change, for, while there is no human way to prevent a king from having a bad heart, there is a human way to prevent a people from having an erroneous opinion. The way is to furnish the whole people, as part of their ordinary education with correct information about their relations to other peoples, about the limitation of their rights, about their duties to respect the rights of others, about what has happened and is happening in international affairs, and about the effect on national life of the things that are done or refused as between nations; so that the people themselves will have the means to test misinformation and appeals to prejudice and passion based upon error.[41]

If we take Root's diagnosis as the standard, public opinion data provide both good news and bad news. There is some evidence that, whatever their lack of knowledge about international affairs and other shortcomings, many Americans have developed a mature outlook about some aspects of foreign affairs. Several surveys of the past two decades have yielded some relevant data on this score. Even after the 9/11 terrorist attacks, a Gallup poll found that 77 percent of Americans agreed that it is patriotic to question "the decisions of our nation's leaders, even when they are trying to rally the country." When a *Newsweek* survey asked "do you think it is patriotic or unpatriotic to raise questions about a possible military campaign against Iraq these days," those who agreed that it is patriotic to do so outnumbered the naysayers by a margin of 67 percent to 15 percent.[42] Responses to revelations about torture and other prisoner abuses in Iraq found that many Americans did not adopt a "my country, right or wrong" posture to the issue. Still other surveys have shown that while substantial majorities among the public reject a withdrawal from world affairs, they also reject a hegemonic "world policeman" role for the United States, preferring cooperation with others and burden sharing for coping with international issues. They also express concern for the decline in America's reputation among publics abroad.[43] Such findings may or may not represent more or less permanent features of public attitudes about foreign affairs and the appropriate ways for this country to confront global challenges and opportunities. To the extent that they do, it would reduce the likelihood of falling prey to myths about the enemies in our midst.

But there is also some bad news. If the best antidote to destructive myths, of which stab-in-the-back explanations are but one example, lies in educating the public about the realities, complexities, and responsibilities arising from the challenges and opportunities posed by global affairs, there are also some grounds for disquiet. The poverty of factual knowledge about the world has already been cited. As noted earlier, there is support for the proposition that the public in the aggregate is capable of "low information rationality." Although that may provide some considerable comfort, is there some point at which there is a danger of slipping into "no information irrationality"?

One disturbing example illustrates the point. Gallup surveys commissioned by the National Geographic Society in 1948 and 1988 revealed that basic geographic knowledge—for example, identification of the largest country in the world or the location of Great Britain on a world map—declined during the 40-year interval between the surveys.[44] Yet this was a period of dramatic increases in educational attainment, whether measured by the percentages of high school diplomas or of undergraduate, graduate, and professional degrees earned by Americans. Those four decades also witnessed greatly increased opportunities for cheap international travel and a dramatic proliferation of information sources. Yet considering that geography has virtually dropped out of school curricula and that many universities have dropped geography departments, the results are not especially surprising. A study in 2006 revealed that among college-age respondents (ages 18–24), 63 percent could not locate Iraq on a map of the Middle East, and 88 percent were unable to locate Afghanistan on a map of Asia; these responses came after United States had been at war in these two countries for three and five years, respectively.[45]

Unfortunately, the lack of basic geographic knowledge is but one area in which there is significant room for improvement of public knowledge and understanding. Two other examples, both relevant to the Iraq War, might be cited. Basic knowledge about other cultures and their histories would provide some basis for questioning such blatant, politically motivated misinformation as the Wolfowitz thesis that post-Saddam Iraq would be peaceful because there was no need to fear conflict between Sunnis, Shiites, and Kurds. No doubt most Americans now understand the fallacy underlying that rosy postwar scenario, but it has been a very costly lesson indeed.

A fuller understanding of when and why American military interventions are likely to be welcomed or opposed by local populations would also be helpful. U.S. forces were warmly greeted by the vast majority of the French population when they joined Allied forces in 1917 and when they liberated France by driving out the Nazi invaders in 1944. The same was true when U.S. troops liberated the Philippines from Japanese occupation in 1945, at least in part because the Philippines had been promised independence after the war. In these instances the United States intervened to liberate countries from foreign occupiers, and American troops were indeed warmly greeted by most of those populations.

However, when the goal was to overthrow authoritarian indigenous regimes, especially in the Third World, the record is much more mixed. Fidel Castro severely disappointed those who had hoped he would bring democracy to Cuba following his successful revolution, but to most Cubans he was a vast improvement over the corrupt and authoritarian Batista regime that he had replaced. CIA agent Howard Hunt, who had been interviewing Cubans just prior to the Bay of Pigs invasion of 1961, found that "all I could find was a lot of enthusiasm for Castro."[46] For many Vietnamese who had fought the Japanese occupiers during World War II and the French after the war to gain independence, the American intervention, even if Washington believed that it was a well-intentioned undertaking that supported the interests of the Vietnamese people as well as vital American security concerns, was another hurdle to be overcome on the path to independence and national unity. There is perhaps a lesson to be learned from the response of a Confederate soldier who was asked by his Union captor why he fought: "Because you are here."[47] That is probably an answer that many Iraqi insurgents would have given if asked to explain the reasons for their attacks on American forces.

The evidence presented here largely sustains the view that, in the aggregate, public opinion on the Iraq War reflected a sensible rather than randomly volatile assessment of events on ground. Whatever the well-documented deficiencies of public knowledge about world affairs, the Iraq War case would seem to add to the growing body of evidence that challenges Lippmann's 1955 depiction of the public as invariably—and dangerously—out of kilter with reality. Indeed, many Americans paid more attention to the course of events in Iraq than to the administration's aggressive public relations campaigns in support of the war.

It is important to point out, however, that even had the American public been better informed about Iraq, it would not have prevented the American invasion because even under the most favorable circumstances, public opinion can only play a circumscribed role in foreign policy decisions; foreign affairs are not conducted by plebiscite. Given the combination of a highly ambitious leadership determined to achieve its goals, repeated assertions by those leaders that such worthy aims could be achieved by the invasion with only very limited cost in blood and treasure, the political and social context following the September 11 terrorist attacks, the fact that Saddam Hussein was the leader that "everyone could love to hate," a vigorous overt and covert public relations campaign by the administration, and prewar media performances that too often ranged between complacent and complicit, there is little reason to believe that even widespread opposition to the invasion could have derailed it.

That said, a public better informed about world affairs is nevertheless intrinsically important, and it should serve as a significant goal for both the educational system and the media. A well-informed public would also serve to reduce the possibility that the Iraq War—or any such future conflict—will give rise to destructive myths about how the evil machinations of enemies at home undermined the achievement of America's most ambitious goals.

Notes

INTRODUCTION

1. John Mueller, *Policy and Opinion in the Gulf War* (Chicago: University of Chicago Press, 1994).

2. Some of the vast numbers of surveys are summarized in Andrew Kohut and Bruce Stokes, *America Against the World: How We Are Different and Why We Are Disliked* (New York: Times Books, 2006); Peter Katzenstein and Robert O. Keohane, *Anti-Americanism in World Politics* (Ithaca: Cornell University Press, 2006); Ole R. Holsti, *To See Ourselves as Others See Us: How Publics Abroad View the United States after 9/11* (Ann Arbor: University of Michigan Press, 2008); and Monti Datta, "The Macro Politics of Anti-Americanism: Consequences for the U.S. National Interest" (PhD diss., University of California at Davis, 2009).

3. Among the best are books by Thomas E. Ricks, *Fiasco: The American Military Adventure in Iraq, 2003–2005* (New York: Penguin, 2006); Ricks, *The Gamble: General David Petraeus and the American Military Adventure in Iraq, 2006–2008* (New York: Penguin, 2009); Ron Suskind, *The Price of Loyalty: George W. Bush, the White House, and the Education of Paul O'Neill* (New York: Simon and Schuster, 2004); Suskind, *The Way of the World: A Story of Truth in the Age of Extremism* (New York: HarperCollins, 2008); Bob Woodward, *Bush at War* (New York: Simon and Schuster, 2002); Woodward, *Plan of Attack* (New York: Simon and Schuster, 2004); Woodward, *State of Denial: Bush at War, Part III* (New York: Simon and Schuster, 2006); Woodward, *The War Within: A Secret White House History, 2006–2008* (New York: Simon and Schuster, 2008); Michael Gordon and Bernard E. Trainor, *Cobra II: The Inside Story of the Invasion and Occupation of Iraq* (New York: Pantheon Books, 2006); and James Risen, *State of War: The Secret History of the CIA and the Bush Administration* (New York: Simon and Schuster, 2006). There have also been a large number of pro- and antiadministration screeds that are long on emotion and rather short on facts or analysis. At this time it is not clear whether the many "lost" e-mails within the administration, if found, will shed additional light on decision making.

4. For example, memoirs by Douglas Feith, *War and Decision: Inside the Pentagon at the Dawn of the War on Terror* (New York: HarperCollins, 2007); Richard N. Haass, *War of Necessity, War of Choice* (New York: Simon and Schuster, 2009); Karl Rove, *Courage and Consequences: My Life as a Conservative in the Fight* (New York: Simon and Schuster, 2010); George W. Bush, *Decision Points* (New York: Crown, 2010); Donald H. Rumsfeld, *Known and Unknown* (New York: Sentinel, 2011); Scott McClellan, *Inside the Bush White House and Washington's Cult of Deception* (New York: Public Affairs, 2008); and Ari Fleischer. *Taking Heat: The President, the Press, and My Years in the White House*

(New York: William Morrow, 2005). The latter two authors served as press secretaries in the White House. Colin Powell is the target of harsh criticism from Bush and Rumsfeld. At this time, there is no indication that Powell is writing memoirs of his four years as secretary of state. A fine summary of Powell's career, including the Iraq War years, is Karen De Young, *Soldier: The Life of Colin Powell* (New York: Knopf, 2006).

5. Arthur M. Schlesinger Jr., "Back to the Womb?" *Foreign Affairs* 74 (1995): 2–8.

CHAPTER 1

1. James Chace, *Acheson: The Secretary of State Who Created the American World* (New York: Simon and Schuster, 1998), 353. Acheson described these events in somewhat less colorful language in his own memoirs, *Present at the Creation* (New York: W. W. Norton, 1969), 679–86. Although his memoirs have generally received very favorable reviews, and the plot against Mossadeq took place after Eisenhower came to office in January 1953, Acheson's brief description of these events—a short section entitled "Eden's Vindication"—fails to mention what was soon thereafter common knowledge—that it had been orchestrated and led by the CIA. Kermit Roosevelt published his own memoirs of the coup. *Countercoup: The Struggle for Control of Iran* (New York: McGraw-Hill, 1979).

2. Quoted in Stephen Kinzer, *Overthrow: America's Century of Regime Change, Hawaii to Iraq* (New York: Henry Holt, 2006).

3. Tim Weiner, *Legacy of Ashes: The History of the CIA* (New York: Doubleday, 2007).

4. Quoted in Weiner, *Legacy of Ashes*, 368. The "Nixon Doctrine" was mentioned in a press conference in Guam on July 25, 1969, and was fully described in "President Nixon's speech on Vietnamization" on November 3, 1969.

5. Weiner, *Legacy of Ashes*, 371.

6. Kenneth M. Pollack, *The Persian Puzzle: The Conflict between Iran and America* (New York: Random House, 2004), quoted in Weiner, *Legacy of Ashes*, 374.

7. Although post-2003 analyses revealed no evidence supporting the Bush administration's repeated assertions of intimate ties between the Saddam Hussein regime and the al Qaeda organization that perpetrated the September 11 terrorist attacks on New York and Washington, there was ample evidence that for years Baghdad had used terrorism as an instrument of state policy. See a highly redacted collection of documents in Kevin M. Woods and James Larey, *Iraq: Perspectives Project. Saddam and Terrorism: Insights from Captured Iraqi Documents*, vol. 1, IDA Paper P-4287 (Alexandria, VA: Institute for Defense Analyses, November 2007).

8. Much of the evidence in the following several paragraphs is drawn from Nathaniel Hurd, *Diplomatic and Commercial Relationships with Iraq, 1980–2 August 1990* (July 15, 2000).

9. Department of State, Action Memorandum from Jonathan T. Howe to Lawrence S. Eagleburger, "Iraqi Use of Chemical Weapons," November 21, 1983. This and other U.S. documents cited below are available from the National Security Archive at George Washington University, www.nsarchive.org.

10. U.S. Embassy in United Kingdom Cable from Charles H. Price to the Department of State, "Rumsfeld Mission: December 20 Meeting with Iraqi President Saddam Hus-

sein," December 21, 1983; and U.S. Embassy in the United Kingdom, "Rumsfeld One-on-One Meeting with Iraqi Deputy Prime Minister," December 21, 1983.

11. Department of State, Action Memorandum from Richard W. Murphy to Lawrence S. Eagleburger, "EXIM Bank Financing for Iraq," December 22, 1983.

12. Department of State Memorandum, "Notifying Congress of [Excised] Truck Sales," March 5, 1984.

13. Department of State Cable from George P. Shultz to the United States Embassy in Lebanon (et al.), "Department Press Briefing, March 30, 1984," March 31, 1984; Department of State, Memorandum from Dick Gromet to Richard T. Kennedy, "U.S. Dual-Use Exports to Iraq: Specific Actions," May 9, 1984; and Defense Intelligence Agency Intelligence Report, "Defense Estimative Brief: Prospects for Iraq," September 25, 1984.

14. White House, *National Security Directive 26*, October 2, 1989.

15. The transcript of the conversation is in the Bush Library at Texas A&M University. It was also published in the *New York Times*, September 23, 1990.

16. Weiner, *Legacy of Ashes*, 426–27.

17. Haass, *War of Necessity, War of Choice*, 84, 94.

18. Haass, *War of Necessity, War of Choice*, 61.

19. George H. W. Bush and Brent Scowcroft, *A World Transformed* (New York: Knopf, 1999), 446.

20. *Conduct of the Gulf War*, Final Report to the U.S. Congress by the Department of Defense, April 1992, Appendix P.

21. Patrick Tyler, "After the War: U.S. Juggling Iraq Policy," *New York Times*, April 26, 1991.

22. Joel Connelly, "In Northwest: Bush-Cheney Flip Flops Cost America in Blood," *Seattle Post-Intelligencer*, July 29, 1994. The Discovery Institute, a self-described nonpartisan public policy organization, champions conservative causes, devoting much of its resources to attacking Charles Darwin and the theory of evolution.

23. Bush and Scowcroft, *A World Transformed*, chap. 19.

24. Public Law 105-138, October 31, 1998.

25. Haass, *War of Necessity, War of Choice*, 167; and Ivo H. Daalder and I. M. Destler, *In the Shadow of the Oval Office: Profiles of the National Security Advisers and the Presidents They Served—From JFK to George W. Bush* (New York: Simon and Schuster, 2009), 249.

26. Ron Suskind, *The Price of Loyalty*.

CHAPTER 2

1. Dick Cheney did not join Rumsfeld and Wolfowitz and 16 other PNAC signatories to this letter, but he had signed PNAC "Statement of Principles." Aside from Cheney, the PNAC group did not include the top officials who had led the United States into the Gulf War against Iraq: George H. W. Bush, James Baker, Brent Scowcroft, Colin Powell, and Richard Haass. For further information about members of the incoming Bush administration's foreign policy team, see James Mann, *The Rise of the Vulcans: The History of Bush's War Cabinet* (New York: Penguin, 2004). Wolfowitz separately asserted that he had told the elder President Bush of the need to oust Saddam, as had others, but "Presi-

dent Bush failed to heed this advice." Wolfowitz, "Rising Up," *New Republic,* December 7, 1998, 12–14.

2. Ron Suskind, *The Price of Loyalty.*

3. White House Fact Sheet, the August 6, 2001, Presidential Daily Briefing entitled "Bin Laden Determined to Strike in U.S.," Declassified and Approved for Release, April 10, 2004. The Richard Clarke memo is available online at the National Security Archive, www.nsarchive.org. For further details, see Richard Clarke's memoir *Inside America's War on Terror—What Really Happened* (New York: Free Press, 2004).

4. Thomas E. Ricks, *Fiasco* (New York: Penguin, 2006); and Department of Defense, "Deputy Secretary Wolfowitz Interview with Sam Tannenhaus, *Vanity Fair,*" May 9, 2003.

5. Quoted in David Rohde and David E. Sanger, "How a 'Good War' in Afghanistan Went Bad," *New York Times,* August 12, 2007.

6. Ahmed Rashid, *Descent into Chaos: The U.S. and the Disaster in Pakistan, Afghanistan, and Central Asia* (New York: Penguin, 2009), 133, 134, 137.

7. David F. Sanger, *The Inheritance: The World Obama Confronts and the Challenges to American Power* (New York: Harmony Books, 2009), 146.

8. Bob Woodward, *State of Denial,* 3.

9. Charles Krauthammer, "Changing of the Guard," *News and Observer,* May 26, 2002, A29.

10. George W. Bush, "State of the Union Address" (January 20, 2003).

11. National Security Strategy of 2002, www.whitehouse.Gov/nsc/nss/2002 .index.html; and Michael Byers, "Preemptive Self-Defense: Hegemony, Equality, and Strategies of Legal Change," *Journal of Political Philosophy* 11 (June 2003): 171–90. Retired marine general Anthony Zinni, whose experience in the Middle East included serving as head of Central Command until his retirement in 2000, asserted, "The first mistake [of the Iraq War] that will be recorded in history: The belief that containment as a policy doesn't work." "Eyes on Iraq: Remarks at the CDI Board of Directors Meeting" (Washington, DC: Center for Defense Information, May 12, 2004). See also Larry Korb and Michael Kraig, "Winning the Peace in the 21st Century. A Task Force Report of the Strategies for US National Security Program," Stanley Foundation, October 2003.

12. Rashid, *Descent into Chaos,* 116. See also Jeffrey Record, "The Bush Doctrine and War with Iraq," *Parameters* (Spring 2003): 4–21. A personal note: At a seminar on the 2002 NSS attended by two persons with close ties to the administration, I attempted to raise a question about the possibility that the reasoning behind the NSS might free others to launch preemptive strikes in cases of suspected threats to their vital interests. I was told that the agenda of the meeting was limited to serious, not "inane" questions.

13. The term "low information rationality" is from Samuel L. Popkin, *The Reasoning Voter: Communication and Persuasion in Presidential Campaigns* (Chicago: University of Chicago Press, 1991). Many other important studies of public opinion and foreign policy include Douglas Foyle, *Counting the Public In: President, Public Opinion, and Foreign Policy* (New York: Columbia University Press, 1999); Richard Sobel, *Public Opinion and Foreign Policy: The Controversy Over Contra Aid* (Lanham, MD: Rowman and Littlefield, 1993); Sobel, *The Impact of Public Opinion on U.S. Foreign Policy since Vietnam: Constraining the Colossus* (New York: Oxford University Press, 2000); Lawrence R. Jacobs

and Robert Y. Shapiro, *Politicians Don't Pander: Political Manipulation and the Loss of Democratic Responsiveness* (Chicago: University of Chicago Press, 2000); Brandice Canes-Wrone, *Who Leads Whom? Presidents, Policy, and the Public* (Chicago: University of Chicago Press, 2006); and a number of studies of specific administrations by Jacobs and Shapiro. An excellent recent synthesis of the question appears in Matthew A. Baum and Philip B. K. Potter, "The Relationship between Mass Media, Public Opinion and Foreign Policy: Toward a Theoretical Synthesis," in *Annual Review of Political Science*, 2008 edition.

14. Because the Iraq War was by far the president's most visible policy undertaking, it comes as no surprise that the correlation between assessments of President Bush and support for the Iraq War is exceptionally high. Gary C. Jacobson, "Perception, Memory, and the Partisan Polarization of Opinion on the Iraq War," *Political Science Quarterly* 125 (Spring 2010): 31–56.

15. During 20 formal interviews and 5 "casual conversations" with the FBI after his capture in December 2003, Saddam readily admitted that had he possessed WMDs, he would have used them against the invading U.S. forces. Texts of the interviews are archived at the National Security Archive at George Washington University and may be accessed at www.nsarchive.org.

16. "Bush Makes Historic Speech Aboard Warship," May 1, 2003. Unedited transcript available at CNN.com/U.S.

17. "Rumsfeld Blames Iraq Problems on 'Pockets of Dead-enders,'" *USA Today*, June 8, 2003. Rumsfeld repeated his "dead-enders" assessment of the insurgents on August 25. Wolfowitz's statement was made to the House of Representatives Armed Services Committee.

18. Further evidence on how the public abroad viewed the U.S. war in Iraq is available in Ole R. Holsti, *To See Ourselves as Others See Us*, 46–53. The impact of foreign views on American publics during the period August 2002–March 2003 is described in Danny Hayes and Matt Guardino, "The Influence of Foreign Voices on U.S. Public Opinion," unpublished manuscript, American University, 2010.

19. Thomas E. Ricks, *The Gamble* (New York: Penguin, 2009), 38.

20. General David H. Petraeus, Report to Congress on the Situation in Iraq (September 10–11, 2007). The best and fullest account of the "surge" and General Petraeus's role is Ricks, *The Gamble*. Ricks credits the military in Iraq; Woodward cites the efforts of National Security Council staffers in Washington. The difference may arise from the fact that although both were on the staff of the *Washington Post*, Ricks was by far the more frequent visitor to Iraq. Disclosure: In a 2006 opinion article, I urged the administration to deploy significantly more troops to both Iraq and Afghanistan as soon as it was politically feasible to do so—that is, right after the midterm elections—in an effort to reverse the deteriorating military situation in both countries, and also to replace defense secretary Donald Rumsfeld. "Bridging Our Wartime Divide," *News and Observer*, July 20, 2006.

21. The quotations in this paragraph are from Feith, *War and Decision*, 238; David Mitchell and Tansa George Massoud, "Anatomy of Failure: Bush's Decision-Making Process and the Iraq War," *Foreign Policy Analysis* 5 (July 2009): 279; Bob Woodward, *The War Within*, 432; and Woodward, *State of Denial*, 226.

22. Stephen F. Hayes, "Case Closed," *Weekly Standard,* November 24, 2003; White House, "President Bush Discusses War on Terror and Operation Iraqi Freedom," Cleveland, OH (March 20, 2006); White House, "President Bush Press Conference" (August 21, 2006); R. Jeffrey Smith, "Hussein Prewar Ties to al Qaeda Discounted," *Washington Post,* April 6, 2007; and Kevin M. Woods, with James Lacey, *Iraqi Perspectives Project. Saddam and Terrorism: Emerging Insights from Captured Iraqi Documents.* Vol. 1 (redacted), IDA Paper P-4287 Washington, DC: Institute for Defense Analyses, 2007.

23. Paul Wolfowitz, Speech to the Veterans of Foreign Wars, March 11, 2003; NBC News, "Interview with Vice-President Dick Cheney," *Meet the Press,* Transcript for March 16, 2003; and John McCain, "The Right War for the Right Reason," *New York Times,* March 12, 2003.

24. Paul Wolfowitz, Interview with Melissa Block, *National Public Radio,* February 19, 2003.

25. T. E. Lawrence, "A Report on Mesopotamia by T. E. Lawrence," *Sunday Times,* August 22, 1920; and Christopher Catherwood, *Churchill's Folly: How Winston Churchill Created Modern Iraq* (New York: Basic Books, 2005). The 1925 League of Nations report is quoted in Roger Cohen, "The Ottoman Swede," *New York Times,* September 13, 2007.

26. James A. Baker, "Getting Ready for the 'Next Time' in Iraq," *New York Times,* February 27, 1998; Brent Scowcroft, "Taking Exception: The Power of Containment in Iraq," *Washington Post,* March 1, 1998; and Lawrence Eagleburger on FSN, August 19, 2002, quoted in Jon Western, *Selling Intervention and War: The President, the Media, and the American Public* (Baltimore: Johns Hopkins University Press, 2005), 175. The latter is an excellent study, not only of selling the invasion of Iraq, but also of several other wars and interventions. Brent Scowcroft, "Don't Attack Saddam," *Wall Street Journal,* August 15, 2002; James A. Baker III, "The Right Way to Change a Regime," *New York Times,* August 25, 2002. Emphasis added to the Baker article. President Bush's reaction to the Scowcroft article is from Craig Unger, *The Fall of the House of Bush* (New York: Scribner's, 2007), 244.

27. James R. Schlesinger and Thomas Pickering, *Iraq: The Day After* (New York: Council on Foreign Relations, 2003). Panel members included General John Shalikashvili, Chairman of the Joint Chiefs of Staff, 1993–1997; and Jeane J. Kirkpatrick, who served in high foreign policy positions in the Reagan administration.

28. Mitchell and Massoud, "Anatomy of Failure," 282; U.S. Department of State, *The Future of Iraq Project.* The report included 17 working groups that met in the second half of 2002 and the opening months of 2003. Eight of the 14 documents were released on February 10, 2006, and 6 others were released with excisions.

29. Carl Kaysen, Steven E. Miller, Martin B. Malin, William D. Nordhaus, and John D. Steinbruner, *War with Iraq: Costs, Consequences, and Alternatives* (Cambridge, MA: American Academy of Arts and Sciences, November 2002); John Diamond, "Prewar Intelligence Predicted Iraqi Insurgency," *USA Today,* October 24, 2004. The Army War College report is quoted in James Fallows, "Blind into Baghdad," *Atlantic Monthly,* January–February 2004.

30. General Eric Shinseki, Testimony before the Senate Armed Services Committee, February 25, 2003. His estimate of troop needs for Iraq was based on *Desert Crossing Seminar, Action Report,* June 28–29, 1999, Declassified July 2, 2004. Available at the Na-

tional Security Archive at George Washington University, www.nsarchive.org; and U.S. Central Command, *OPLAN 1003-98*, published within the Pentagon October 31, 2002.

31. Paul Wolfowitz, Testimony before the House Budget Committee, February 27, 2003. He also stated that oil exports would pay for the reconstruction of postwar Iraq. "If we liberate Iraq those [oil] resources will belong to the Iraqi people, that they will be able to develop them and borrow against them." House Budget Committee, *Hearings on FY 2004 Defense Budget Request*, February 27, 2003. A month later he repeated the point. "We are dealing with a country that can really finance its own reconstruction and relatively soon." *Hearings of the Defense Subcommittee of the House Appropriations Committee*, March 27, 2003. It is difficult to estimate the final cost of an ongoing war precisely, if only because future medical costs for those suffering physical and psychiatric traumas are necessarily uncertain. In 2007 the Democratic-led Joint Economic Committee estimated that by 2009 the costs would total $1.6 trillion, and economists Joseph E. Stiglitz and Linda Bilmes put the figure at $3 trillion. Stiglitz and Bilmes, *The Three Trillion Dollar War* (New York: W. W. Norton, 2008). A recent study by the Congressional Research Office found that post-9/11 congressional appropriations for the wars in Iraq and Afghanistan were well in excess of $1 trillion. Stephen Daggett, *Cost of Major U.S. Wars* (Washington, DC: Congressional Research Office, June 29, 2010). Whatever the final correct figure, it will certainly make Wolfowitz's prediction seem like another exercise in fantasy. The Lindsey interview appears in the *Wall Street Journal*, September 15, 2002.

32. Woodward, *Plan of Attack*, 150; and Woodward, "10 Take Aways from the Bush Years," *Washington Post*, January 18, 2009.

33. Ricks, *Fiasco*, 22. See also Robert Jervis, "War, Intelligence, and Honesty: A Review Essay," *Political Science Quarterly* 123 (Winter 2008–9): 645–75; and David Barstow et al., "The Nuclear Card: The Aluminum Tube Story—A Special Report; How White House Embraced Suspect Arms Intelligence," *New York Times*, October 3, 2004. On the "Curveball" episode, see Ricks, *Fiasco*, 91; Jervis, "War, Intelligence, and Honesty"; David Barstow, "Doubts on Sources for Key Piece of Data We Suppressed, Report Says," *New York Times*, April 1, 2005; Bob Drogin, *Curveball, Lies, and the Con Man Who Caused a War* (New York: Random House, 2007); and Thomas E. Ricks, "'Curveball': Yeah, I Lied—You Suckers!" *The Best Defense: Foreign Policy Website*, February 11, 2011.

34. Vice President Cheney, *Larry King Live*, June 20, 2005.

35. National Security Council, *A National Strategy for Victory in Iraq*, November 30, 2005. Congressman Murtha's comments are from Eric Schmitt, "Fast Withdrawal of G.I.'s Is Urged by Key Democrat," *New York Times*, November 18, 2005.

36. George W. Bush, "Address at the United States Naval Academy," Annapolis, MD (November 30, 2005).

37. Richard N. Haass, *War of Necessity, War of Choice*, 262.

38. David E. Sanger, "Bush Shifts Terms for Measuring Progress in Iraq," *New York Times*, September 5, 2007; and David M. Herszenhorn, "Democrats Aim to Reframe Iraq Debate," *New York Times*, September 5, 2007.

39. The term *global war on terrorism* has evoked considerable criticism, not the least because terrorism is a tactic, not an enemy. A member of the State Department, Philip Zelikow, suggested that it be replaced with "the global struggle against violent extremism" but was "publicly slapped down" for doing so. As a symbolic way of distancing him-

self from Tony Blair, his predecessor at 10 Downing Street, Gordon Brown, the new British prime minister, has dropped the term. Philip Stephens, "How to Defeat the Jihadis in Something Other than a War," *Financial Times*, July 6, 2007, 9.

40. David Kay, "Statement by David Kay on the Interim Progress Report on the Activities of the Iraq Survey Group Before the House Permanent Committee on Intelligence," October 2, 2003; "Kay: No Evidence Iraq Stockpiled WMDs," CNN.com (January 26, 2004); Julian Borger, "Admit WMD Mistake, Survey Chief Tells Bush," *Guardian*, March 3, 2004; and Charles Duelfer, *Comprehensive Report of the Special Adviser to Director of Central Intelligence on Iraq's Weapons of Mass Destruction*, 3 vols. (September 30, 2004). See also Joseph Cirincione, Jessica T. Matthews, and George Perkovich, *WMD in Iraq: Evidence and Implications* (Washington, DC: Carnegie Endowment, January 2004).

41. For example, in an interview with Juan Williams on National Public Radio, January 22, 2004.

42. Samia Nakhoul, "Bin Laden Labels Saddam an Infidel—Jezeera TV," Reuters, February 11, 2003.

43. Warren P. Strobel, "After Two Days, No Answers to 'How This Ends,'" McClatchy Newspapers, September 11, 2007.

44. Declassified Key Judgments of the National Intelligence Estimate "Trends in Global Terrorism: Implications for the United States," dated April 2006, 2; and Mark Mazzetti and David Sanger, "Al Qaeda Threatens; U.S. Frets," *New York Times*, July 22, 2007.

45. "Bring Them On, Bush Says of Iraq Attacks," Reuters, July 2, 2003.

46. Thomas E. Ricks, *Fiasco*, 115–17. An almost equally critical appraisal appears in Joseph J. Collins, *Choosing War: The Decision to Invade Iraq and Its Aftermath*, Occasional Paper 5 (Washington, DC: Institute for National Strategic Studies, National Defense University, April 2008). The author, a retired army colonel who served for three years as the Deputy Assistant Secretary of Defense for Stability Operations, received the Defense Department's highest civilian award for Distinguished Public Service in 2004. The opening sentence of his detailed study sets the stage for his analysis: "Measured in blood and treasure, the war in Iraq has achieved the status of a major war and a major debacle." For an excellent analysis of the flawed postwar administration of Iraq, see Nora Benhasel, "Mission Not Accomplished: What Went Wrong with Iraqi Reconstruction," *Journal of Strategic Studies* 29 (2006): 453–73.

47. Ricks, *Fiasco*, 102. That Rumsfeld's invasion plans were driven largely by an effort to discredit the Powell Doctrine was confirmed in a conversation with another longtime Pentagon correspondent in April 2006.

48. However, the surge strategy has been criticized by an expert on the Middle East and former member of the National Security Council for fostering tribalization, encouraging the growth of warlordism, and worsening sectarianism. Thus, the short-run gain in reducing violence may be reducing the long-term chances of building a viable Iraqi state. Steven Simon, "The Price of the Surge," *Foreign Affairs*, May–June 2008.

49. The text of the agreement may be found on the McClatchy website: www.Mcclatchy.com. See also R. Chuck Mason, *U.S.-Iraq Status of Forces Agreement: Issues for Congressional Oversight*, Congressional Research Service, December 12, 2008.

50. Barack Obama, "Speech on Iraq," Fort Bragg, NC, March 19, 2009. Although

Obama and his presidential campaign rival John McCain differed on many issues, McCain had described the 16-month withdrawal plan as "a pretty good timetable." Elisabeth Bumiller, "Bush-McCain Divergences on Foreign Policy Shown in Recent Moves," *New York Times*, July 26, 2008.

51. AP-GfK Roper Public Affairs and Media poll, April 16–20, 2009; *Newsweek* poll conducted by Princeton Research Associates International, March 4–5, 2009; Pew Research Center poll, March 9–12, 2009; CNN/Opinion Research Corporation polls, March 12–15, 2009, and April 3–5, 2009; ABC/*Washington Post* poll, January 13–16, 2009; Gallup poll, June 30, 2009; and CNN/Opinion Research survey, September 1–2, 2010.

52. Sam Dagher, "Iraq Wants the U.S. Out," *Wall Street Journal*, December 28, 2010.

53. CNN/Opinion Research Corp. surveys, July 27–29, 2008, and December 1–2, 2008; and a *Newsweek* poll conducted by Princeton Research Associates, April 1–2, 2009.

54. "Obama Changing the Way Germans See US," *World Public Opinion Poll*, June 4, 2009. Full study is available at worldpublicopinion.org; and Richard Auxier, "Few in NATO Support Call for Additional Forces in Afghanistan," Pew Research Center, August 31, 2009.

55. Associated Press, "Petraeus: Afghan Violence at Peak Levels Last Week," June 11, 2009; Thom Shanker and Eric Schmitt, "U.S. Commander in Afghanistan Given More Leeway," *New York Times*, June 10, 2009, A1; and Shanker and Schmitt, "General Given Pick of Military in Afghanistan," *New York Times*, June 11, 2009, A1.

56. Bob Woodward, "McChrystal: More Forces or 'Mission Failure'; Top U.S. Commander for Afghan War Calls Next 12 Months Decisive," *Washington Post*, September 21, 2009. McChrystal's memo to Gates is available at www.washingtonpost.com. Intra-administration debates on dealing with the war in Afghanistan are described in considerable detail by Bob Woodward, *Obama's Wars* (New York: Simon and Schuster, 2010). The survey responses to the request for additional forces to Afghanistan are from ABC News/*Washington Post* poll, October 15–18, 2009; and *USA Today*/Gallup poll, October 6, 2009.

57. George F. Will, "Time to Get Out of Afghanistan," *Washington Post*, September 1, 2009; Will, "Is It 1966 in Washington?" *Newsweek*, October 5, 2009, 25; Will, "The Clock's Ticking," *Washington Post*, May 6, 2010; Will, "McChrystal Had to Go," *Washington Post*, June 24, 2010; Bob Herbert, "Reliving the Past," *Washington Post*, September 5, 2009; Nicholas Kristof, "The Afghanistan Abyss," *New York Times*, September 5, 2009; and Doyle McManus, "Afghanistan Isn't Obama's Vietnam—Yet," *Los Angeles Times*, September 6, 2009. Kristol's rejoinder to Will, entitled "No Will, No Way," also appeared in the *Washington Post*, September 1, 2009. During the same week, the syndicated *Doonesbury* comic strip featured a battle-scarred veteran of eight years in Afghanistan who depicted the war as an almost perfect replay of Vietnam.

The veteran military analyst Anthony H. Cordesman proposed a strategy that might but is not guaranteed to succeed, in *The Afghanistan Campaign: Can We Win?* (Washington, DC: Center for Strategic and International Studies, July 22, 2009). Counterinsurgency specialist David Kilcullen also deals with Afghanistan (as well as Iraq), in *The Accidental Guerilla: Fighting Small Wars in the Midst of a Big One* (New York: Oxford University Press, 2009). For a more pessimistic assessment of the situation in Afghanistan by a RAND Corporation expert on that country, see Seth Jones, *The Grave-*

yard of Empires (New York: Norton, 2009); also Andrew J. Bacevich, "The War We Can't Win," *Harper's,* November 2009, 15–20; Richard N. Haass, "We're Not Winning. It's Not Worth It," *Newsweek,* July 26, 2010, 30–35; and Bing West, *The Wrong War: Grit, Strategy, and the Way Out of Afghanistan* (New York: Random House, 2011).

58. President Obama's speech to the nation on Afghanistan, December 1, 2009. The text is available at www.nytimes.com. His Nobel Prize speech is available in "Obama's Nobel Remarks," *New York Times,* December 10, 2009.

59. Joseph Berger, "U.S. Commander Describes Marja Battle as the First Salvo of Campaign," *New York Times,* February 21, 2010.

60. Michael Hastings, "The Runaway General," *Rolling Stone,* July 8–22, 2010. In a very generous gesture, President Obama allowed General McChrystal to retire at the 4-star rank, even though he had not served sufficient time at that rank.

CHAPTER 3

1. Arthur H. Vandenberg Jr., ed., *The Private Diaries of Senator Vandenberg* (Boston: Houghton Mifflin, 1952), 1.

2. Among many others, see John Zaller, *The Nature and Origin of Mass Opinion* (Cambridge: Cambridge University Press, 1992); Richard A. Brody and Catherine R. Shapiro, "Policy Failure and Public Support: The Iran-Contra Affair and Public Assessment of President Reagan," *Political Behavior II* (1989): 353–69.

3. Barry B. Hughes, *The Domestic Context of American Foreign Policy* (San Francisco: Freeman, 1978), 128.

4. Barry M. Goldwater, *Conscience of a Conservative* (Washington, DC: Regnery, 1960).

5. Ole R. Holsti and James N. Rosenau, *American Leadership in World Affairs: Vietnam and the Breakdown of Consensus* (London: Allen and Unwin, 1984). For an effort by a moderate Republican senator to revive bipartisanship, see Charles Percy, "The Partisan Gap," *Foreign Policy,* no. 45 (1981–82): 3–15. However, Percy (R-IL) was defeated in his next reelection bid, in part because his ultraconservative Republican Senate colleague Jesse Helms (R-NC) helped to raise funds for Percy's opponent, Paul Simon, a liberal Democrat.

6. Commencement address at Notre Dame University, May 22, 1977, *Public Papers of the Presidents of the United States: Jimmy Carter,* vol. 1 (1977), 954; and Jimmy Carter, "The President's Proposed Energy Policy," April 18, 1977. *Vital Speeches of the Day* 43 (May 1, 1977): 418–20.

7. Speech to the British House of Commons, June 8, 1982.

8. Ole R. Holsti, *Public Opinion and American Foreign Policy,* rev. ed. (Ann Arbor: University of Michigan Press, 2004), 173, table 5.3. For much fuller discussions of public opinion and the Gulf War, see John Mueller, *Policy and Opinion in the Gulf War;* and W. Lance Bennett and David Paletz, eds., *Taken by Storm: The Media, Public Opinion, and U.S. Foreign Policy in the Gulf War* (Chicago: University of Chicago Press, 1994).

9. I. M. Destler, Leslie H. Gelb, and Anthony Lake, *Our Own Worst Enemy: The Unmaking of American Foreign Policy* (New York: Simon and Schuster, 1984). Further discussions of partisanship may be found in Alan Abramowitz and Kyle Saunders, "Why

Can't We All Just Get Along? The Reality of a Polarized America," *Forum* 3, no. 2 (2005), article 1; Gary C. Jacobson, "Polarized Politics and the 2004 Elections," *Political Science Quarterly* 120 (Summer 2005): 199–218; Jacobson, *Divider, Not Uniter: George W. Bush and the American People* (New York: Longman, 2006); Ronald Brownstein, *The Second Civil War* (New York: Penguin, 2007); Robert Y. Shapiro and Yaeli Bloch-Elkon, "Political Polarization and the Rational Public," paper for the Annual Conference of the American Association of Public Opinion Research, Montreal, May 10, 2006; Shapiro and Bloch-Elkon, "Ideological Partisanship and American Public Opinion Toward Foreign Policy," in *Power and Superpower: Global Leadership and Exceptionalism in the 21st Century*, ed. M. H. Halperson et al. (New York: Century Foundation Press, 2007), 49–68; and Joseph Bafumi and Robert Shapiro, "A New Partisan Voter," undated manuscript, Columbia University, New York.

10. As noted above, leadership opinion can have a significant impact on the general public, especially if there is agreement among leaders of the two major parties, but there is also some evidence that publics can at times independently develop opinions on foreign policy issues. See Maxine Isaacs, "Two Different Worlds: The Relationship between Elite and Mass Opinion on American Foreign Policy," *Political Communication* 15 (1988): 323–45.

11. Gary C. Jacobson, "Perception, Memory, and the Partisan Polarization of Opinion on the Iraq War," *Political Science Quarterly* 125 (Spring 2010): 31–56.

12. A careful study of bipartisanship since the late nineteenth century in the Congress revealed that the level of external threat is the most important determinant of bipartisanship. Peter Trubowitz and Nicole Mellow, "Going Bipartisan: Politics by Other Means," *Political Science Quarterly* 120 (Fall 2005): 433–53. In an earlier (August 2003) conference draft of the article, the authors presciently predicted that the post-9/11 bipartisan consensus would be likely to erode over the Iraq War.

13. Steven Kull, Clay Ramsey, and Evan Lewis, "Misperception, the Media, and the Iraq War," *Political Science Quarterly* 118 (Winter 2003–4): 569–98. Also see Clay Ramsey, Steven Kull, Evan Lewis, and Stefan Subia, "Misinformation and the 2010 Election." Available at www.worldpublicopinion.org. December 10, 2010.

14. Recently available tapes revealed that President Johnson told Secretary of Defense Robert McNamara that he doubted that the alleged North Vietnamese attack on U.S. ships in the Gulf of Tonkin had in fact taken place.

15. Amy Lorentzen, "Cheney: Kerry Victory Will Lead to Another Terrorist Attack on U.S.," Associated Press, September 7, 2004.

16. Richard W. Stephenson, "Bush Contends Partisan Critics Hurt War Effort," *New York Times*, November 12, 2005, A1.

17. For the full transcript of Rove's speech, see "Remarks of Karl Rove at the New York Conservative Party," *Washington Post*, June 22, 2005.

18. Wilson committed a number of other blunders that ultimately undermined his goal of American membership in the League of Nations. The most serious was Wilson's demand that his supporters in the Senate vote *against* the final draft of the Versailles Treaty because it included Senator Lodge's and some other "reservations" that he refused to accept. Despite that, the treaty was approved by the Senate on March 19, 1920, by a vote of 49–35, falling short of the constitutional requirement of a two-thirds majority by

just 7 votes. Wilson's hope that the 1920 election would provide a "solemn referendum" on the Versailles Treaty was also wholly misguided as was his hope that Democrats would nominate him for a third term. For an excellent analysis, see Thomas A. Bailey, *Woodrow Wilson and the Peacemakers* (New York: Macmillan, 1947). Wilson's behavior and judgment may have been affected by a major stroke suffered in 1919. Kenneth Crispell and Carlos Gomez, *Hidden Illness in the White House* (Durham: Duke University Press, 1989).

19. Although General Jones's partisan preferences, if any, are unknown, an overwhelming majority of military officers identify with the Republican Party. Ole R. Holsti, "A Widening Gap between the U.S. Military and Civilian Society? Some Evidence, 1976–1996," *International Security*, no. 23 (1998): 5–42.

CHAPTER 4

1. Hadley Cantril, *The Human Dimension: Experiences in Policy Research* (New Brunswick: Rutgers University Press, 1967), 74.

2. Arthur M. Schlesinger Jr., "Back to the Womb?"

3. For example, two pillars of post–World War II liberal internationalism, George F. Kennan and Senator J. William Fulbright, turned into leading critics of the war in Vietnam and called for a sharply reduced conception of America's role in the world. Kennan, *The Cloud of Danger* (Boston: Little, Brown, 1977); Kennan, "An Appeal to Thought," *New York Times Magazine*, May 7, 1978; Fulbright, *The Arrogance of Power* (New York: Random House, 1967); and Fulbright, *The Crippled Giant* (New York: Random House, 1972). Others who have been vocal proponents of a reduced U.S. role include 1992 and 1996 presidential candidates Ross Perot and Patrick Buchanan.

4. Kenneth Waltz, "The Emerging Structure of World Politics," *International Security*, no. 18 (Fall 1993): 76.

5. Pew Research Center, *America's Place in the World, 2009.*

6. For example, the widely read syndicated columnist Charles Krauthammer, "The Unipolar Moment," *Foreign Affairs* 70 (1990–91): 23–43. During the subsequent two decades, Krauthammer has continued to be a vocal proponent of American foreign policy unilateralism in foreign affairs as the only appropriate role for the world's sole superpower as it is in the best interests of the world. Because he argued that others seem to lack the wisdom and intestinal fortitude to appreciate that self-evident truth, he has rarely lost the opportunity to deride those who do not take their marching orders from Washington. These views also appear in frequent opinion articles by John Bolton, who served as interim U.S. ambassador to the United Nations in the second George W. Bush administration.

7. In a column justifying the "Bush Doctrine" of meeting suspected threats by preemptive military action, Charles Krauthammer asserted that "we are not just any hegemon. We are a uniquely benign imperium. This is more than self-congratulation, it is a fact manifest in the way others welcome our power." "The Bush Doctrine," *Weekly Standard* (June 4, 2001). Extensive evidence on how the United States and its policies are viewed abroad does not fully support Krauthammer's claim. See Peter Katzenstein and Robert O. Keohane, *Anti-Americanism in World Politics* (Ithaca: Cornell University

Press, 2006); Steven Brooks, *As Others See Us: The Causes and Consequences of Foreign Perceptions of America* (Petersborough, ON: Brookview Press, 2006); Andrew Kohut and Bruce Stokes, *America Against the World* (New York: Times Books, 2006); Ole R. Holsti, *To See Ourselves as Others See Us;* and Monti Datta, "The Macro Politics of Anti-Americanism: Consequences for the U.S. National Interest" (PhD diss., University of California at Davis, 2009).

8. For example, Fouad Ajami, "The Falseness of Anti-Americanism," *Foreign Policy* (September–October 2003): 52–61; Ajami, "Anti-Americanism Is Mostly Hype," *Wall Street Journal,* June 23, 2008: A17: Hillel Fradkin, *National Review Online,* http://nationalreview.com; and Paul Johnson, "Anti-Americanism Is Racist Envy," July 31, 2003, http://forbes.com. Ajami, a scholar at Johns Hopkins University, served as a consultant to Vice President Cheney during the run-up to the invasion in Iraq.

9. President Bush's press conference, July 12, 2007; Sheryl Gay Stolberg and Jeff Zeleny, "A Firm Bush Tells Congress Not to Dictate Policy on War," *New York Times,* July 13, 2007, A1. Indeed, it is not even clear that Iraqis always helped the U.S. effort. For example, in July 2007 American troops and air power had to be used against a rogue Iraqi police unit. Stephen Farrell, "U.S. Troops Battle Iraqi Police in East Baghdad," *New York Times,* July 14, 2007, A5. In April 2008 Prime Minister Nuri al-Maliki had to fire 1,300 soldiers and police for refusing to fight or for changing sides during a crackdown on Muqtada al Sadr's Mahdi army.

10. Steven Lee Myers and Marc Santora, "Premier Casting U.S. Withdrawal as Iraqi Victory," *New York Times,* June 26, 2009, A1. The 1920 uprising was the occasion for the T. E. Lawrence critique of British policy described in chapter 2.

11. Thom Shanker, "Warning Against Wars Like Iraq and Afghanistan," *New York Times,* February 25, 2011.

12. Ole R. Holsti, "Public Opinion and Human Rights in American Foreign Policy," in *The United States and Human Rights: Looking Inward and Outward,* ed. David P. Forsythe (Lincoln: University of Nebraska Press, 2000); Holsti, "Democracy Promotion as Popular Demand?" in *American Democracy Promotion: Impulses, Strategies, and Impacts,* ed. Michael Cox, G. John Ikenberry, and Takashi Inogushi (New York: Oxford University Press, 2000); Bruce W. Jentleson, "The Pretty Prudent Public: Post-Vietnam American Opinion on the Use of Military Force," *International Studies Quarterly* 36 (1992): 49–73; and Jentleson and Rebecca L. Britton, "Still Pretty Prudent: Post–Cold War American Public Opinion on the Use of Force," *Journal of Conflict Resolution* 42 (1998): 395–417.

13. Nicholas Kristof, "Diplomacy at Its Worst," *New York Times,* April 29, 2007; Glenn Kessler, "In 2003, U.S. Spurned Iran's Offer of Dialogue," *Washington Post,* June 18, 2006, A16; and Ryan Crocker, "Eight Years On," *Newsweek,* September 14, 2009, 31–41. The text of the Iranian proposal can be found at ipsnews.net/iranletterfacsimile.pdf.

14. Data from the following surveys conducted in the fall of 2009: NBC/*Wall Street Journal,* October 22–25; CNN/Opinion Research, October 16–18; ABC/*Washington Post,* October 15–18; Ipsos/McClatchy, October 1–5; CNN/Opinion Research, October 26–28.

15. Rachel Weiner, *Huffpost Reports,* June 12 and 14, 2009.

16. Pew Research Center, *America's Place in the World, 2009.*

17. Schlesinger, "Back to the Womb?"

18. Letter to Thomas Jefferson, May 25, 1798, *Letters and Other Writings of James Madison*, vol. 2 (1865): 141.

19. Thom Shanker, "Pentagon Says Iraq Effort Limits Ability to Fight Other Conflicts; Chairman of Joint Chiefs Tells Congress of Risks," *New York Times*, May 5, 2005, A1. Retired general Barry McCaffrey, who opposed an immediate withdrawal from Iraq, had an even gloomier assessment: "There is no argument of whether the US Army is rapidly unraveling." Gordon Lubold, "Is US Army Bent to the Breaking Point?" *Christian Science Monitor*, April 3, 2007; Barry R. McCaffrey, "No Choice: Stay the Course in Iraq," *Los Angeles Times*, April 3, 2007; and Joseph L. Galloway, "A Fading Fighting Force," McClatchy-Tribune Information Service (October 28, 2007). The psychological toll paid by veterans of deployments in Afghanistan and Iraq is analyzed in Terri Tanielian and Lisa H. Jaycox, editors, *Invisible Wounds of War* (Monica, CA: Rand Corporation, 2008); Lizette Alvarez, "After the Battle, Fighting the Bottle at Home," *New York Times*, July 8, 2008; Alvarez, "Suicides of Soldiers Reach High of Nearly 3 Decades," *New York Times*, January 30, 2009; James Dao, "Vets' Mental Health Diagnoses Rising," *New York Times*, July 17, 2009; Karen H. Seal, Daniel Bertenthal, Christian R. Miner, Saunak Sen, and Charles Marmar, "Bringing the War Back Home; Mental Health Disorders among 103,788 U.S. Veterans Returning from Afghanistan and Iraq Seen at VA Facilities," *Archives of Internal Medicine*, no. 167 (2007): 476–82; and Karen Seal, T. J. Meltzer, Shira Maguen, and Charles R. Marmar, "Growing Prevalence of Mental Disorders among Iraq and Afghanistan Veterans: Trends and Risk Factors for Mental Health Diagnoses in New Users of VA Health Care, 2002–2008," *American Journal of Public Health* (2009). In order to meet recruitment quotas, the army has loosened standards on criminal backgrounds, fitness, and education, and the upper age limit has been raised from 35 to 42 years. Army and Marine Corps waivers for recruits with criminal records rose sharply in 2007. Eighteen percent of army recruits during the year ending on September 30, 2007, had records of felonies and misdemeanors. Some felony waivers were granted for such major crimes as terrorist threats, kidnapping, rape, sexual abuse, and indecent acts or liberties with children. Lizette Alvarez, "Army and Marine Corps Grant More Felony Waivers," *New York Times*, April 22, 2008. Army desertions increased steadily from 2,357 in fiscal year 2004 to 2,543 and 3,196 in the following two fiscal years. During the first quarter of fiscal year 2007, 871 soldiers deserted. Ian Urbina, "Even as Loved Ones Fight, War Doubts Arise," *New York Times*, July 15, 2007. Military suicides reached a record level in 2007. "U.S. Suicides Highest in 2007," Reuters, May 28, 2008. A 300-page army report, released on July 29, 2010, summarized the results of a 15-month study on the increasingly serious problems of suicide and other forms of risky behavior. *Army. Health Promotion, Risk Reduction and Suicide Prevention. Report 2010*. The full report is available at www.army.mil.

CHAPTER 5

1. Robert Novak, "No Midyear Crisis for Bush: Dubious Poll Results Aside, Bush Has Delivered on a Major Campaign Issue—Tax Cuts," *Chicago Sun-Times*, July 2, 2001; and Joshua Green, "The Other War Room," *Washington Monthly*, April 2002.

2. Walter Lippmann, *Public Opinion* (New York: Macmillan, 1922).

3. Lippmann, *Essays in the Public Philosophy* (Boston: Little, Brown, 1955), 20. Lipp-

mann later did a rather sharp about-face, as he came to see an increasingly critical pub lic as more enlightened than the administration in Washington on the Vietnam War.

4. George F. Kennan, *American Diplomacy, 1900–1950* (New York: Mentor Books, 1951); Thomas A. Bailey, *The Man in the Street: The Impact of Public Opinion on Foreign Policy* (New York: Macmillan, 1948); and Gabriel Almond, *The American People and Foreign Policy* (New York: Harcourt Brace, 1950). The role of public opinion was a part of vigorous postwar debates between proponents of realist and liberal perspectives on international affairs.

5. Ole R. Holsti, "Public Opinion and Foreign Policy: Challenges to the Almond-Lippmann Consensus," *International Studies Quarterly* 36 (1992): 439–66. See also the many studies cited in note 4, chapter 2 above.

6. Douglas Foyle, *Counting the Public In: Presidents, Public Opinion, and Foreign Policy* (New York: Columbia University Press, 1999).

7. "But in fact, the Bush administration is a frequent consumer of polls, though it takes extraordinary measures to appear that it isn't." Joshua Green, "The Other War Room," 12.

8. Telephone interviews conducted November 6 and 9, 2006. In accordance with a promise of anonymity, the interviewee's name and position will not be identified.

9. Bob Woodward, *State of Denial*, 11. The president's self-description as a "gut player" also appears in Scott McClellan's memoir, *What Happened*.

10. According to the Government Accounting Office, between fiscal year 2003 and the first quarter of FY2005, seven federal departments (including the Department of Defense) spent $1.62 billion on contracts with advertising agencies, public relations firms, media organizations, and individual members of the media. GAO Report-06-305 to Congressional Requesters, January 13, 2006.

11. According to Paul O'Neill, secretary of the treasury until he was fired in December 2002 for doubting the need for additional tax cuts and failing to exhibit sufficient enthusiasm for the impending invasion of Iraq, the first meeting of the National Security Council discussed ways of ousting Saddam Hussein. Ron Suskind, *The Price of Loyalty: George W. Bush, The White House, and the Education of Paul O'Neill* (New York: Simon and Schuster, 2004). On this point, see also Scott McClellan, *What Happened*.

12. Ron Suskind, "Faith, Certainty, and the Presidency of George W. Bush," *New York Times Magazine*, October 17, 2004.

13. The quotations in this paragraph are drawn from James Sandrolini, "Propaganda: The Art of War," *Chicago Media Watch Report* (Fall 2002): 1. For further evidence on the prewar role of the media, see Steven Kull, Clay Ramsey, and Evan Lewis, "Misperception, the Media, and the Iraq War," *Political Science Quarterly*, no. 118 (2003–4): 569–98.

14. Quoted in Jonathan Merman, "The Media's Independence Problem," *World Policy Journal* (Fall 2004): 67.

15. Thomas Ricks, *Fiasco*, 35; and Michael Gordon and Judith Miller, "Threats and Responses: The Iraqis; U.S. Says Hussein Intensifies Quest for A-Bomb Parts," *New York Times*, September 8, 2002, A1.

16. Ricks, *Fiasco*, 57; and Michael Gordon and Bernard Trainor, *Cobra II* (New York: Pantheon Books, 2006).

17. "The Times and Iraq," *New York Times*, May 26, 2004, 18.

18. Quoted in Michael Massing, "Now They Tell Us," *New York Review of Books* 51 (February 26, 2004).

19. Massing, "Now They Tell Us."

20. Brian Stelter, "Was Press a War 'Enabler'? 2 Offer a Nod from the Inside," *New York Times,* May 30, 2008.

21. Howard Kurtz, "The Post on WMDs: An Inside Story: Prewar Articles Questioning Threat Often Didn't Make Front Page," *Washington Post,* August 12, 2004, A01.

22. Jonathan S. Landay, "Lack of Hard Evidence of Iraqi Weapons Worries Top U.S. Officials," McClatchy News Bureau, September 6, 2002. This was not an isolated effort by McClatchy reporters to assess the validity of administration assertions about important foreign and defense policy issues. Much more recently, an article found that a Dick Cheney speech defending the administration's use of "enhanced interrogation techniques" contained at least ten factual errors. Landay and Warren P. Strobel, "Cheney's Speech Ignored Some Inconvenient Truths," McClatchy News Bureau, May 21, 2009.

23. Joe Strupp, "McClatchy's D.C. Bureau Claims It's Barred from Defense Secretary Planes," *Editor and Publisher,* May 23, 2007.

24. Kurtz, "The Post on WMDs."

25. Thomas E. Ricks, *Fiasco,* 88. Ricks was not alone in his criticism of the media on the Iraq issue. See, among many others, Andrew J. Bacevich, "War and the Failure of the Fourth Estate," *Raritan* 26, no. 2 (Fall 2006): 24–34; Mark Danner, "The Secret War: The Downing Street Memo and the Iraq War's Buried History," *New York Review of Books* 52, no. 10 (June 9, 2005); Danner, "Words in a Time of War," *Los Angeles Times,* June 1, 2007; Greg Palast, "U.S. Media Have Lost the Will to Dig Deep," *Los Angeles Times,* April 27, 2007; Stefan Halper and Jonathan Clarke, *The Silence of the Rational Center* (New York: Basic Books, 2007); Tom Fenton, *Bad News: Decline of Reporting, the Business of News, and the Danger to Us All* (New York: Regan Books, 2005); John R. MacArthur, "The Lies We Bought," *Columbia Journalism Review* 42 (May–June 2003): 62–63; Jonathan Mermin, "The Media's Independence Problem," *World Policy Journal,* no. 21 (2004): 67–71; Daniel Okrent, "Weapons of Mass Destruction? Or Mass Distraction?" *New York Times,* May 30, 2004; Michael Massing, "Now They Tell Us," *New York Review of Books* 51, February 26, 2004; Robert Entman, *Projections of Power: Framing News, Public Opinion, and U.S. Foreign Policy* (Chicago: University of Chicago Press, 2003); Michael Massing, "The Press: The Enemy Within," *New York Review of Books,* 52 (December 15, 2005): 36–44; Steve Schifferes, "Who Won the Media War," *BBC News Online,* April 18, 2003; Andrew Flibbert, "The Road to Baghdad," *Security Studies* 15 (2006): 310–52; Kevin Coe et al., "No Shades of Gray," *Journal of Communication* 54 (2004): 234–52; Scott Althus and Devon Largio, "When Osama Became Saddam," *PS: Political Science and Politics* 37 (2004): 795–99; Richard Perez-Pena, "The War Endures, but Where's the Media?" *New York Times,* March 28, 2008; Chaim Kaufman, "Threat Inflation and the Marketplace of Ideas: The Selling of the Iraq War," *International Security* 29 (Summer 2004): 5–48. For a critique and rejoinder on the latter study, see Ronald R. Krebs and Chaim Kaufman, "Correspondence: Selling the Market Short? Marketplace of Ideas and the Iraq War," *International Security* 29 (Spring 2005): 196–207.

26. McClellan, *What Happened?* Not surprisingly, McClellan's book has not been well received by members of the Bush administration and its cheerleaders. Some questioned

his mental health, and the *Wall Street Journal* even suggested that the book is a part of an intricate left-wing conspiracy: "We'd merely note that [McClellan's] publisher is Public Affairs, an imprint founded by left-wing editor Peter Osnos and which has published six books by George Soros. Public Affairs is owned by Perseus Books, which is owned by Perseus LLC, a merchant bank whose board included Democrats Richard Holbrooke and Jim Johnson, who is now doing Barack Obama's vice presidential vetting. One of Perseus' investment funds, Perseus-Soros Biopharmaceutical, is co-managed with Mr. Soros." Quoted in Tim Rutten, "No Swans in This Sewer," *Los Angeles Times*, May 31, 2008.

27. For example, George W. Bush, "Speech to the U.S. Congress" (September 20, 2001); and press conference with French president Jacques Chirac, November 5, 2001.

28. Kate Phillips, "Clinton Critiques Defense Department for Reply on Her Request," *New York Times*, July 20, 2007, A11.

29. Charlie Savage, "Obama Looks to Limit Impact of Tactic Bush Used to Sidestep New Laws," *New York Times*, March 9, 2009. For a fuller discussion of the signing statement issues, see Christopher S. Kelly, "The Unitary Executive and the Presidential Signing Statement" (PhD diss., Miami University of Ohio, 2003). According to Kelly's follow-up research, the number of presidential challenges to legislation in signing statements varies quite widely: Reagan (149), George H. W. Bush (246), Clinton (153), George W. Bush (1,168), and Obama (30 through July 4, 2009). The latter figure indicates that Obama has not completely abandoned the use of signing statements. Data from Kelly's website at Miami University.

30. Signing statement on HR 2863, December 30, 2005.

31. American Bar Association, *Blue-Ribbon Task Force Finds President Bush's Signing Statements Undermine Separation of Powers*, Press Release, July 24, 2006.

32. Jack Goldsmith, *The Terror Presidency: Law and Judgment Inside the Bush Presidency* (New York: Norton, 2007). Sheryl Gay Stolberg and Jeff Zeleny, "A Firm Bush Tells Congress Not to Dictate Policy on War," *New York Times*, July 13, 2007, A1. A spirited defense of virtually unlimited executive powers appears in John Yoo, *Crisis and Command* (New York: Kaplan, 2009).

33. George W. Bush, "State of the Union Address," January 29, 2002; and George W. Bush, "Graduation Address at the U.S. Military Academy," West Point, NY, June 1, 2002.

34. The memo was not published until almost three years later in the *Sunday Times*, May 1, 2005.

35. Douglas Foyle, "Leading the Public to War? The Influence of American Public Opinion on the Bush Administration's Decision to Go to War in Iraq," *International Journal of Public Opinion Research* 6, no. 3 (2004): 269–94.

36. Elizabeth Bumiller, "War Public Relations Machine Is Put on Full Throttle," *New York Times*, February 8, 2003, A17. The details of this campaign are described in considerable detail in *What Happened?* by now-repentant White House press secretary Scott McClellan, who served in that position between 2003 and 2006.

37. A memo summarizing the Bush-Blair meeting became available in 2006. Richard Norton-Taylor, *Guardian*, February 3, 2006. The information became available only much later in the American media. Don Van Natta, "Bush Was Set on Path to War, British Memo Says," *New York Times*, March 27, 2007.

38. Henry A. Kissinger, "The Lessons of Vietnam," *Los Angeles Times,* May 31, 2007. See also Jeremy Brecher and Brendan Smith, "The 'Stab in the Back' Trap," *Truthout,* April 27, 2007.

39. Christopher Gelpi, Jason Reiffler, and Peter Feaver, "Iraq the Vote: Retrospective and Prospective Foreign Policy Judgments on Candidate Choice and Casualty Tolerance," *Political Behavior* 29, no. 2 (June 2007): 151–74. Respondents were asked a hypothetical question—how many future casualties they would accept, on a five-point scale of 0 to 50,000—rather than whether existing casualty levels were acceptable. For a comparison with other conflicts, see Richard Sobel and David Nelson, "Trying to Steer Public Opinion?" *Baltimore Sun,* January 22, 2006.

40. Paul R. Abramson, John H. Aldrich, Jill Rickershauser, and David W. Rohde, "Fear in the Voting Booth: The 2004 Presidential Election," *Political Behavior* 29, no. 2 (June 2007): 197–220.

41. Dana Milbank, "Curtains Ordered for Media Coverage of Returning Coffins," *Washington Post,* October 21, 2003; and Milbank, "What the Family Would Let You See, the Pentagon Obstructs," *Washington Post,* April 24, 2008. The media ban was instituted by then–defense secretary Dick Cheney during the run-up to the Gulf War in 1991. A fuller discussion of this issue appears in Jim Sheeler, *Final Salute: A Story of Unfinished Lives* (New York: Penguin, 2008). Sheeler won a Pulitzer Prize for the essays that ultimately led to this book. That policy has been reversed by the Obama administration.

42. Quoted in Frank Rich, "The Petraeus-Crocker Show Gets the Hook," *New York Times,* April 13, 2008.

43. Further details may be found in a report from the House of Representatives Committee on Oversight and Government Reform, *Misleading Information from the Battlefield: The Tillman and Lynch Episodes,* July 17, 2008. See also Jon Krakauer, *Where Men Win Glory: The Odyssey of Pat Tillman* (New York: Doubleday, 2009).

44. National Security Council, *National Strategy for Victory in Iraq,* November 2005.

45. "The Angry One," *GQ,* January 2007. Hagel's views are more fully spelled out in his book (with Peter Kammsky) *America: Our Next Chapter* (New York: Ecco, 2008).

46. The financial and economic data were obtained from the *Wall Street Journal* at www.wsj.com.

47. CNN Election Center, November 4, 2008, 11:43 p.m. EST, www.cnn.com; and the Pew Research Center, "Inside Obama's Sweeping Victory," November 5, 2008, www.pew peoplepress.com. The best comprehensive analysis of the 2008 election is Kate Kenski, Bruce W. Hardy, and Kathleen Hall Jamieson, *The Obama Victory: How Media, Money, and Message Shaped the 2008 Election* (New York: Oxford University Press, 2010).

48. John Mueller, "The Iraq Syndrome," *Foreign Affairs* 84 (November–December 2005). For a rejoinder and rebuttal see Christopher Gelpi and John Mueller, "How Many Casualties Will Americans Tolerate?" *Foreign Affairs* 85 (January–February 2006).

49. Ricks, *Fiasco,* 386; and Richard Cheney, "Cheney Blasts Media on al Qaeda-Iraq Link," CNN.com (June 18, 2004). Figures on media deaths in Vietnam and Iraq are from Ricks, *Fiasco,* 424.

50. Private communication, May 28, 2008. The relative impotence of MoveOn and Americans Against Escalation in Iraq (AAEI) is described in Michael Crowley, "Can Lobbyists Stop the War?" *New York Times,* September 9, 2007.

51. Telephone interviews with an administration official, November 6 and 9, 2006.

52. U.S. Department of Defense, "News Transcript of DoD Briefing with Secretary Rumsfeld and Gen. Pace" (March 7, 2006). Other pro-administration and pro-Iraq war critics of the media include former press secretary Ari Fleisher, *Taking Heat: The President, the Press, and My Years in the White House* (New York: William Morrow, 2005); and Jim A. Kuypers, *Bush's War: Media Bias the Justification for War in a Terrorist Age* (Lanham, MD: Rowman and Littlefield, 2006).

53. Tommy Franks, *American Soldier* (New York: HarperCollins, 2004), quoted in Ricks, *Fiasco,* 156.

54. Mike Allen, "Bush Courts Columnists, Hill," *Politico,* July 18, 2007; and David Brooks, "Heroes and History," *New York Times,* July 17, 2007.

55. Information in this and the preceding paragraphs on the covert Pentagon program is drawn from David Barstow, "Message Machine: Behind Military Analysts, the Pentagon's Hidden Hand," *New York Times,* April 20, 2008; Barstow, "Pentagon Suspends Briefing for Analysts," *New York Times,* April 26, 2008; Barstow, "One Man's Military-Industrial-Media Complex," *New York Times,* November 29, 2008; Barstow, "Inspector General Sees No Misdeeds in Pentagon's Effort to Make Use of TV Analysts," *New York Times,* January 17, 2009; and Barstow, "Inspector at Pentagon Says Report Was Flawed, *New York Times,* May 6, 2009. Barstow, who won the 2009 Pulitzer Prize for investigative reporting for these stories, had to win a legal battle to gain access to the evidence because the Pentagon originally refused to release many of the relevant documents.

CHAPTER 6

1. Thomas W. Graham, "The Pattern and Importance of Public Knowledge in the Nuclear Age," *Journal of Conflict Resolution* 32 (1988): 19–34; Stephen Earl Bennett, "Trends in Americans' Political Information, 1967–1987," *American Politic Quarterly* 17 (1989): 422–35; Bennett, "Is the Public's Ignorance Trivial?" *Critical Review* 15 (2003): 307–38; Michael Delli Carpini and Scott Keeter, *What Americans Know about Politics and Why It Matters* (New Haven: Yale University Press, 1996); M. Kent Jennings, "Political Knowledge Over Time," *Public Opinion Quarterly,* no. 60 (1996): 228–52; Michael A. Dimock and Samuel L. Popkin, "Political Knowledge in a Comparative Perspective," in *Do the Media Govern?* ed. Shanto Iynegar and Richard Reeves (Thousand Oaks, CA: Sage, 1986), 217–24; and Pew Research Center, "Public Knowledge of Current Affairs Little Changed by the Revolutions. What Americans Know: 1989–2007," April 15, 2007.

2. Gabriel A. Almond, *The American People and Foreign Policy* (New York: Praeger, 1950).

3. See the studies cited in note 13, chapter 2. For a more general assessment of problems arising from the "most important problem" survey questions, see Christopher Wlezien, "On the Salience of Political Issues: The Problem with 'Most Important Problem,'" *Electoral Studies* 24 (2005): 555–79.

4. Samuel Popkin, *The Reasoning Voter: Communication and Persuasion in Presidential Campaigns* (Chicago: University of Chicago Press, 1991); and many other recent studies.

5. Peter Trubowitz and Nicole Mellow, "Going Bipartisan: Politics by Other Means," *Political Science Quarterly* 120 (Fall 2005): 433–53.

6. Charles Lindbergh, Speech at America First rally, Des Moines, IA, September 11, 1941. Available at www.pbs.org/wgbh/lindbergh/filmmore/reference/primary/des moinesspeech.html.

7. Ricks, *The Gamble*, 324; Ricks, "Understanding the Surge in Iraq and What's Ahead," Philadelphia: Foreign Policy Institute, May 29, 2009; and Zinni, "Eyes on Iraq."

8. Steven Kull, Clay Ramsay, and Evan Lewis, "Misperception, the Media, and the Iraq War," *Political Science Quarterly* 118 (2003–4): 569–98; and Gary C. Jacobson, "Perception, Memory, and the Partisan Polarization of Opinion on the Iraq War," *Political Science Quarterly* 125 (Spring 2010): 31–56.

9. Matthew Baum, "Going Private: Public Opinion, Presidential Rhetoric, and the Domestic Politics of Audience Costs in U.S. Foreign Policy Crises," *Journal of Conflict Resolution* 48 (October 2004): 603–31.

10. U.S. Department of Defense, "News Transcripts: Paul Wolfowitz interview with Sam Tannenbaum of *Vanity Fair*" (May 9, 2003).

11. Thomas Jefferson to Colonel Edward Harrington, January 16, 1787. In Adrienne Koch and William Peden, eds., *The Life and Selected Writings of Thomas Jefferson* (New York: Modern Library, 1944), 411–12.

12. Carl Bernstein and Bob Woodward, *All the President's Men* (New York: Simon and Schuster, 1974). For the citations to the David Barstow articles about the Bush administration's covert program to hire and train retired military officers to promote the Iraq War on television, see note 55, chapter 5.

13. Thomas Jefferson to John Norwell, June 11, 1807, in Koch and Peden, *Life and Selected Writings*, 581.

14. The Nixon quote on Vietnam is from William M. Hammond, *Reporting Vietnam: Media and Military at War* (Lawrence: University Press of Kansas, 2007), 249; and James Blitz, "Blair Labels British Media a 'Feral Beast,'" *Financial Times*, June 13, 2007, 4.

15. Michale O'Brien, *John F. Kennedy: A Biography* (New York: St. Martin's Press, 2005), 529.

16. W. Lance Bennett, "Toward a Theory of Press-State Relations in the United States," *Journal of Communication* 40 (Spring 1990): 103–25.

17. Max Boot, "The Media Aren't the Enemy in Iraq: Blaming the Press for the Problem in Iraq Deflects the Blame from Where it Belongs," *Los Angeles Times*, January 10, 2007. For more detailed rebuttals on the media and the Vietnam War, see Hammond, *Reporting Vietnam*; and Daniel C. Hallin, *The "Uncensored" War: The Media and Vietnam* (New York: Oxford University Press, 1986).

18. Kull, Ramsey, Clay Ramsay, and Evan Lewis, "Misperception, the Media, and the Iraq War"; and Pew Research Center, "Public Knowledge of Current Affairs."

19. Boot, "The Media Aren't the Enemy in Iraq."

20. Newspaper Association of America based on data from *Editor and Publisher International Yearbook*, 2008.

21. *Editor and Publisher International Yearbook*.

22. Michael Emery, "An Endangered Species: The International News Hole," *Gannett Center Journal* 3 (1989): 151–64; Pippa Norris, "The Restless Searchlight: Network News Framing of the Post–Cold War Period," *Political Communication* 12 (1995): 357–70; Gar-

rick Utley, "The Shrinking of Foreign News: From Broadcast to Narrowcast," *Foreign Affairs*, March–April 1997; and Luca Robinson and Steven Livingston, "No News and Foreign News: U.S. Media Coverage of the World," paper presented at the Annual Convention of the International Studies Association, Portland, OR, February 2003. According to Utley, time devoted to foreign news declined from 3,733 minutes in 1989 to 1,838 minutes in 1991 on ABC, and the comparable figures for NBC were 3,351 minutes and 1,175 minutes.

23. Kevin Baker, "Stabbed in the Back! The Past and Future of a Right-Wing Myth," *Harper's*, June 2006; and Jeffrey P. Kimball, "The Stab-in-the-Back Legend and the Vietnam War," *Armed Forces and Society* 14 (1988): 434.

24. Paul E. Vallely and Michael A. Aquino, "From PSYOP to Mind War: The Psychology of Victory" (San Francisco: Headquarters of the 7th Psychological Operations Group, 1980), 4. After his retirement as a brigadier general, Vallely was a very active member of the group of retired officers recruited by the Pentagon to sell the Iraq War on television.

25. Quoted in Kimball, "The Stab-in-the-Back Legend," 439, 441. See also "Time Essay: The Army and Vietnam: The Stab-in-the-Back Complex," *Time*, December 12, 1969.

26. Glenn Greenwald, "John McCain's Vietnam-based View," *Salon*, May 12, 2008.

27. Walter Cronkite broadcast, February 27, 1968.

28. John Mueller, *War, Presidents, and Public Opinion* (New York: Wiley, 1973), is the classic study of the impact of casualties on public opinion in the Korean and Vietnam Wars.

29. Henry A. Kissinger and Arnaud de Borchgrave, "Straight Talk from Kissinger," *Current*, no. 210 (February 1979): 51–58; and Kissinger, "The Lessons of Vietnam," *Los Angeles Times*, May 31, 2007. A 2008 Gallup poll in Vietnam revealed that, by a margin of 44 percent to 16 percent, the Vietnamese approved of the job performance of U.S. leadership.

30. For example, Thomas E. Ricks, *The Gamble;* Steven Biddle, "Seeing Baghdad, Thinking Saigon," *Foreign Affairs*, March–April 2006; and Kenneth Pollock, "Five Myths About the Iraq Troop Withdrawal," *Washington Post*, August 22, 2010.

31. For example, David Petraeus, "Report to Congress on the Situation in Iraq" (April 8–9, 2008); and Petraeus, "Iraq Progress 'Fragile and Reversible' after Bombing Petraeus Warns," FoxNews.com (April 24, 2009). General Ray Odierno, commanding general of U.S. forces in Iraq, repeated that assessment on September 17, 2009.

32. Hanna Fischer, "Iraq Civilian Casualty Estimates," Congressional References Service, January 12, 2009; and United Nations High Commission for Refugees, "Iraq Operations at a Glance," January 1, 2009. The estimates on Iraqi civilian death vary widely: The Brookings Institution figure is 108,707; the World Health Organization's is 151,000; and that of the medical journal *Lancet* is a range of 426,000 to 795,000.

33. A classic study of the frustration-aggression hypothesis found a significant correlation between the lynching of African-Americans in the South and falling cotton prices. Carl I. Hovland and Robert Sears, "Minor Studies of Aggression: Correlation of Economic Indices with Lynchings," *Journal of Psychology* 9 (1940): 301–10. This study has given rise to some critiques of the statistical analysis but the basic data have escaped challenge.

34. Frank Gaffney, "America's First Muslim President?" *Washington Times*, June 9,

2009; Jerome Corsi, "Shooter Advised Obama Transition," *WorldNetDaily,* November 6, 2009; Dinesh D'Souza, "How Obama Thinks," *Forbes,* September 27, 2010; and a Princeton Research Associates International survey conducted for *Newsweek,* August 25–26, 2010.

35. The Perry article is archived on www.talkingpointsmemo.com.

36. James Q. Wilson, "The Press at War: The Patriot Reporter Is Passé," *City Journal,* Autumn 2006. To the extent that his analysis presents data on Iraq War coverage, it focuses on the three traditional television networks—ABC, CBS, and NBC—and excludes any information about Fox News and other media outlets that have strongly supported the Bush administration and the Iraq War. Wilson also includes some obligatory anecdotal critiques of the *New York Times* but makes no mention of the highly conservative *Wall Street Journal* or the very strong editorial support of the *Washington Post* for the Iraq War.

37. John P. Hannah, "Is the Job Done?" *Los Angeles Times,* June 29, 2009; and Rich Lowry, "Obama's South Vietnam?" *National Review On-Line,* August 20, 2010.

38. Rush Limbaugh, Interview on "Fox News Sunday with Chris Wallace," November 1, 2009; and Limbaugh Show, January 16, 2009.

39. Dick Cheney, Speech to the American Enterprise Institute (May 21, 2009). The text is available at www.FoxNews.com; and Jonathan S. Landay and Warren P. Strobel, "Cheney's Speech Ignored Some Inconvenient Truths," McClatchy News Bureau, May 21, 2009. For a detailed assessment and rebuttal of former vice president Cheney's attacks on the Obama administration policy for dealing with terrorism, see Jack Goldsmith, "The Cheney Fallacy," *New Republic,* May 18, 2009. Goldsmith served the Bush administration as assistant attorney general.

40. Dick Cheney, speech when accepting the award from the Center for Security Policy, October 21, 2009.

41. Elihu Root, "A Requisite for the Success of Popular Diplomacy," *Foreign Affairs* 1 (1922): 5.

42. Miroslav Nincic and Jennifer Ramos, "The Dynamics of Patriotism: Survey and Experimental Evidence," paper presented at the Annual Meeting of the American Political Science Association, Toronto, September 2009.

43. The data are drawn from Steven Kull, Clay Ramsay, Stefan Subias, Stephen Weber, and Evan Lewis "Americans on Detention, Torture, and the War on Terrorism," Program on International Policy Attitudes, July 22, 2004; Council on Foreign Relations, "Public Opinion on Global Issues," November 2009; and World Public Opinion, "American Attitudes: Americans and the World," August 3, 2007, www.WorldPublicOpinion.org.

44. National Geographic Society, 1988.

45. National Geographic-Roper Public Affairs, *Final Report: 2006 Geographic Literacy Study,* May 2006. A brief summary of the main findings appears in John Roach, "Young Americans Geographically Illiterate, Survey Suggests," *National Geographic News,* May 2, 2006.

46. Howard Hunt, in "Cold War," CNN, 1988.

47. Quoted in John Keegan, *The American Civil War: A Military History* (New York: Knopf, 2009).

Bibliography

Note: Newspaper articles and articles from the Internet are listed in the notes.

Abrahamson, Paul R., John H. Aldrich, Jill Rickerhauser, and David W. Rhode. "Fear in the Voting Booth: The 2004 Election." *Political Behavior* 29, no. 2 (June 2007): 197–220.

Abramowitz, Alan, and Kyle Saunders. "Why Can't We All Just Get Along? The Reality of a Polarized America." *Forum* 3, no. 2 (2005), Article 1.

Acheson, Dean G. *Present at the Creation.* New York: Norton, 1969.

Ajami, Fouad. "The Falseness of Anti-Americanism." *Foreign Policy* (September–October 2003): 52–61.

Allen, Mike. "Bush Courts Columnists, Hill." *Politico* (July 18, 2007).

Almond, Gabriel. *The American People and Foreign Policy.* New York: Harcourt Brace, 1950.

Althus, Scott, and Devin Largio. "When Osama Became Saddam." *PS: Political Science and Politics* 37 (2004): 795–99.

American Bar Association. *Blue Ribbon Task Force Finds President Bush's Signing Statements Undermine Separation of Powers.* Press Release (July 24, 2006).

Auxier, Richard. "Few in NATO Support Call for Additional Forces in Afghanistan." Pew Research Center, August 31, 2009.

Bacevich, Andrew J. "War and the Failure of the Fourth Estate." *Raritan* 26, no. 2 (Fall 2006): 24–34.

Bacevich, Andrew J. "The War We Can't Win." *Harper's* (November 2009): 15–20.

Bafumi, Joseph, and Robert Y. Shapiro. "A New Partisan Voter." Undated manuscript. Columbia University, New York.

Bailey, Thomas A. *The Man in the Street: The Impact of Public Opinion on Foreign Policy.* New York: Macmillan, 1948.

Bailey, Thomas A. *Woodrow Wilson and the Peacemakers.* New York: Macmillan, 1947.

Baker, Kevin. "Stabbed in the Back! The Past and Future of a Right-Wing Myth." *Harper's* (June 2006).

Baum, Matthew. "Going Private: Public Opinion, Presidential Rhetoric, and the Domestic Politics of Audience Costs in U.S. Foreign Policy Crises." *Journal of Conflict Resolution* 48 (October 2004): 603–31.

Baum, Matthew, and Philip B. K. Potter. "The Relationship between Mass Media, Public Opinion, and Foreign Policy: Toward a Theoretical Synthesis." *Annual Review of Political Science* (2008).

Benhasel, Nora. "Mission Not Accomplished: What Went Wrong with Iraqi Reconstruction." *Journal of Strategic Studies* 29 (2006): 453–73.

Bennett, Stephen Earl. "Is the Public's Ignorance Trivial?" *Critical Review* 15 (2003): 307–38.

Bennett, Stephen Earl. "Trends in Americans' Political Information, 1967–1987." *American Politics Quarterly* 17 (1989): 422–35.

Bennett, W. Lance. "Toward a Theory of Press-State Relations in the United States." *Journal of Communication* 40 (Spring 1990): 103–25.

Bennett, W. Lance, and David Paletz, eds. *Taken by Storm: The Media, Public Opinion, and U.S. Foreign Policy in the Gulf War.* Chicago: University of Chicago Press, 1994.

Bernstein, Carl, and Bob Woodward. *All the President's Men.* New York: Simon and Schuster, 1974.

Biddle, Steven. "Seeing Baghdad, Thinking Saigon." *Foreign Affairs* (March–April 2006).

Boulton, Marshall, and Benjamin Page. *Worldviews 2002: American Public Opinion and Foreign Policy.* Chicago: Chicago Council on Foreign Relations (CCFR), 2000.

Brecher, Jeremy, and Brendan Smith. "The 'Stab in the Back' Trap." *Truthout* (April 27, 2007).

Brody, Richard A., and Catherine R. Shapiro. "Policy Failure and Public Support: The Iran-Contra Affair and Public Assessment of President Reagan." *Political Behavior* 11 (1989): 353–69.

Brookings Institution. *Iraq Index.*

Brooks, Stephen. *As Others See Us: The Causes and Consequences of Foreign Perceptions of America.* Petersborough, ON: Brookview Press, 2006.

Brownstein, Ronald. *The Second Civil War.* New York: Penguin, 2007.

Bush, George H. W., and Brent Scowcroft. *A World Transformed.* New York: Knopf, 1999.

Bush, George W. "Address at the United States Naval Academy." Annapolis, MD, November 30, 2005.

Bush, George W. *Decision Points.* New York: Crown, 2010.

Bush, George W. "Graduation Address at the U.S. Military Academy." West Point, NY, June 1, 2002.

Bush, George W. "Press Conference." July 12, 2007.

Bush, George W. "Press Conference with French President Jacques Chirac." November 5, 2001.

Bush, George W. "Signing Statement on House of Representatives Bill 2863." December 30, 2005.

Bush, George W. "Speech to U.S. Congress." September 20, 2001.

Bush, George W. "State of the Union Address." January 29, 2002.

Bush, George W. "State of the Union Address." January 20, 2003.

Byers, Michael. "Preemptive Self-Defense: Hegemony, Equality, and Strategies of Legal Change." *Journal of Political Philosophy* 11 (June 2003): 171–90.

Canes-Wrone, Brandice. *Who Leads Whom? Presidents, Policy, and the Public.* Chicago: University of Chicago Press, 2006.

Cantril, Hadley. *The Human Dimension: Experiences in Policy Research.* New Brunswick: Rutgers University Press, 1967.

Carter, Jimmy. "Commencement Address at Notre Dame University, May 22, 1977." *Public Papers of the Presidents of the United States: Jimmy Carter.* Vol. 1 (1977).

Carter, Jimmy. "The President's Proposed Energy Policy." April 18, 1977. *Vital Speeches of the Day* 43 (May 1, 1977): 418–20.

Catherwood, Christopher. *Churchill's Folly: How Winston Churchill Created Modern Iraq.* New York: Basic Books, 2005.

Chase, James. *Acheson: The Secretary of State Who Created the American World.* New York: Simon and Schuster, 1998.

Cheney, Dick. *Larry King Live.* June 20, 2005.

Cheney, Dick. "NBC Interview." *Meet the Press,* March 16, 2003.

Cheney, Dick. Speech when accepting an award from the Center for Security Policy. October 21, 2009.

Chicago Council on Foreign Relations. *Global Views 2004: American Public Opinion and Foreign Policy: Topline Data from U.S. Public Survey: U.S. Leaders Survey.* Chicago: CCFR, 2004.

Chicago Council on Foreign Relations. *Global Views 2006.* Chicago: CCFR, 2006.

Chicago Council on Global Affairs. *Global Views 2008.* Chicago: CCGA, 2008.

Cirincione, Joseph, Jessica T. Matthews, and George Perkovich. *WMD in Iraq: Evidence and Implications.* Washington, DC: Carnegie Endowment, January 2004.

Clarke, Richard. *Inside America's War on Terror—What Really Happened.* New York: Free Press, 2004.

Coe, Kevin, David Domke, Erica S. Graham, Sue Lockett John, and Victor W. Pickard. "No Shades of Gray." *Journal of Communication* 54 (2004): 234–52.

Collins, Joseph J. *Choosing War: The Decision to Invade Iraq and Its Aftermath.* Occasional Paper 5. Washington, DC: Institute of National Strategic Studies, National Defense University, April 2008.

Cordesman, Anthony H. *The Afghanistan Campaign: Can We Win?* Washington, DC: Center for Strategic and International Studies, July 22, 2009.

Crispell, Kenneth, and Carlos Gomez. *Hidden Illness in the White House.* Durham: Duke University Press, 1989.

Crocker, Ryan. "Eight Years On." *Newsweek* (September 14, 2009): 31–41.

Cronkite, Walter. Broadcast. February 27, 1968.

Daalder, Ivo, and I. M. Destler. *In the Shadow of the Oval Office: Profiles of the National Security Advisers and the Presidents They Served—From JFK to George W. Bush.* New York: Simon and Schuster, 2009.

Daggett, Stephen. *Cost of Major U.S. Wars.* Washington, DC: Congressional Research Office, June 29, 2010.

Danner, Mark. "The Secret War: The Downing Street Memo and the Iraq War's Buried History." *New York Review of Books* 52, no. 10 (June 9, 2005).

Datta, Monti. *The Macro Politics of Anti-Americanism: Consequences for the U.S. National Interest.* PhD diss., University of California at Davis, 2009.

Delli Carpini, Michael, and Scott Keeter. *What Americans Know about Politics and Why It Matters.* New Haven: Yale University Press, 1996.

Destler, I. M., Leslie H. Gelb, and Anthony Lake. *Our Own Worst Enemy: The Unmaking of American Foreign Policy.* New York: Simon and Schuster, 1984.

De Young, Karen. *Soldier: The Life of Colin Powell.* New York: Knopf, 2006.

Dimock, Michael A., and Samuel L. Popkin. "Political Knowledge in a Comparative Perspective." In *Do the Media Govern?*, edited by Shanto Iynegar and Richard Reeves. Thousand Oaks, CA: Sage, 1986.

Drogin, Bob. *Curveball, Lies, and the Con Man Who Caused a War.* New York: Random House, 2007.

D'Souza, Dinesh. "How Obama Thinks." *Forbes* (September 24, 2010).

Duelfer, Charles. *Comprehensive Report of the Special Adviser to the Director of Central Intelligence on Iraq's Weapons of Mass Destruction.* 3 vols. Washington, DC, September 30, 2004.

Editor and Publisher. International Yearbook. 2008.

Emery, Michael. "An Endangered Species: The International News Hole." *Gannett Center Journal* 3 (1989): 151–64.

Entman, Robert. *Projections of Power: Framing News, Public Opinion, and U.S. Foreign Policy.* Chicago: University of Chicago Press, 2003.

Fallows, James. "Blind into Baghdad." *Atlantic Monthly* (January–February 2004).

Feith, Douglas. *War and Decision: Inside the Pentagon at the Dawn of the War on Terror.* New York: HarperCollins, 2007.

Fenton, Tom. *Bad News: Decline of Reporting, the Business of News, and the Danger to Us All.* New York: Regan Books, 2005.

Fischer, Hanna. "Iraq Civilian Casualty Estimates." Washington, DC: Congressional Reference Services, January 12, 2009.

Fleischer, Ari. *Taking Heat: The President, the Press, and My Years in the White House.* New York: William Morrow, 2005.

Flibbert, Andrew. "The Road to Baghdad." *Security Studies* 15 (2006): 310–52.

Foyle, Douglas. *Counting the Public In: Presidents, Public Opinion, and Foreign Policy.* New York: Columbia University Press, 1999.

Foyle, Douglas. "Leading the Public to War? The Influence of American Public Opinion on the Bush Administration's Decision to Go to War in Iraq." *International Journal of Public Opinion Research* 6, no. 3 (2004): 269–94.

Franks, Tommy. *American Soldier.* New York: HarperCollins, 2004.

Fulbright, J. William. *The Arrogance of Power.* New York: Random House, 1967.

Fulbright, J. William. *The Crippled Giant.* New York: Random House, 1972.

Gelpi, Christopher, and John Mueller. "How Many Casualties Will Americans Tolerate?" *Foreign Affairs* 85 (January–February 2006).

Gelpi, Christopher, Jason Reiffler, and Peter Feaver. "Iraq, the Vote: Retrospective and Prospective Foreign Policy Judgments on Candidate Choice and Casualty Tolerance." *Political Behavior* 29, no. 2 (June 2007): 151–74.

Goldsmith, Jack. "The Cheney Fallacy." *New Republic* (May 18, 2009).

Goldsmith, Jack. *The Terror Presidency: Law and Judgment Inside the Bush Presidency.* New York: Norton, 2007.

Goldwater, Barry M. *Conscience of a Conservative.* Washington, DC: Regnery, 1960.

Gordon, Michael, and Bernard Trainor. *Cobra II: The Inside Story of the Invasion and Occupation of Iraq.* New York: Pantheon Books, 2006.

Graham, Thomas W. "The Pattern and Importance of Public Knowledge in the Nuclear Age." *Journal of Conflict Resolution* 32 (1988): 19–34.

Green, Joshua. "The Other War Room." *Washington Monthly* (April 2002).

Greenwald, Glenn. "John McCain's Vietnam-based View." *Salon* (May 12, 2008).

Haass, Richard N. *War of Necessity, War of Choice.* New York: Simon and Schuster, 2009.

Haass, Richard N. "We're Not Winning. It's Not Worth It." *Newsweek* (July 26, 2010): 30–35.

Hagel, Chuck, with Peter Kammsky. *America: Our Next Chapter.* New York: Ecco, 2008.

Hagel, Chuck. "The Angry One." *GQ* (January 2007).

Hallin, Daniel C. *The "Uncensored" War: The Media and Vietnam.* New York: Oxford University Press, 1986.

Halper, Stefan, and Jonathan Clarke. *The Silence of the Rational Center.* New York: Basic Books, 2007.

Hammond, William M. *Reporting Vietnam: Media and Military at War.* Lawrence: University Press of Kansas, 2007.

Hastings, Michael. "The Runaway General." *Rolling Stone* (July 8–22, 2010).

Hayes, Danny, and Matt Guardino. "The Influence of Foreign Voices on U.S. Public Opinion." Unpublished manuscript. Washington, DC: American University, 2010.

Hayes, Stephen F. "Case Closed." *Weekly Standard* (November 24, 2003).

Holsti, Ole R. "Democracy Promotion as Popular Demand?" In *American Democracy Promotion: Impulses, Strategies, and Impacts,* edited by Michael Cox, G. John Ikenberry, and Takashi Inoguchi. New York: Oxford University Press, 2000.

Holsti, Ole R. *Public Opinion and American Foreign Policy.* Rev. ed. Ann Arbor: University of Michigan Press, 2004.

Holsti, Ole R. "Public Opinion and Foreign Policy: Challenges to the Almond-Lippmann Consensus." *International Studies Quarterly* 36 (1992): 439–66.

Holsti, Ole R. "Public Opinion and Human Rights in American Foreign Policy." In *The United States and Human Rights: Looking Inward and Outward,* edited by David P. Forsythe. Lincoln: University of Nebraska Press, 2000.

Holsti, Ole R. *To See Ourselves as Others See Us: How Publics Abroad View the United States after 9/11.* Ann Arbor: University of Michigan Press, 2008.

Holsti, Ole R. "A Widening Gap between the U.S. Military and Civilian Society? Some Evidence, 1976–1996." *International Security,* no. 23 (1998): 5–42.

Holsti, Ole R., and James N. Rosenau. *American Leadership in World Affairs: Vietnam and the Breakdown of Consensus.* London: Allen and Unwin, 1984.

Hovland, Carl I., and Robert Sears. "Minor Studies of Aggression: Correlation of Economic Indices with Lynchings." *Journal of Psychology* 9 (1940): 301–10.

Hughes, Barry B. *The Domestic Context of American Foreign Policy.* San Francisco: Freeman, 1978.

Hunt, Howard. "Cold War." CNN, 1988.

Hurd, Nathaniel. *Diplomatic and Commercial Relationships with Iraq, 1980–2 August 1990.* Third World Traveler, July 15, 2000.

Iraq Casualty Count. www.uscasualties.org.

Isaacs, Maxine. "Two Different Worlds: The Relationship between Elite and Mass Opinion on American Foreign Policy." *Political Communication* 15 (1988): 323–45.

Jacobs, Lawrence, and Robert Y. Shapiro. *Politicians Don't Pander: Political Manipulation and the Loss of Democratic Responsiveness.* Chicago: University of Chicago Press, 2000.

Jacobson, Gary C. *Divider, Not Uniter: George W. Bush and the American People.* New York: Longman, 2006.

Jacobson, Gary C. "Perception, Memory, and the Partisan Polarization of Opinion on the Iraq War." *Political Science Quarterly* 125 (Spring 2010): 31–56.

Jacobson, Gary C. "Polarized Politics and the 2004 Elections." *Political Science Quarterly* 120 (Summer 2005): 199–218.

Jennings, M. Kent. "Political Knowledge over Time." *Public Opinion Quarterly* 60 (1996): 228–52.

Jentleson, Bruce W. "The Pretty Prudent Public: Post–Vietnam American Opinion on the Use of Force." *International Studies Quarterly* 36 (1992): 49–73.

Jentleson, Bruce W., and Rebecca L. Britton. "Still Pretty Prudent: Post–Cold War American Public Opinion on the Use of Force." *Journal of Conflict Resolution,* no. 42 (1998): 395–417.

Jervis, Robert. "War, Intelligence, and Honesty: A Review Essay." *Political Science Quarterly* 123 (Winter 2008–9): 645–75.

Jones, Seth. *The Graveyard of Empires.* New York: Norton, 2009.

Katzenstein, Peter, and Robert O. Keohane. *Anti-Americanism in World Politics.* Ithaca: Cornell University Press, 2006.

Kaufman, Chaim. "Threat Inflation and the Marketplace of Ideas: The Selling of the Iraq War." *International Security,* no. 29 (Summer 2004): 5–48.

Kay, David. "Statement by David Kay on the Interim Progress Report on the Activities of the Iraq Survey Group Before the House Permanent Committee on Intelligence." October 2, 2003.

Keegan, John. *The American Civil War: A Military History.* New York: Knopf, 2009.

Kelly, Christopher S. *The Unitary Executive and the Presidential Signing Statement.* PhD diss., Miami University of Ohio, 2003.

Kennan, George F. *American Diplomacy, 1900–1950.* New York: Mentor Books, 1951.

Kennan, George F. "An Appeal to Thought." *New York Times Magazine* (May 7, 1978).

Kennan, George F. *The Cloud of Danger.* Boston: Little, Brown, 1977.

Kenski, Kate, Bruce W. Hardy, and Kathleen Hall Jamieson. *The Obama Victory: How Media, Money, and Message Shaped the 2008 Election.* New York: Oxford University Press, 2010.

Kilcullen, David. *Accidental Guerilla: Fighting Small Wars in the Midst of a Big One.* New York: Oxford University Press, 2009.

Kimball, Jeffrey P. "The Stab-in-the-Back Legend and the Vietnam War." *Armed Forces and Society* 14 (1988).

Kinzer, Stephen. *Overthrow: America's Century of Regime Change, Hawaii to Iraq.* New York: Henry Holt, 2006.

Kissinger, Henry A., and Arnaud de Borchgrave. "Straight Talk from Kissinger." *Current* 210 (February 1979): 51–58.

Koch, Adrienne, and William Peden, eds. *The Life and Selected Writings of Thomas Jefferson.* New York: Modern Library, 1944.

Kohut, Andrew, and Bruce Stokes. *America Against the World: How We Are Different and Why We Are Disliked.* New York: Times Books, 2006.

Korb, Larry, and Michael Kraig. "Winning the Peace in the 21st Century: A Task Force

Report of the Strategies for US National Security Program." Stanley Foundation, October 2003.

Krakauer, Jon. *Where Men Win Glory: The Odessey of Pat Tillman*. New York: Doubleday, 2009.

Krauthammer, Charles. "The Bush Doctrine." *Weekly Standard* (June 4, 2001).

Krauthammer, Charles. "The Unipolar Moment." *Foreign Affairs* 70 (1990–91): 23–43.

Krebs, Ronald, and Chaim Kaufman. "Correspondence: Selling the Market Short? Marketplace of Ideas and the Iraq War." *International Security*, no. 29 (Spring 2005): 196–207.

Kull, Steven, Clay Ramsay, and Evan Lewis. "Misperception, the Media, and the Iraq War." *Political Science Quarterly* 118 (Winter 2003–4): 569–98.

Kull, Steven, Clay Ramsay, Stefan Subias, Stephen Weber, and Evan Lewis. "Americans on Detention, Torture, and the War on Terrorism." Program on International Policy Attitudes, July 22, 2004.

Kuypers, Jim A. *Bush's War: Media Bias and Justifications for War in a Terrorist Age*. Lanham, MD: Rowman and Littlefield, 2006.

Limbaugh, Rush. "Interview on 'Fox News Sunday' with Chris Wallace." November 1, 2009.

Lindbergh, Charles. "Speech at America First Rally." Des Moines, IA, September 11, 1941.

Lippmann, Walter. *Essays in the Public Philosophy*. Boston: Little, Brown, 1955.

Lippmann, Walter. *Public Opinion*. New York: Macmillan, 1922.

MacArthur, John R. "The Lies We Bought." *Columbia Journalism Review* 42 (May–June 2003): 62–63.

Madison, James. "Letter to Thomas Jefferson, May 25, 1798." *Letters and Other Writings of James Madison*. Vol. II, 1865.

Mann, James. *The Rise of the Vulcans: The History of Bush's War Cabinet*. New York: Penguin, 2004.

Mason, R. Chuck. *U.S.-Iraq Status of Forces Agreement: Issues for Congressional Oversight*. Washington, DC: Congressional Research Service, December 12, 2008.

Massing, Michael. "Now They Tell Us." *New York Review of Books* 51 (February 26, 2004).

Massing, Michael. "The Press: The Enemy Within." *New York Review of Books* 52 (December 15, 2005): 36–44.

McClellan, Scott. *Inside the Bush White House and Washington's Cult of Deception*. New York: Public Affairs, 2008.

Merman, Jonathan. "The Media's Independence Problem." *World Policy Journal* (Fall 2004).

Mitchell, David, and Tansa George Massoud. "Anatomy of Failure: Bush's Decision-Making Process and the Iraq War." *Foreign Policy Analysis* 5 (July 2009).

Mueller, John. "The Iraq Syndrome." *Foreign Affairs* 84 (November–December 2005).

Mueller, John. *Policy and Opinion in the Gulf War*. Chicago: University of Chicago Press, 1994.

Mueller, John. *War, Presidents, and Public Opinion*. New York: Wiley, 1973.

Nakhoul, Samia. "Bin Laden Labels Saddam an Infidel—Jezeera TV." *Reuters*, February 11, 2003.

National Geographic-Roper Public Affairs. *Final Report: 2006 Geographic Literacy Study*. May 2006.

Nincic, Miroslav, and Jennifer Ramos. "The Dynamics of Patriotism: Survey and Experimental Evidence." Paper presented at the Annual Meeting of the American Political Science Association, Toronto, September 2009.

Norris, Pippa. "The Restless Searchlight: Network News Framing of the Post–Cold War Period." *Political Communication* 12 (1995): 357–70.

Obama, Barack. "Speech on Iraq." Fort Bragg, NC, March 19, 2009.

O'Brien, Michale. *John F. Kennedy: A Biography.* New York: St. Martin's Press, 2005.

Percy, Charles. "The Partisan Gap." *Foreign Policy* 45 (1981–82): 3–15.

Petraeus, David. "Report to Congress on the Situation in Iraq." September 10–11, 2007.

Petraeus, David. "Report to Congress on the Situation in Iraq." April 8–9, 2008.

Pew Research Center. *America's New International Point of View.* Washington, DC, December 2001.

Pew Research Center. *America's Place in the World.* Washington, DC, 2009.

Pew Research Center. "Inside Obama's Sweeping Victory." Washington, DC, November 5, 2008.

Pew Research Center. *More See America's Loss of Global Respect as Major Problem,* Washington, DC, June 16, 2008.

Pew Research Center. *Public Knowledge of Current Affairs Little Changed by the Revolution. What Americans Know, 1989–2007.* Washington, DC, April 15, 2007.

Pollack, Kenneth M. *The Persian Puzzle: The Conflict between Iran and America.* New York: Random House, 2004.

Popkin, Samuel L. *The Reasoning Voter: Communication and Persuasion in Presidential Campaigns.* Chicago: University of Chicago Press, 1991.

Rashid, Ahmed. *Descent into Chaos: The U.S. and the Disaster in Pakistan, Afghanistan, and Central Asia.* New York: Penguin, 2009.

Reagan, Ronald W. "Speech to the British House of Commons." June 8, 1982.

Record, Jeffrey. "The Bush Doctrine and War with Iraq." *Parameters* (Spring 2003): 4–21.

Reilly, John E., ed. *American Public Opinion and U.S. Foreign Policy, 1999.* Chicago: CCFR, 1999.

Ricks, Thomas E. "'Curveball': Yeah, I Lied—You Suckers!" *The Best Defense: Foreign Policy Website.* February 11, 2011.

Ricks, Thomas E. *Fiasco: The American Military Adventure in Iraq, 2003–2005.* New York: Penguin, 2006.

Ricks, Thomas E. *The Gamble: General David Petraeus and the American Military Adventure in Iraq, 2006–2008.* New York: Penguin, 2009.

Ricks, Thomas E. "Understanding the Surge in Iraq and What's Ahead." Philadelphia: Foreign Policy Research Institute, May 29, 2009.

Risen, James. *State of War: The Secret History of the CIA and the Bush Administration.* New York: Simon and Schuster, 2006.

Roach, John. "Young Americans Geographically Illiterate, Survey Suggests." *National Geographic News* (May 2, 2006).

Robinson, Luca, and Steven Livingston. "No News and Foreign News: U.S. Media Coverage of the World." Paper presented at the Annual Convention of the International Studies Association, Portland, OR, February 2003.

Roosevelt, Kermit. *Countercoup: The Struggle for Control of Iran.* New York: McGraw-Hill, 1979.

Root, Elihu. "A Requisite for Success of Popular Diplomacy." *Foreign Affairs* 1 (1922): 1–10.

Rove, Karl. *Courage and Consequences: My Life as a Conservative in the Fight.* New York: Simon and Schuster, 2010.

Rumsfeld, Donald H. *Known and Unknown.* New York: Sentinel, 2011.

Sandrolini, James. "Propaganda: The Art of War." *Chicago Media Watch Report* (Fall 2002).

Sanger, David. *The Inheritance: The World Obama Confronts and the Challenges to American Power.* New York: Harmony Books, 2009.

Schlesinger, Arthur M., Jr. "Back to the Womb?" *Foreign Affairs* 74 (1995): 2–8.

Schlesinger, James R., and Thomas Pickering. *Iraq: The Day After.* New York: Council on Foreign Relations, 2003.

Seal, Karen H., Daniel Bertenthal, Charles R. Miner, Saunak Sen, and Charles Marmar. "Bringing the War Back Home: Mental Health Disorders among 103,788 U.S. Veterans Returning from Afghanistan and Iraq, Seen at VA Facilities." *Archives of Internal Medicine,* no. 167 (2007): 476–82.

Seal, Karen H., T. J. Meltzer, Shira Maguen, and Charles R. Marmar. "Growing Prevalence of Mental Disorders among Iraq and Afghanistan Veterans: Trends and Risk Factors for Mental Health Diagnoses in New Users of VA Health Care, 2002–2008." *American Journal of Public Health* (2009).

Shapiro, Robert Y., and Yaeli Bloch-Elkon. "Ideological Partisanship and American Public Opinion toward Foreign Policy." In *Power and Superpower: Global Leadership and Exceptionalism in the 21st Century,* edited by M. H. Halperson, Jeffrey Laurenti, Peter Rundlet, and Spencer C. Boyer, 49–68. New York: Century Foundation Press, 2007.

Shapiro, Robert Y., and Yaeli Bloch-Elkon. "Political Polarization and the Rational Public." Paper for the Annual Conference of the American Association of Public Opinion Research, May 10, 2006.

Sheeler, Jim. *Final Salute: A Story of Unfinished Lives.* New York: Penguin, 2008.

Shinseki, Eric. "Testimony before the Senate Armed Services Committee." February 25, 2003.

Simon, Steven. "The Price of the Surge." *Foreign Affairs* 88 (May–June 2008).

Sobel, Richard. *The Impact of Public Opinion on U.S. Foreign Policy since Vietnam: Constraining the Colossus.* New York: Oxford University Press, 2000.

Sobel, Richard. *Public Opinion and Foreign Policy: The Controversy over Contra Aid.* Lanham, MD: Rowman and Littlefield, 1993.

Stiglitz, Joseph E., and Linda Bilmes. *The Three Trillion Dollar War.* New York: Norton, 2008.

Strupp, Joe. "McClatchy's D.C. Bureau Claims It's Barred from Defense Secretary's Plane." *Editor and Publisher* (May 23, 2007).

Suskind, Ron. "Faith, Certainty, and the Presidency of George W. Bush." *New York Times Magazine* (October 17, 2004).

Suskind, Ron. *The Price of Loyalty: George W. Bush, the White House, and the Education of Paul O'Neill.* New York: Simon and Schuster, 2004.

Suskind, Ron. *The Way of the World: A Story of Truth in an Age of Extremism.* New York: HarperCollins, 2008.

Tanielian, Terri, and Lisa H. Jaycox, eds. *Invisible Wounds of War.* Santa Monica, CA: Rand Corporation, 2008.

Time Essay. "The Army and Vietnam: The Stab-in-the-Back Complex." *Time* (December 12, 1969).

Trubowitz, Peter, and Nicole Mellow. "Going Bipartisan: Politics by Other Means." *Political Science Quarterly* 120 (Fall 2005): 433–53.

Unger, Craig. *The Fall of the House of Bush.* New York: Scribner's, 2007.

United Nations High Commission on Refugees. "Iraq Operations at a Glance." January 1, 2009.

U.S. Army. *Army. Health Promotion, Risk Reduction, and Suicide Prevention Report 2010.*

U.S. Casualties in Iraq. www.global.securities.org/militaries/Iraq_casualties.htm.

U.S. Central Command. *OPLAN 1003–98.* Washington, DC, October 31, 2002.

U.S. Department of Defense. *Conduct of the Gulf War.* Final Report to the U.S. Congress. Appendix P. April 1992.

U.S. Department of Defense. "Deputy Secretary Wolfowitz Interview with Sam Tannenhaus, *Vanity Fair.*" May 9, 2003.

U.S. Department of Defense. *Desert Crossing Seminar: Action Report.* Washington, DC, June 28–29, 1999.

U.S. Department of Defense. "News Transcript of DoD Briefing with Secretary Rumsfeld and Gen. Pace." March 7, 2006.

U.S. Department of State. "Action Memorandum from Jonathan T. Howe to Lawrence S. Eagleburger: Iraqi Use of Chemical Weapons." November 21, 1982.

U.S. Department of State. Action Memorandum from Richard W. Murphy to Lawrence S. Eagleburger. "EXIM Bank Financing for Iraq." December 22, 1983.

U.S. Department of State. *The Future of Iraq Project.* Washington, DC, 2003.

U.S. Department of State. Memorandum. "Notifying Congress of [Excised] Truck Sales." March 5, 1984.

U.S. Embassy in the United Kingdom. Cable from Charles H. Price to the Department of State. "Rumsfeld Mission: December 20 Meeting with Iraqi President Saddam Hussein." December 21, 1983.

U.S. Embassy in the United Kingdom. "Rumsfeld One-on-One Meeting with Iraqi Deputy Prime Minister." December 21, 1983.

U.S. Government Accounting Office. Report-06-305 to Congressional Requesters. January 13, 2006.

U.S. House of Representatives. Committee on Oversight and Government Reform. *Misleading Information from the Battlefield: The Tillman and Lynch Episodes.* July 17, 2008.

U.S. National Security Council. *A National Strategy for Victory in Iraq.* Washington, DC, November 30, 2005.

U.S. Public Law 105-138. October 31, 1998.

Utley, Garrick. "The Shrinking of Foreign News: From Broadcast to Narrowcast." *Foreign Affairs* 76 (March–April 1997).

Vallely, Paul E., and Michael A. Aquino. "From PSYOP to Mind War: The Psychology of Victory." San Francisco: Headquarters of the 7th Psychological Operations Group, 1980.

Vandenberg, Arthur H., Jr., ed. *The Private Diaries of Senator Vandenberg.* Boston: Houghton Mifflin, 1952.

Waltz, Kenneth. "The Emerging Structure of World Politics." *International Security,* no. 18 (Fall 1993): 44–79.

West, Bing. *The Wrong War: Grit, Strategy, and the Way Out of Afghanistan.* New York: Random House, 2011.

Weiner, Tim. *Legacy of Ashes: The History of the CIA.* New York: Doubleday, 2007.

Western, Jon. *Selling Intervention and War: The President, the Media, and the American Public.* Baltimore: Johns Hopkins University Press, 2005.

White House. *National Security Directive 26.* October 2, 1989.

White House. "President Bush Discusses War on Terror and Operation Iraqi Freedom." Cleveland, OH, March 20, 2006.

White House. "President Bush Press Conference." August 21, 2006.

White House Fact Sheet. The August 6, 2001 Presidential Daily Briefing. "Bin Laden Determined to Strike in U.S." Declassified and Approved for Release, April 10, 2004.

Will, George. "Is It 1966 in Washington?" *Newsweek* (October 5, 2009).

Will, George. "McChrystal Had to Go." *Washington Post* (June 24, 2010).

Wilson, James Q. "The Press at War: The Patriot Reporter Is Passé." *City Journal* (Autumn 2006).

Wlezien, Christopher. "On the Salience of Political Issues: The Problem with 'Most Important Problem.' " *Electoral Studies* 24 (2005): 555–79.

Wolfowitz, Paul. "Interview with Melissa Block." *National Public Radio,* February 19, 2003.

Wolfowitz, Paul. "Rising Up." *New Republic* (December 7, 1998): 12–14.

Wolfowitz, Paul. "Speech to the Veterans of Foreign Wars." March 11, 2003.

Wolfowitz, Paul. "Testimony before House Budget Committee." *Hearings on FY 2004 Defense Budget Request,* February 27, 2003.

Woods, Kevin M., and James Larey. *Iraq: Perspectives Project. Saddam and Terrorism: Insights from Captured Iraqi Documents.* Vol. I. IDA Paper P-4287. Alexandria, VA: Institute for Defense Analyses, November 2007.

Woodward, Bob. *Bush at War.* New York: Simon and Schuster, 2002.

Woodward, Bob. *Obama's Wars.* New York: Simon and Schuster, 2010.

Woodward, Bob. *Plan of Attack.* New York: Simon and Schuster, 2004.

Woodward, Bob. *State of Denial: Bush at War, Part III.* New York: Simon and Schuster, 2006.

Woodward, Bob. *The War Within: A Secret History of the White House, 2006–2008.* New York: Simon and Schuster, 2008.

World Public Opinion. *American Attitudes: Americans and the World.* August 3, 2007.

World Public Opinion Poll. *Obama Changing the Way Germans See U.S.* June 4, 2009.

Yoo, John. *Crisis and Command.* New York: Kaplan, 2009.

Zaller, John. *The Nature and Origin of Mass Opinion.* Cambridge: Cambridge University Press, 1992.

Zinni, Anthony. "Eyes on Iraq: Remarks at the CDI Board of Directors Meeting." Washington, DC: Center for Defense Information, May 12, 2004.

Index